BEYOND HOMOPHOBIA

BEYOND HOMOPHOBIA

Centring LGBTQ Experiences in
the Anglophone Caribbean

EDITED BY

Moji Anderson and Erin C. MacLeod

The University of the West Indies Press
Jamaica • Barbados • Trinidad and Tobago

The University of the West Indies Press
7A Gibraltar Hall Road, Mona
Kingston 7, Jamaica
www.uwipress.com

A catalogue record of this book is available from the National
Library of Jamaica.

ISBN: 978-976-640-744-5 (paper)
978-976-640-745-2 (Kindle)
978-976-640-746-9 (ePub)

Cover photograph: *Not Your Slave*; produced by
Karib F.U.N.Q and Simone Harris @360Artistsja;
directed by Lee Rose @lee.rose_9rs; styled by
Emani Edwards @emanithegenderlessstylist
and Lee Rose; photographer, Shasta-Lee Smith
@SMKSPhotography; assistant photographer,
Chadrick Barnes.

Cover design by Richard Rawlins

Printed in the United States of America

Contents

Foreword

Perhaps, nigh on twenty-odd years ago when, on a quiet afternoon in Kingston, the Jamaica Forum for Lesbians, All-Sexuals and Gays (J-FLAG) was formed, it wasn't possible, at least for those of us in J-FLAG's small but determined and dedicated founding group, to envisage an anthology like this one, centred on the ideal of moving – literally, intellectually, artistically and politically – *beyond* the grim and grinding realities of anti-queer bigotry that many of us had come to know (and sometimes chosen to ignore or forget about but very often chosen to resist fiercely) in our varying parts of the Caribbean region and beyond, including our many diasporas and even beyond them, far out across this ever vaster-than-vast world.

Perhaps, concerned as we were in those days with what one might call "triage" work in Jamaica's hostile environment (and any honest person scornful of revisionist, blissful nostalgia, especially any who lived in Jamaica at that time or worked with J-FLAG or our then-host, the manna-from-heaven Jamaica AIDS Support organization, will know and recall exactly what I mean), we couldn't even begin to think of such future possibilities, although preoccupied as we were with the daunting business of clearing more Jamaican and Caribbean space in which we and future generations could simply breathe, become and (blessedly or otherwise) *be*, we may well have been dreaming of what then might have seemed unenvisionable. And so it may also have been, dream-wise, for the redoubtable (and always unflappable) Larry Chang twenty years before us, when he, virtually on his own, founded Jamaica's first-ever queer organization, the Gay Freedom Movement, in 1978, a mere sixteen years after Jamaica's 1962 independence from Great Britain: the colonial power that, apart from its ongoing obsession with rawhide whips, genocide and rape, was also largely responsible for the Christian-based cruelty and ignorance, including hatred and fear of gender nonconformity and sexual difference, that had long throttled its colonized realms. In the late twentieth century, but still twenty years before our turn-of-the-century J-FLAG time, Larry Chang may indeed have been dreaming with the intention of bequeathing his dreams to us and those who came after. But how could any of us know? For here we are now, at the annunciated birth of this anthology *Beyond Homophobia*. And so it is.

When regarding this collection and its preceding Jamaica-located queer gatherings, celebrations, ceremonies and conferences, we might well feel a range of emotions similar to those we register when we observe the progress of history and of humanity in general. For as we know, even at this time in the early twenty-first century, the emergence of an anthology such as this one and the political struggles and humanistic work that cleared innumerable paths and engendered – provoked and demanded – increasingly more broad-minded and imaginative Caribbean gender- and sexuality-related discourses exorcised of fundamentalist dogma and general narrowness, cannot and *must not* be taken for granted, any more than the incisive work contained in this volume can or should be taken for granted. This anthology braves more steps, in fact more leaps, in reminding us by way of its reflective contents that we must not risk dishonouring our present, our very selves and the (now more than ever) increased possibilities of our futures by *disremembering*, to invoke Toni Morrison's piercing word, the fiercely engaged on-the-ground struggles of our past, during which a collection such as this one and the conferences that preceded it might well have been considered luxuries beyond imagining. Yet we also know that nearly everything that has not been entirely imagined, including human beings, can always be envisaged and breathed into exis-tence, as when our own primordial sun, indifferent to millennia of grousing rumbles far beneath it, declined for its own reasons to imagine the formation of particular islands and even entire archipelagos of desire, until the fury of volcanoes blasted them (and to some degree us) out of the sea.

So it was no doubt remembering that flaming-but-aloof sun and the irate volcanoes, while also recalling the immortal sea out of which we each once crawled, either on two legs or four, and to which on similar legs we shall someday return, that on a cool January evening in 2017, on the campus of the University of the West Indies (UWI) at Mona, while awaiting Rinaldo Walcott's keynote address, attendees of the Beyond Homophobia conference and others sat together as an audience and listened. We listened to the univer-sity's walrus-voiced Principal Archibald McDonald's welcoming remarks, during which he stated that the UWI at Mona unequivocally "support[s] this conference . . . [that] drives home the idea that hate and discrimina-tion do *not* belong within our society, especially within a learning institution that is aligned with global ideals of inclusion, diversity and understanding". The gathered people listened as he insisted that "as an institution, we are committed to diversity and inclusion, and . . . [to] support[ing] our fellow scholars and colleagues regardless of how they identify their gender or sexu-ality". We listened as he stressed that "the message that we wish to impart as a learning institution is that we are one community . . . [and that] sex, gender or sexual identity should not exclude anyone from our group". We listened as he thanked several university departments and J-FLAG for their work that had made the conference (and now, by extension, this anthology) possible. Did any of us in the new-born J-FLAG twenty years ago ever dream that we would one day hear the esteemed principal publicly welcome the presence of a queer conference on Jamaican soil, convened at the exalted UWI, no less? UWI's campus, less than a mile from the University of Technology on the campus of which only five years earlier, in 2012, two male students had been beaten almost to death by their enraged fellow students and by campus security guards (as can still, as of this writing, be viewed in online videos) who believed the two men were homosexuals who had been having sex in a public campus bathroom. Did some of us absorbing the walrus-voiced principal's words, recalling the UTech violence and local reactions that had ranged from frank approval to outrage and condemnation of it, tremble slightly in both joy and sadness – and maybe with a little disbelief – as we listened to his warm welcome and wished, sometimes with tightly closed eyes, that those who we had known and loved, who one quiet night might have been machete-chopped up or shot dead, or who had taken their own lives during the long years of struggle, but also those who had celebrated and triumphed with us but weren't present on that cool January evening, could have been there to hear for themselves? For surely the principal's words brought to mind then, and conjure still, Jamaica's much-quoted but often (sometimes brutally) disregarded motto, "out of many, one people", applied in this regard to all of our Caribbean. Applied to everyone. To all of us. Everywhere.

In application to everyone everywhere, and especially to those most vulnerable, must the lofty Jamaican words be made flesh linked with spirit, solidified into and through the sacred terrains of safeguarded and honoured flesh. For it is and can only be through such honouring and safeguarding, as attested to and illustrated throughout this anthology's pages and for which its presence and title claim fully deserved human space – the invaluable space of speaking and self-naming that undergird and *are* self-declaration – that the living, breathing bodies of the nation and the territory, the bodies that traverse daily life across and through the mountains and the cities and the rain forests and the villages, the bodies that are inimitably our own and those of innumerable others, are *valued*, brought into clear vision and actualized in the centring of LGBTQ experiences within and beyond the Caribbean: experiences lived and narratives recounted beyond gender binaries and the pitfalls of ignorance that make human stupidity and retrogression possible.

Yet far beyond retrogression and ignorance beckon once more the words "honouring" and "safeguarding": useful tools for the journey onward through our era and all those to follow.

In preparation for its own journey, regard how easily this book rises to its feet and, unrestrained by glares or glances or even raised eyebrows of the past, walks forward, all the while craning its neck upward as if seeking somewhere in the eternal firmament a shower of cooling stars, a rainfall of silver light or perhaps merely yet another shower of remarkably brazen flowers, their eyelids once more painted the outrageous gold that remains beloved by those who, similarly prepared, have always known the source of both the colour and the gleam. This book, all of its pages. Walking forward. Now walking faster. Now *running* –

Thomas Glave
Birmingham, England

Introduction

MOJI ANDERSON AND ERIN C. MacLEOD

The purpose of this edited volume is to challenge and change the conventional narratives that shape representations of Caribbean LGBTQ people.[1] LGBTQ people in the Caribbean are talked about directly and indirectly, inside and outside the region, with much authority and little room for debate. This book brings together academic papers, prose and poetry presented at the Beyond Homophobia symposium (2015) and conference (2017) at the University of the West Indies (UWI). These events aimed to contest two particularly powerful narratives that claim to represent the truth about Caribbean LGBTQ people and their lives. The first, propagated by Euro-American rights organizations and international media, strips LGBTQ people in the Caribbean of their agency by presenting them as subject to a monolithic homophobia. Thus, in the region, and especially in Jamaica – "the worst offender" (Padgett 2006) – they are "hated to death" (Schleifer 2004) in the "most homophobic place on earth" (Padgett 2006). This narrative pervades the global popular imagination, shaping people's (mis)perceptions of the region. For example, in late 2017, when visiting African American journalist Shaun King tweeted a picture of a popular Jamaican restaurant, expressing his excitement at returning to the island, some readers responded by asserting and condemning the country's intractable homophobia. As one woman said, "Looks great! Unfortunately, I (a lesbian) cannot safely travel to Jamaica, so I'll have to take your word for it." Challenged by another tweeter, she brooked no argument: "It's not gay friendly. That's just that."[2]

The second narrative circulates within the Caribbean, condemning LGBTQ people as immoral, pathological interlopers. As M. Jacqui Alexander (1994) argues, citizenship in the Caribbean is premised on heterosexuality: LGBTQ people are therefore noncitizens. Without legitimate claim to belonging, they are intruders. Thus the leader of a Jamaican anti-gay organization's admonition to the advocacy group J-FLAG for staging Pride week during the national emancipation and independence celebrations: "instead of competing with Jamaica, celebrate Jamaica" ("J-FLAG Should Celebrate Emancipendence not Homosexuality", *Jamaica Observer*, 27 July 2016), as if the assertion of LGBTQ identities placed them outside the bounds of the nation. This alienness is established and reinforced in St Lucia by the print media that illustrates the few LGBTQ-related stories with stock photographs of white people and in Guyana by the judge who repeatedly barred a transgender woman from his courtroom (IGLHRC 2015, 41; "SASOD, GEF Protest over Barring of Transgender Woman from Court", *Stabroek News*, 12 March 2017).³ LGBTQ people's immorality is considered contagious and pathological. Thus, the labelling of a Grenadian gay rights organization as "agents of Satan" (IGLHRC 2015, 25), the accusation that an LGBTQ film festival in Guyana would corrupt the youth ("Gays Should Live on an Island by Themselves – Inter-Religious Organisation Vice-Chair Says", *Stabroek News*, 9 June 2014) and the frequent description of homosexuality as a disease by "experts" cited in the media across the region (IGLHRC 2015, 13).

The tweeter's comment about homophobia in Jamaica is of course partly right: there are many more examples of homophobia and transphobia in other Caribbean countries to add to those in the paragraph above. However, the finality and factuality of the phrase "that's just that" does its own type of violence to the lives and selves of LGBTQ Jamaicans. "That's just that" ignores the regular and increasingly popular gaycations organized out of New York to Jamaica. "That's just that" erases the annual Pride events in Kingston and Montego Bay. "That's just that" silences the empirical evidence that levels of homophobia in fact vary, particularly with degree of contact with LGBTQ Jamaicans (West and Hewstone 2012).

This volume not only challenges popular Euro-American discourses of the Caribbean as a uniformly homophobic region but also attempts to expand the approach to homophobia by engaging with lived experiences in queer Anglo-Caribbean spaces. In the edited collection *Homophobias: Lust and Loathing across Time and Space*, Suzanne LaFont (2009) and David Murray (2009b) discuss the nature of homophobia in Jamaica and Barbados respectively. However, the anthology is more an ethnography of homophobia than an analysis of LGBTQ life. Another volume, *Global Homophobia: States, Movements, and the Politics of Oppression* (2013), is a macrolevel, cross-cultural analysis of resistance across states and legal contexts but without reference to the Caribbean.

Assertions of homophobia or immorality cannot do justice to the complexities inherent in Caribbean LGBTQ people's navigation of their environments. Understanding their realities requires nuance in recognizing them as fully actualized humans who are agents, not objects and, as a corollary, recognizing the complexity of homophobias in the Caribbean (see King et al. 2012). This in turn requires a refusal to be "captives of others' narratives", as Trinidadian writer and activist Colin Robinson writes in this volume.

Although far from complete, that work is being done. Caribbean LGBTQ organizations are well aware of the need for nuance in their advocacy. For example, J-FLAG's fight for the rights of LGBTQ Jamaicans is combined with acknowledgement of the stories about positive experiences and hope "that beyond the homophobia and transphobia that are perpetrated, there are possibilities for respect, tolerance, and acceptance", as Jaevion Nelson, the executive director of J-FLAG, put it ("New Sense of National Pride", *Gleaner,* 5 August 2017). Accordingly, they have staged events to which politicians were invited to express support for J-FLAG's work and at which fathers, mothers, brothers and sisters celebrated their LGBTQ child or sibling.

The push for nuance often pits organizations in the region against the Euro-American gay rights establishment and what Savannah Shange (2012) calls "homonormative media outlets". For example, in 2017, the Eastern Caribbean Alliance for Diversity and Equality (ECADE) urged foreign media to consult with regional advocacy organizations when reporting on the region, after *Pink News,* a UK-based newspaper, headlined a story about St Lucia with "Stonewall Auctions Luxury Holiday to Country Where Gays Are Imprisoned". ECADE pointed out the real dangers and the potential victims of this absolutism: "misrepresentation of the situation of LGBTQ people in St Lucia can be deleterious to our advocacy, undermining the work and our credibility" ("Rights Group Urge International Media to Use Local Sources", *St Lucia Times,* 1 April 2017). Bahamian activist Erin Greene (2012) agrees that foreign LGBTQ rights organizations ignore local realities, priorities and activism. Colin Robinson (2012) has a similar complaint, arguing that "queer internationalism" de-emphasises local organizing in favour of reliance on external advocacy and funding, which reinforces the pre-existing perception of the alienness of local LGBTQ communities. Savannah Shange (2012) sees Puar's (2007) "homonation-alism" at work, with its depiction of non-"Western" states as uniquely, irre-deemably homophobic, necessarily asserting Euro-American activism as a "modernizing intervention" in the affairs of the benighted region.

Although Linden Lewis complained in his 2003 edited volume that "not much sustained and systematic treatment of sexuality in the schol-arly literature of the region exists" and that "sexual orientation is very much a taboo subject . . . and is therefore not always considered impor-tant enough for academic analysis", there has been an increasing amount of work in this area over the years (9, 10).[4] Many scholars (and activists, and scholar-activists) have reflected the concerns of activists noted above, taking issue with "over-generalising statements" about LGBTQ people and homophobia in the Caribbean (Murray 2009a, 17) and pointing out that "there is a complex range of viewpoints and attitudes that must be accounted for in our defining of homophobias" (King and Nixon 2012). Haitian activist Steve Laguerre (2012) says that "when I'm outside of Haiti, I see that Haiti is not a homophobic country" and that Christian churches and its middle-class worshippers are to blame for stigmatizing homosexuality, unlike the indigenous religion, Vodou, which allows for sexual fluidity. Class functions differently in other Caribbean contexts: so, for example, Suzanne LaFont (2009) and Rafael Ramírez (2003) note that experiences of homophobia by Jamaican LGBTQ and Puerto Rican gay men, respectively, can be buffered by class, while Rosamond King's (2014, 64) discussion of the LGBTQ Caribbean adds place and gender expression as insulators against homophobia. Gloria Wekker's (2006) scholarship on "mati work" in Suriname reveals that specific, discrete sexual or gender identification is not a concern for working-class women sexually intimate with both women and men. David Murray (2009a, 4) describes the diverse expressions of sexual and gender identities in Martinique and Barbados, describing the Bajan "sexscape" as both similar and different to that of Euro-America (see also Murray 2002). Karen Carpenter's 2017 edited collection discusses sexual and gender identities from a psychological perspective, addressing the tension between cultural expectations and lived realities.

These and other researchers have made explicit the failings of the conventional apprehension of sexual and gender identities. Linden Lewis (2003, 12) brings attention to the güevedoches in the Dominican Republic studied by Herdt: "neither male nor female, they inhabit a different category that complicates the binarism of male and female in Caribbean society". Carla Moore (2014) explores the lives of men who have sex with men (MSM) in Jamaica and rejects Euro-American assumptions about LGBTQ identity, positing Jamaican MSM as representing variations in LGBTQ expression rather than being "victims of (naturalized) internalized (black) homophobia" (11). Mark Padilla (2007) also discusses challenges to these non-Caribbean assumptions about sexuality and identity within the community of male sex workers in the Dominican Republic. Murray (2002, 9) states that Caribbean subjectivities are particularly complicated because of the colonization project's "sediment of ruptured, violent, disenfranchised and dehumanizing histories where policies and actions based on 'fixed identity categories' were once enacted to erase, assimilate and/or subordinate". Therefore, he posits Caribbean LGBTQ identities as "everchanging, everparadoxical and evercontradictory" (9). Lawrence La Fountain-Stokes's (2009) work in Puerto Rico leads him to posit the "open secret" rather than the Euro-American-derived "closet" as the primary dynamic governing LGBTQ identity negotiation. King (2014, 64) agrees, saying that the "'secret' is not fully hidden . . . [it] is both known and (relatively) tolerated by those around the individual", while according to Steve Laguerre (2012), Haitians "know [others' sexuality]. But it's just that no one talks about it". Omise'eke Tinsley (2011) also dismisses "the closet", stating that it "is not always the place to find same-sex desire". She proposes an "epistemology of the garden" and posits that, rather than navigating opposites (inside/outside), Caribbean sexual and gender identities thrive on the *intersection* of inside and outside and find expression at the "interface between race, class, culture and sexuality" (249). In an earlier work, she rejects the heteronormative and the patriarchal, focusing instead on female Caribbean writers' and poets' attention to the erotic worlds created by and among women in the region (Tinsley 2010). Moore (2014, 128) talks of the discovery of "ways of queerly *being* that *may* more comfortably fit Afro-Caribbean subjects while interrupting the homohegemony of white-western-middle class queerness" (emphasis in original). One way in which it interrupts is, for example, conceptualizing same-sex relations as activity rather than identity (Moore 2014; Kempadoo 2009). What activists and scholars are calling for and engaging in, then, are analyses of Caribbean LGBTQ people from their own perspectives: centring them in their own narratives.

Scholars also engage the macrolevel to critique Caribbean nation-states under the thrall of Euro-American imperialism in its many forms and its longevity in the region that posit nonheterosexual identities and practices as outside of true citizenship and discuss the complicated ways that the region's premiere source of revenue – tourism – engages (and does not engage) the reality of diverse sexualities in the region.[5] Kamala Kempadoo (2004, 2), for example, points to the wide range of sexual practices that have resulted from the combination of "colonial and neo-colonial ideas about the region [and] West African, East Indian, Amerindian, and other non-Western traditions and legacies". However, she also indicates, following Alexander (2006), that heteropatriarchy and the putative hypersexuality of Caribbean people have stigmatized nonheterosexuals as "outlaws and noncitizens" (Kempadoo 2004, 9). Angelique Nixon (2015), through her description and analysis of cultural products in the Caribbean, presents examples of resistance to the commodifying and marginalizing effects of paradise-making in favour of tourism that more accurately reflects the sexual, class and racial realities of its citizens.

Scholars and activists in the region join those conducting research in other parts of the world that increasingly gives the lie to Euro-American-derived epistemologies and ontologies. For example, Boyce, Engebretsen, and Posocco's (2017) special issue of the journal *Sexualities* entitled "Anthropology's Queer Sensibilities" presents ethnographic research from Africa, Asia and among migrants in Europe to demonstrate "experimental thinking in ethnographically informed investigations of gender and sexual differences" and the need for "relativizing 'Western' paradigmatic knowledge in the study of gender and sexual diversity" (1, 5). Similarly, there are lessons to be learned from sexual and gender identities in the Caribbean that, crucially, can be of interest and even of use further afield, as models of the multiplicity of ways of not being heterosexual and of activism. Indeed, in this volume Rinaldo Walcott presents what he calls a particularly Caribbean understanding of queerness expressed in his native Barbados: "being so". He considers this a "recognition of nonheterosexuality . . . not necessarily deployed in the service of homophobia" that has the potential to challenge the state, root Caribbean LGBTQ people in their own unique ontological realities and guide their futures.

This type of thinking underpinned and guided the symposium Beyond Homophobia: Exploring Identities and Sexualities in Jamaica and the biennial conference it spawned, Beyond Homophobia: Centring LGBT Experiences in the Caribbean (the second iteration, Beyond Homophobia: Navigating the State, was held in January 2019). The criteria for inclusion were simple: that participants move beyond hackneyed discourses and stereotypes to focus on the lived realities and diverse ways in which LGBTQ people in the Caribbean experience love, respect, (in)tolerance and acceptance, with the presumption that LGBTQ people *act* and are not only acted upon. The aim was to hear LGBTQ people speak for themselves, in the expectation that taking up this space will redound not just to their benefit, but to wider society as well, by confronting the latter with the long obvious but long obscured reality that LGBTQ people are fully functioning agents of their own destiny, not hapless victims of circumstance.

The conference, although the first regional conference initiated by the UWI to focus on LGBTQ people in this way, builds on the previous work of academics and activists. There has been important collaborative work over the years: workshops and meetings, some on UWI campuses, that have led to significant publications, advocacy groups, online resources and networks, and even legal action. For example, the Caribbean Region of the

International Resource Network organized the Sexualities Gathering at UWI, Mona, Jamaica in 2009, which brought together thirty scholars, activists and community workers from ten countries in the region and further afield. This event was particularly important for concentrating explicitly on understanding the variegated nature of homophobia in the region and led to the production of a multimedia collection of artistic works, activist reports, prose, scholarly articles and interviews in 2011 entitled *Theorizing Homophobias in the Caribbean: Complexities of Place, Desire and Belonging* (King et al. 2012). Another meeting bringing together academics and activists held in 2008 entitled Rights and Regulation in the Anglo-Caribbean was held at UWI's Cave Hill, Barbados campus and led the following year to the establishment of the UWI Rights Advocacy Project in the Faculty of Law, which works with civil society organizations to promote human rights through constitutional litigation. Further collaboration between activists and scholars led to an edited volume in 2009 entitled *Sexuality, Social Exclusion and Human Rights: Vulnerability in the Context of HIV*.

An important antecedent of this volume is *Our Caribbean: A Gathering of Lesbian and Gay Writing from the Antilles* (2008), which brings together different types of writing – fiction, poetry and personal reflections – that reflect a range of ways to explore the meanings and expressions of LGBTQ identities in the region. Its editor, Thomas Glave (2008, 10), believed that the collection heralded "an ending of silences and invisibilities". As he says in the foreword of this volume, the present collection takes us further down that path.

There has also been important work in various journals, such as *Sargasso* (particularly the issue entitled "Love, Hope, Community: Sexualities, and Social Justice"), *Gay and Lesbian Quarterly* and *Caribbean Review of Gender Studies*. The Caribbean Sexualities Working Group, which convenes every year at the Caribbean Studies Conference (and throughout the year online), is also working to add and encourage scholarship in this area. This edited volume will add to this growing field of English-language Caribbean sexuality studies.

The Book

Providing a range of different perspectives, the scope of this text is wide, although it must be noted that, geographically speaking, it is confined to the larger countries of the English-speaking Caribbean.[6] The volume contains academic treatments of the lived experiences of LGBTQ Caribbean people, as well as poems, prose and commentary. A discussion about the role of art and activism vis-à-vis academia underpinned the organizational approach to the conference itself, and this volume reflects the aim to honour creativity and variety. This book, although compiled by academics, rejects the notion that academic study is the only means of understanding and representing phenomena. Rather, the collection adopts a holistic approach that acknowledges and welcomes the contribution of the arts and activism in forging, understanding and presenting selves and issues important for the continued battle to negotiate space for Caribbean LGBTQ people and communities. Indeed, some contributors represent this intersection of the various streams (for example, activist-academics Colin Robinson and Rinaldo Walcott and poet-activist Andre Bagoo). This innovative combination is one of the strengths of this collection, similar to Thomas Glave's heterodox volume *Our Caribbean*.

The purposefully multidisciplinary approach to the expression and analysis of and reflection on LGBTQ lives and identities mirrors Caribbean LGBTQ individuals' and communities' refusal to be trapped within conventional categories and taxonomies. This volume shows that there are multiple ways of representing homophobia, gender and sexual diversity, and activism in the Caribbean, and that some of them even contradict each other. This should come as no surprise, given the very fluidity that, as we have seen, scholars and activists have highlighted.

Bookending this collection are brief pieces from two well-known Jamaican writer-poets: Thomas Glave's foreword, in which his glee and amazement at the success of and institutional support for Beyond Homophobia leap off the page, and the afterword by Kei Miller, who calls for us to honour the space of truth-telling and agency created by Beyond Homophobia. In between are four sections that represent elements of queer lived experience in the Caribbean. Practical approaches to centring the queer in daily life as well as in the context of research and the education system is the topic of the first section. The second considers artistic practice: beginning with an analysis of calypso and the sacred and ending with a discussion of dancehall and marronage, this section demonstrates the queer in creative work. This is followed, in the third section, by some examples of this creativity in poetry and prose. The final section comprises specific discussions of activism, ending with Rinaldo Walcott's keynote address at the 2017 conference.

Centring Praxis

Working together and engaging with the practicalities of praxis, Krystal Ghisyawan, Nikoli Attai, Rajanie Preity Kumar and Carla Moore consider the process of research that centres queer perspectives. Through a multi-sited approach that deals with Jamaica, Barbados, Trinidad and Tobago, Guyana, and Canada, the authors discuss researching LGBTQ issues. How can this type of research be best conducted? What is best practice for engaging with lived experiences? By confronting the myths and precon-ceived notions about conducting sexuality research in the Caribbean, ethical dilemmas posed in research and adjustments to these myths and dilemmas through methodological negotiations, the authors propose a self-reflexive, decolonial process in the interest of more honest research. The essay accounts for the types of relationships developed through interac-tions with subjects and includes considerations of vocabulary and naming as well as positionality in the strategy of participant observation and the negotiation of insider and outsider positions.

In a first step toward creating "safe, positive spaces for LGBTQ students", Carol Hordatt Gentles and Vileitha Davis-Morrison focus on the Jamaican education system. Their essay, part of a larger project to propose ways for the education system to encourage inclusivity, focuses on a revealing survey completed by Jamaican educators. Discovering that a significant proportion of teachers do not wish to work toward inclusivity of LGBTQ students, Gentles and Davis-Morrison suggest strategies for encouraging tolerance and acceptance.

Keith E. McNeal tells the story of a young Trinidadian who killed himself and the creation of an organization called the Silver Linings Foundation that engages in advocacy as well as provides safe spaces for LGBTQ Trin-bagonians. McNeal describes how people can "adapt and craft lives char-acterized by complex and dynamic experiences and perspectives", given that being out is a "privilege" that only some people pursue. Some are out and some are not or somewhere in-between, some experience homophobia more than others, and homophobia is itself complicated and contested. LGBTQ individuals in the Caribbean imagine and fashion alternative free-doms in various ways; these must be recognized because they have impor-tant implications for the achievement of social justice.

Queering the Artistic

Lyndon Gill's essay connects faith to the queer, recognizing the spiritual life of queer people and specifically the role of same sex–desiring people in the Spiritual Baptist movement. He traces the life of Calypso Rose as singer, lesbian and Spiritual Baptist Mother, demonstrating the link between the sensual and the sacred. Gill sees possibility in syncretic Christian tradi-tion. Contrary to the assumption that Christianity forbids homosexuality, a variety of practices within the Caribbean and throughout the Americas provide access to spaces of acceptance of nonconformity.

Anna Kasafi Perkins, through a discussion of Man Booker Prize-winning Jamaican author Marlon James's first novel *John Crow's Devil*, demonstrates a perspective on spirituality quite different from Gill's. As she writes, "James makes a trenchant critique of religion that mirrors his own distancing from dogmatic Christianity." Here, unlike in Gill's work, the role of spirituality in enforcing gender norms and denying the lived experiences of those who do not conform is highlighted. Obedience to faith requires adherents to deny elements of themselves and others, enforcing specific expectations and insisting on the reality of sin. Religion, however, cannot be attacked – it is immune because of the very nature of faith as well as the ways in which religion relies upon charismatic leadership.

Nick Marsellas also engages with fiction, arguing that in *Kingston by Starlight*, the author Christopher John Farley challenges the concept of Jamaica as naturally straight until "the imposition of Western queerness" in all its whiteness, thus also challenging religious, evangelical interpretations of the history of the island. Marsellas states that Farley's representations of gender ambiguity push "the more popular 'out of many, one people' version of history" beyond its familiar territory of ethnicity and into rather more dangerous terrain that questions conventional assumptions and assertions about the heterosexual, "queerphobic" imaginations of the nation.

Further challenges to monolithic notions of homophobia and LGBTQ life in the Caribbean are made by O'Neil Lawrence in his work on the homoerotic photography of Archie Lindo. Lawrence contextualizes Lindo as a photographer of his time (he worked mainly in the 1950s and 1960s) but also ahead of his time in terms of some of his experiments with the presentation of Jamaican black masculinity. Comparing Lindo's photographs with the work of other artists, Lawrence wonders about the potential connections between homoerotic and homosexual imagery in Jamaica and other locations in the diaspora. Presenting mid-twentieth century images that challenge traditional and stereotypical presentations of gender, Lawrence joins Marsellas in providing an analysis of how the queer has long existed in Jamaica.

So too does Carla Moore, who provides a perspective on the location of the queer in Jamaica by looking at queerness in the dancehall and the ways in which a space presumed to be homophobic may not in fact be as virulently so as imagined. Asking the question, "How do queerness and the dancehall (not so) secretly meet and shape each other?", Moore provides specific examples provided by queer participants in dancehall culture. There is a range of opportunities and identities available to MSM in the dancehall; Moore identifies "a type of modern-day queer marronage". The challenges to masculinity in the dancehall are plural, and Moore's enumeration of different instances of queerness allows her to see a level of liberatory possibility in spaces often considered to be irredeemably homophobic.

Telling Stories, Finding Self

Thomas Glave's prose piece also raises questions of possibility but through a revisiting and revisioning of history. Engaging with the dead and with memory, Glave asks readers to consider what it means to inherit genes from a white man – a slave owner – and how the past is always part of the present. Glave reminds us that sex, history and race are interlinked in Jamaica and that stories help us speak the memories that exist.

As a reaction to the Pulse nightclub mass shooting of 2017, Andre Bagoo asks how to connect the specific with the universal. His use of poetry not only helps him cope with this tragedy but to demonstrate the repercussions of the denial of subtextual homosexual desires.

Dorothea Smartt's poetry also focuses on denial of the homosexual, presenting blind, stubborn heterosexual desire in the face of homosexual love. Her female characters are in love, but a male character is confident in his ability to change this reality, even though the lesbian affair is accepted by the main character's family. As a story, it asserts homosexuality, it questions homophobia, but it also shows the heteronormativity at play that makes a man think it is possible to convince lesbians out of their homosexuality.

Activism and Action

Adwoa Onuora and Ajamu Nangwaya present an argument for queer activism, taking into consideration the history of this activism in Jamaica. Their perspective is that of a working-class queer agenda focused on "the fight to rid the world of class exploitation and capitalism". The authors recognize that the majority of queer individuals in Jamaica are working class, and therefore there is a need to consider a Marxist perspective. Onuora and Nangwaya suggest ways to encourage heterosexual solidarity and allyship by recognizing emancipation for one group leading to freedom for all.

With a similar desire to encourage practical action, academic and activist Colin Robinson considers how to elicit change and insists that it has to be on Caribbean LGBTQ people's own terms, based on their lived experiences, whether or not they accord with those of more powerful others. His contribution is in effect a call to action for LGBTQ movements across the region to transform and challenge assumptions about sexuality and gender.

The final paper is Rinaldo Walcott's keynote address. Speaking to the specificity of queer experience in the Caribbean, Walcott discusses the concept of *so*. As he puts it, "To be *so* was to invoke in a nondemeaning fashion that one's sexuality and gender was nonhegemonic. Thus one would hear adults refer to someone as *being so*, said in a fashion not to demean them." This speaks to a wider sense of sexual nonconformity in spaces like Barbados where queer people live in caring communities, communities that complicate and problematize perceptions of Caribbean homophobia. The concept of "being so" allows Walcott to assert a way of being outside the concept of Eurocentric humanity as enforced through colonialism. Calling for activism within the Caribbean and the diaspora that takes into consideration the specificities of Caribbean, black and African nonhetero-sexual practices and nonhegemonic gender performativity, Walcott speaks of *so* as "ontological restitution" against the names given queers, marking a collective ethical ontological condition that requires a different register of love and care, a register uniquely Caribbean.

Walcott's words provide an opportunity to consider more ideas, activism and scholarship. His call to appreciate the uniqueness of Caribbean queer-ness is also a call for more thinking through of these specific LGBTQ reali-ties. Ideally, this text will be a springboard for not just more conversation but also real action and, ultimately, greater understanding and apprecia-tion for the *being so* that is the lived experience beyond homophobia.

Notes

1. Throughout this volume a range of acronyms that are variations on LGBTQ are used. In this introduction, we have chosen to use LGBTQ, but we recognize that in different countries across the Caribbean region the standard differs based on local terminology.

2. Shaun King's tweet can be found at www.twitter.com/ShaunKing/status /942598376326971392.

3. In a victory for LGBTQ rights advocates, the Caribbean Court of Justice ruled in November 2018 that the Guyanese law criminalizing cross-dressing was unconstitutional.

4. Lewis does acknowledge exceptions to this statement, some of which are presented in Lewis (2003), specifically in the chapter "Exploring the Intersections of Gender, Sexuality and Culture in the Caribbean: An Introduction" (1–21).

5. See, for example, Kempadoo (2004), Alexander (2006), Smith (2011), Nixon (2015).

6. This is a limitation of this volume, and one that reflects the disproportionate influence of Jamaica within the Caribbean, as well as the location of the conference. The second conference boasted wider representation: from countries as northerly as Bermuda and as southerly as Brazil. The organizers have developed plans to expand the scope of future conferences.

References

Alexander, M. Jacqui. 1994. "Not Just (Any)Body Can Be a Citizen: The Politics of Law, Sexuality and Postcoloniality in Trinidad and Tobago and the Bahamas". *Feminist Review* 48:5–23.

———. 2006. *Pedagogies of Crossing: Meditations on Feminism, Sexual Politics, Memory, and the Sacred*. Durham, NC: Duke University Press.

Boyce, Paul, Elisabeth Engebretsen, and Silvia Posocco. 2017. "Introduction: Anthropology's Queer Sensibilities". *Sexualities* 21 (5–6): 843–52. doi:10.1177/1363460717706667.

Carpenter, Karen. 2017. *Interweaving Tapestries of Culture and Sexuality in the Caribbean*. London: Palgrave Macmillan.

Greene, Erin. 2012. "History of Rainbow Alliance Bahamas – Activist Report". In *Theorizing Homophobias in the Caribbean: Complexities of Place, Desire and Belonging*, edited by Rosamond King, Angelique Nixon, Colin Robinson, Natalie Bennett and Vidyaratha Kissoon. http://www.caribbeanhomophobias.org/node/6.

International Gay and Lesbian Human Rights Commission (IGLHRC) and United and Strong. 2015. "Homophobia and Transphobia in Caribbean Media: A Baseline Study in Belize, Grenada, Guyana, Jamaica and St Lucia". New York. Accessed 22 January 2020. https://unitedandstrongstlucia.files.wordpress.com /2015/08/final-baselineaugust102015-2.pdf.

Kempadoo, Kamala. 2004. *Sexing the Caribbean: Gender, Race and Sexual Labour*. New York: Routledge.

———. 2009. "Caribbean Sexuality: Mapping the Field". *Caribbean Review of Gender Studies* 3:1–24.

King, Rosamond. 2014. *Island Bodies: Transgressive Sexualities in the Caribbean Imagination*. Gainesville: University Press of Florida.

King, Rosamond, and Angelique Nixon. 2012. Introduction to *Theorizing Homophobias in the Caribbean: Complexities of Place, Desire and Belonging*, edited by Rosamond King, Angelique Nixon, Colin Robinson, Natalie Bennett and Vidyaratha Kissoon. http://www.caribbeanhomophobias.org/node/6.

King, Rosamond, Angelique Nixon, Colin Robinson, Natalie Bennett and Vidyaratha Kissoon, eds. 2012. *Theorizing Homophobias in the Caribbean: Complexities of Place, Desire and Belonging*. http://www.caribbeanhomophobias .org/node/6.

LaFont, Suzanne. 2009. "Not Quite Redemption Song: LGBT-Hate in Jamaica". In *Homophobias: Lust and Loathing across Time and Space*, edited by David Murray, 105–22. Durham, NC: Duke University Press.

La Fountain-Stokes, Lawrence. 2009. *Queer Ricans: Cultures and Sexualities in the Diaspora.* Minneapolis: University of Minnesota Press.

Laguerre, Steve. 2012. "LGBT Activism in Haiti Through SEROvie – Interview with Angelique V. Nixon". In *Theorizing Homophobias in the Caribbean: Complexities of Place, Desire and Belonging,* edited by Rosamond King, Angelique Nixon, Colin Robinson, Natalie Bennett and Vidyaratha Kissoon. http://www.caribbeanhomophobias.org/node/6.

Lewis, Linden, ed. 2003. *The Culture of Gender and Sexuality in the Caribbean.* Gainesville: University Press of Florida.

Moore, Carla. 2014. "Wah Eye Nuh See, Heart Nuh Leap: Queer Marronage in the Jamaican Dancehall". Master's thesis, Queen's University, Kingston, Ontario.

Murray, David. 2002. *Opacity: Gender, Sexuality, Race, and the "Problem" of Identity in Martinique.* New York: Peter Lang.

———. 2009a. "Bajan Queens, Nebulous Scenes: Sexual Diversity in Barbados". *Caribbean Review of Gender Studies* 3:1–20.

———. 2009b. "Spectral Sexuality and the Good Citizen in Barbadian Media". In *Homophobias: Lust and Loathing across Time and Space,* edited by David Murray, 146–61. Durham, NC: Duke University Press.

Nixon, Angelique V. 2015. *Resisting Paradise: Tourism, Diaspora and Sexuality in the Caribbean.* Jackson: University of Mississippi Press.

Padgett, Tim. 2006. "The Most Homophobic Place on Earth?" *Time.* http://content.time.com/time/world/article/0,8599,1182991,00.html.

Padilla, Mark. 2007. *Caribbean Pleasure Industry: Tourism, Sexuality, and AIDS in the Dominican Republic.* Chicago: University of Chicago Press.

Puar, Jasbir. 2007. *Terrorist Assemblages: Homonationalism in Queer Times.* Durham, NC: Duke University Press.

Ramírez, Rafael. 2003. "Masculinity and Power in Puerto Rico". In *Culture of Gender and Sexuality in the Caribbean,* edited by Linden Lewis, 234–50. Gainesville: University Press of Florida.

Robinson, Colin. 2012. "The Work of Three-Year Old Caiso – Reflections at the MidPoint: Activist Report (Trinidad and Tobago)". In *Theorizing Homophobias in the Caribbean: Complexities of Place, Desire and Belonging,* edited by Rosamond King, Angelique Nixon, Colin Robinson, Natalie Bennett and Vidyaratha Kissoon. http://www.caribbeanhomophobias.org/node/6.

Schleifer, Rebecca. 2004. *Hated to Death: Homophobia, Violence and Jamaica's HIV/AIDS Epidemic.* New York: Human Rights Watch.

Shange, Savannah. 2012. "Mediated (Be)Longing: Consumer Citizenship and Queer Caribbean Diaspora". In *Theorizing Homophobias in the Caribbean: Complexities of Place, Desire and Belonging,* edited by Rosamond King, Angelique Nixon, Colin Robinson, Natalie Bennett, and Vidyaratha Kissoon. http://www.caribbeanhomophobias.org/node/6.

Smith, Faith, ed. 2011. *Sex and the Citizen: Interrogating the Caribbean.* Charlottesville: University of Virginia Press.

Tinsley, Omise'eke N. 2010. *Thiefing Sugar: Eroticism between Women in Caribbean Literature.* Durham, NC: Duke University Press.

————. 2011. "What Is a *Uma?* Women Performing Gender and Sexuality in Paramaribo, Suriname". In *Sex and the Citizen: Interrogating the Caribbean,* edited by Faith Smith, 241–25. Charlottesville: University of Virginia Press.

Wekker, Gloria. 2006. *Politics of Passion: Women's Sexual Culture in the Afro-Surinamese Diaspora.* New York: Columbia University Press.

West, Keon, and Miles Hewstone. 2012. "Culture and Contact in the Promotion and Reduction of Anti-Gay Prejudice: Evidence from Jamaica and Britain". *Journal of Homosexuality* 59 (1): 44–66.

Part 1.

Centring Praxis

1.

Tales from the Field
Myths and Methodologies for Researching
Same Sex–Desiring People in the Caribbean

NIKOLI ATTAI, K. NANDINI GHISYAWAN, RAJANIE PREITY KUMAR
AND CARLA MOORE

The Caribbean region has been framed by the Global North as dangerous and "unsafe" for queer people, and much of the discourse produced about homophobia has fixed queer subjects as dying and at-risk of dying in their homelands because of their aberrant practices and desires. Caribbean feminist researchers Kamala Kempadoo and Halimah DeShong (2013, 1) suggest that research on gender and sexualities within the Caribbean must be "grounded in Caribbean cultural, social, or political experiences" in order to think more critically about people's nuanced and multiple realities. While Caribbean feminist research shares a number of objectives with Western feminism(s), including different methods, what makes Caribbean feminist research distinct is its evolution out of Caribbean epistemologies. Regardless of the method(s) used in our own individual research, as researchers both inside and outside of the region we have grounded our work in the specificities of Caribbean history and experiences. We are also attentive to the fact that "[t]he field is not a pre-existing thing that we go to, but it is something we define. It is something that we make through our interactions with participants, and in a collaborative defining of boundaries. By saying 'okay this is what I am going to research, and these are the people I am interested in meeting', we set the field up as a space" (Ghisyawan, Roundtable, January 2017; hereafter cited as "Roundtable").

This chapter is formulated from a roundtable discussion of the same title presented at the Beyond Homophobia conference in Mona, Jamaica, January 2017. Utilizing qualitative research methods, including interviews, participant observation and subjective mapping, each discussant in this roundtable had conducted research on same-sex/gender desire in a Caribbean territory where sodomy acts, read as homosexual acts, were outlawed at the time of the fieldwork being conducted.[1] We collaborated to explore common themes emerging from our respective work, particularly the methodological challenges posed by having to negotiate misconceptions of the field, such as the depiction of the region as violent and unsafe for same sex–loving people, the labelling or naming of these groups of people, the need for self-reflexivity in research practice, and ethical responsibilities in the field. Beginning with a brief summary of our individual work in different sites in the Caribbean, we reflect on the various myths about homophobia in the Caribbean and our different methodological approaches to navigating these issues in diverse research sites.

Our Work

In 2012 Carla Moore interviewed three same gender–desiring men who are a part of Jamaica's dancehall culture to find out how they bridged the separation between black Jamaican-ness, which theoretically should never be queer, and queerness, which is theoretically read as white. She realized that while same-gender desire was not new to Jamaica, LGBTQ identity politics was. More than that, straight and same gender–desiring black Caribbean sexualities, especially the kind put on display in the dancehall, were always already queer in that they did not or could not conform to white heteronormative expectations of the right way to do sex and gender. Moore pinpoints this as the context in which Jamaica's notorious homophobia arises.

Work pertaining to Jamaican homophobia and same-gender desire (in this case queerness as out-of-the-closet same-gender desire) often positions the queer body in one of two ways: dying in Jamaica (and/or dying to leave Jamaica by any means necessary) or thriving in the diaspora (in particular Global North refugee havens such as Canada and the Netherlands). These narratives reify the idea of queerness and Jamaican-ness as incompatible and the queer body as a white body or a body located in an ideologically white space. They also ignore the important work done by local queers to survive and delegitimize survival techniques premised on staying in rather than getting out. This gives rise to what Moore (2012) calls homohegemony, in which white, queer liberalism serves a neocolonizing function by instructing Global South and Third World countries on the right way to be queer.

Similar to Moore, Nikoli Attai's "decidedly happy critiques" of queer liberation politics in the Caribbean speak back to the deleterious discourses of queerness and queer liberation in white academia, by white and diaspora NGO elites, and some Caribbean advocates located within and outside the region. His multi-sited research over the last five years (in Jamaica, Guyana, Barbados, and Trinidad and Tobago) has been geared toward, first, interrogating these problematic narratives, and second, privileging the alternative ways that nonheterosexual people have been resisting phobias and reimagining autonomy, citizenship and belonging. He explores the stakes of using the logic of dying, or as Moore puts it, "dying to leave", to liberate bullers;[2] how trans people create communities of exile in the Caribbean and specifically in Trinidad, a development that disrupts the allure of "safe havens" like Canada, the United States and the Netherlands; and how Trinidad and Tobago's carnival provides a useful space for gay Caribbean men to resist the tenets of heteromasculinity as they actively participate in it, create space for themselves and maintain connections with each other.

Rajanie Preity Kumar and K. Nandini Ghisyawan both work with same sex–desiring women, in Guyana and Trinidad and Tobago, respectively, starting from the question of how manifestations of heteronormativity and heteropatriarchy in family, religion, legal systems, education systems and media shape the lives of these women.

Ghisyawan's project entitled "Queering Cartographies of Caribbean Sexuality and Citizenship: Mapping Female Same-Sex Desire, Identity and Belonging in Trinidad" (2016), shows how same sex–loving women refashion notions of Caribbeanness, sexual identity and citizenship through their discursive navigations of heteronormativity and same-sex desire to produce "queer safe spaces". This research sought to challenge the invisibility of female same-sex desire in the region, particularly in Trinidad, and to reassert this desire into the contexts from which it has been actively erased by colonial heteronormative power structures and discourses, such as religion and ethnic nationalisms. This project connects the spatial and the social, incorporating subjective mapping exercises as a decolonial queer methodological tool that can reveal about the place and position of same sex–loving women, their same-sex desire and their agency in Trinidadian society, and the ways in which their practices engage with and challenge colonial and neocolonial discourses pertaining to Caribbean femininities, genders and sexualities.

Although beginning from the same point of inquiry, Kumar's work focuses on the ways in which sociocultural attitudes of Guyanese women's sex and sexuality may or may not exist in tension with current LGBT discourses, human rights and movements flowing from the Global North. Her multi-sited ethnography examines Berbice (rural) and Georgetown (urban), focusing on four key areas: (1) questions of home, (2) the urban-rural binary as it intersects with religious, racial and class backgrounds to impact sexual practices, (3) women's experiences and continuums of violence, and (4) queer activism and citizenship. She also pays attention to how Guyanese women enact resistance and carve out alternative ways of existing and belonging.

(Re)Thinking Violence

As noted in our introduction, the Caribbean is often imagined by the Global North as a space that is inherently dangerous and unsafe for queer subjects and researchers. This has resulted in producing a homophobic narrative that queer subjects are either dying in their countries or dying to leave their nation for "safer" life in the North. As a result of this narrative, a second misconception has led to the Caribbean being conceptualized as a site that is also unsafe for researchers to conduct research. Moore notes, "When I started my research my mother told me that they go kill me cause she's like 'this is the most unsafe research that any human has tried to do' and 'why will you try to do it?'" (Roundtable).

This perception of an unsafe region is largely perpetuated by rights discourses disseminated through extensive human rights campaigns about discrimination, homophobic legislation, HIV and AIDS and the precarious existence of at-risk groups like trans sex workers and same sex–desiring men. Places like Toronto have become a hub for these interventions and have produced powerful and problematic material to emphasize Canada's "*obligations* to protect human rights and to provide a sanctuary for people fleeing persecution due to their sexual orientation, gender identity or gender expression" (Canada Research Team 2015, 10; emphasis added). Such politics diverts attention from the more complicated realities in the countries that we study, but as our collective research and findings indicate, activists and groups, researchers inside and outside of the region and our participants often resist and disrupt this narrative. In defining our fields of research, we deliberately refuse to portray the Caribbean as homogeneously homophobic and destructive for same sex–loving and gender-nonconforming people. Our research projects show Caribbean space as nuanced and complicated, and as one that fosters diversity and resilience.

Violence, including homophobic violence, is systemic and unavoidable. However, both research participants and researchers have actively negotiated threats to safety in creative ways. For the subjective mapping exercises used in Ghisyawan's research, she asked participants to draw a map of where they felt safe to express themselves regarding their sexuality. This activity engages the idea of the constancy of violence by raising questions of safety and thus the inverse: danger. The women exhibited what Zygmunt Bauman (2006, 3) refers to as "derivative fear", or the fear of being susceptible and vulnerable to danger even without the presence of a direct threat. Dangers and threats to safety ranged from discomfort around certain family members, ostracism from religious communities, hateful rhetoric in various community spaces including religious and political arenas, to fears of confrontation and physical altercations in public spaces. Participants spoke of explicit acts of interpersonal violence that they had dealt with, mainly citing sexual assaults in early childhood to more recent incidents of rape (Ghisyawan 2013). The women felt these attacks were not directly related to their sexual orientation given the time and manner in which they occurred, yet acknowledged that violence was pervasive and discursive, making spaces "safe enough" some of the time (Ghisyawan 2016). In drawing the maps, some participants struggled to identify safe spaces and opted instead to draw the spaces they felt were particularly unsafe. One participant, Sandy, mused over the exercise, calling it "interesting", adding "maybe 'nowhere' will be my response, but I will draw something for you". "You don't want to be lesbian Krystal. You might as well kill yourself. It very fucked up, especially in the Caribbean. Maybe I don't want to be in the Caribbean, period. I should draw that," Sandy said as she started drawing what looked like walls (Ghisyawan 2016).

Another assumption is that researchers will adversely affect the field of research or harm participants through their research practices but are themselves exempt from violence because of their prestigious title, their resources and supposed location outside of the field. But as mentioned earlier, often researchers simultaneously inhabit insider and outsider positions to their field of work that can leave them vulnerable to threats from within and outside of the research sites. Kumar's encounters with violence in the field reveal the ways in which gendered and sexual violence is insidious, present everywhere and inescapable within the heteronormative patriarchal structure of Guyana. A common preconceived idea is that violence occurs "out there" somewhere in public as a result of interacting with sexual- and gender-nonconforming Guyanese women or from being seen in a public space with them (expanded on below). Yet Kumar's experiences of violence in the field occurred within the walls of her living accommodations. In Berbice, Kumar experienced sexual advances from a male family friend, blurring not only the familial boundaries but violating her personal safety and space. Another moment of experiencing violence in the field was discovering that her Georgetown landlord had murdered his wife and buried her underneath Kumar's flat. In both of these settings, Kumar felt unsafe and was forced to seek alternative living accommodations in order to find personal safety during her fieldwork.

If we only presume that violence will be encountered specifically within one field or site, or only when in contact with sexual minorities, then we miss the critical and nuanced ways in which violence is already present, embodied and existing in other sites in the field. For this reason, Moore acknowledges that researchers must always (re)think how they can ensure a safe and productive environment for themselves and their research participants:

> If you have done one interview anywhere in public media, and people now know that you do research on queerness, then just being seen with you is an indictment. Because you mix up with the girl that do the sup'm with de gay ting! Right? So where do you meet them, and that's one of the hardest things I had to navigate, is figuring out just how to get space, right? . . . For me that whole issue of where to do the interview and my own safety, but also because I was pretty visible before I started doing this research; how to keep people safe when they had to be seen talking with me and when there was no actually perceivable reason to be talking to me other than this? (Roundtable)

A useful approach adopted by Attai to ensure safety and comfort during research interactions has been to meet participants "where they are", in environments where they are comfortable to interact and speak. This sometimes means visiting the spaces and places that research participants occupy. For example, researchers may find it more useful to meet trans women at or close to their homes, or in the places that they socialize like during drag pageant rehearsals or at night in clubs or other areas where they party. This was the case for an interview conducted with Monique, a trans woman from east Trinidad; she felt safe in a small park close to her home early in the morning before her neighbours began moving about. As Attai noted during the roundtable, "I remember Monique telling me that she had just started taking hormone replacements so her body was changing. She did not like to be out during the day, but when she had to, she would move around early, before 10:00 a.m. Monique was comfortable in her small working-class neighbourhood because she knew most of the people there and felt unthreatened by their opinions of her trans-ness" (Roundtable).

Even when much of the stigma and discrimination is internalized, it is important for researchers to be mindful that their respondents' perceptions of their safety are as important as the actual threat, and take necessary steps to meet their participants where they are at, as suggested by Attai. It is equally important that researchers as well, both inside and outside of the region, be cognizant of their location, the ways in which they navigate personal boundaries and feelings of unsafety, especially when violence is manifested subtly. This is especially applicable in the region where there is little state protection or recourse for people at the receiving end of discrimination and violence.

Naming the Field: "Queering"

In many of the islands, we hear these stories about "yeah it always had one". So in my community we had bullerman Matthew. He served as this reminder of what I couldn't be, or what young men in the area couldn't be. I wasn't really effeminate, but playing with dollies growing up is like "oh you will come out like bullerman Matthew". So growing up with girls or not being able to play sports or not liking sports, there was always this reminder that you may become like bullerman Matthew if you don't change your ways. I remember once my cousin, she went to a prestigious Catholic girls' high school, was always transported to school and stuff. One day she had to travel and she bounce up bullerman Matthew on the road walking, and she jumps in a drain and hide because she was afraid of what bullerman Matthew would have done. And that was the kind of imagery that we grew up with in our community of what we couldn't become. . . . So getting into my research I always went in with this appreciation, that I need to meet people where they are, understand how you identify, what you feel comfortable as and stuff . . . even in academia you will hardly see people using the terms that gays use. So for instance, in my work I privilege the use of these once derogatory terms like *bullerman* and *panty man*, because what I've found is that a lot of the people in the communities flip these terms on their head and use it as markers of endearment . . . so you'd hear gay men in Trinidad saying things like "big bullerman like me, you cyar come round me"; it means something to them. (Attai, Roundtable)

As Attai notes, naming practices in the region are situated within larger histories of sexual difference where there are implicit and explicit attitudes toward people who exhibit non-normative sexual and gender traits. The challenge of academia and activism today is naming these groups that were either unnamed or referred to with derogatory terms like "bullerman" and "panty man". Much of the work done by activists and academics in anglophone regions has relied heavily on a received language, like LGBTQI and MSM, adopted globally by North American and European queer movements and large international human rights agencies like the United Nations. While terms like these are useful for identifying a group of people who describe themselves as such, they "produce and police sexuality on singular terms forcing sexual minorities into a one size fits all model" (Walcott 2015, viii). Even the concept of "queerness" as both a language and set of practices is often uncritically understood to be universal and applicable in the same manner across all contexts and locations. But naming has implications for practices of state and nongovernmental agencies, for media and public dialogue, for activists and academics, in that it shapes their manners of relating to these different groups (in legislation, discourse, representation and other means of interaction). In resisting the homogenizing tendencies of queerness, we outline the complicated politics and practices of "naming" in the field, including our mobilizations of "queer" and "queerness".

In our work we think critically about the violence that is enacted through naming or withholding a name from groups in the Caribbean. We also privilege the development of a language that is reflective of the people with whom we conduct research in the field. How do we meet people "where they are"? How do we appreciate the ways that they identify and understand themselves? And quite frankly, how do we use the terms that our research participants use to describe themselves? Caribbean feminist academics Angelique Nixon and Rosamond King gesture toward developing "embodied theories" supported by "local knowledge(s)" because "[l] abels [like LGBT and MSM] are inaccurate; at worst, they enact an epistemic violence upon Caribbean subjects by denying their own agency to name and define (or not name or define) themselves and/or their behavior. . . . It is important to consider how people name themselves and describe their own behavior, as well as expressions found in regionally specific language" (King and Nixon 2013, 9).

King and Nixon's work, along with other Caribbean feminist work, has been seminal in highlighting the centrality of research participants' autonomy as they actively manoeuvre and resist prevailing normativity. We frame our politics, following Mimi Sheller's (2012, 3–4) reasoning, through a "far more savvy contextualization of when, how, and where subaltern subjects appear, [or] are silenced", to document the experiences of same sex and same gender–loving men and women, trans and gender fluid people, and people who may call themselves "bullers" and "hoes", "zami" and other wide-ranging terms.

Moore's research in Jamaica provides a concrete example of the importance of "naming" the field, especially in situations where researchers need to construct a language that is reflective of local realities. This, she posits, is reflective of the longstanding absence of an indigenous language for queer experiences. While terms like LGBTQI and MSM have been popularized in the island (and region), they have produced a discourse about types of behaviours and remain bounded by a complicated medicalized history that presents the region as an HIV/AIDS capital of the world. Andil Gosine (2004, 60) argues that "queerness cannot be confined to limiting acronyms like LGBTQI", because "histor[ies] and all other possibilit[ies are] surrendered to the supposed superiority of the western (specifically, Anglo-American) model[s]" imported through development and human rights work. At the time of Moore's (2012) research, other self-identifying terms like "queer" were not being taken up in Jamaica and, therefore, felt unnatural to spaces and places like the dancehall where a heteronormative performance of masculinity informed her queer research participants' aesthetics. Having continuously grappled with the importance of defining the population, she has discovered that it is more useful to adopt descriptive terms like "same-gender desiring" in order to avoid requiring individuals to take up labels or identify with problematic frameworks. This helps us address what has been happening on the ground for years – people having sex with whom they are having sex. Their lives and identities are not shaped by these praxes, but rather remain a matter of whom they desire.

Unlike Moore, Ghisyawan has adopted the term "same-sex loving" in order to emphasize the visibility and experiences of women as female bodies that love each other, how they present themselves across spaces, how they are read in these spaces, and how they live and embody this nonhegemonic desire. Borrowing from Kamala Kempadoo (2009, 2), Ghisyawan interrogates how a focus on same sex–loving praxes "capture[s] the way in which sexuality is made visible through behaviours, activities and interactions between people, in relations, and in the ways in which desires are actualized".

Similarly, Kumar's naming of the field and her participants sits uncomfortably within two domains. She mobilizes the indigenous language of "women who love women" as an analytic to mark out the distinctions between gender and sexual nonconformativity in women's praxis (Kempadoo 2009), while on the other hand, recognizing the ways in which other participants have adopted "LGBT" as a way to also describe their sexual practices. In addition to self-identified terminology, Kumar argues that in our desire to embrace local languages and histories, we must also be open to and speak of the tensions that arise within our work and in the process of naming. Therefore, critical attention must be paid to the ways in which intersections of family, age, class, ethnicity and location factor into how a participant names themselves.

Attai identifies a similar discomfort in naming his research participants and argues for the need to understand people's nuanced, multivalent lives. He privileges the use of localized terms adopted by queer people themselves in order to theorize their capacity to disrupt dominant hegemony. For example, it is important to understand how many gay Trinidadian men use terms like "bullerman" and "ho" as markers of identity. Terms like these have generally been used pejoratively to signal a failed masculinity and the unbecoming practice of undesirable penetrative anal sex, which is akin to the degrading framing of jamettes and sketels in Caribbean societies (King 2014). Instead, bullers and hoes have reclaimed and reworked the terms as markers of endearment and as a mechanism of claiming alternative forms of citizenship and belonging in Trinidadian society. Ghisyawan (2016) explores these dynamics in her work on same-sex love in the Caribbean and theorizes how these terms are not necessarily identity categories but rather names of same sex–loving practices (11).

In our work, we offer these terms to describe the field. While we appreciate their value, we argue that researchers must exercise due diligence when adopting them to speak about populations that they are a part of representing. But what does it mean to be able to interact with and write about self-identified bullers, trans people, or same sex/gender–desiring people without making them targets of violence in their communities and countries? How do we ensure that our work adds valuable insight about the real concerns of these communities without infantilizing them or at worst, encouraging homophobic backlash? How do we ensure that the terms we use do not replicate the baggage associated with those terms? While we attempt to address some of these questions in our self-reflexivity section, we continue to grapple with these questions as we move forward with our work.

Our Positionality: Self-Reflexive Praxis in the Field

Over the years, organizers, activists and researchers have elected to use terms like "LGBT" and "MSM" while tackling issues like HIV/AIDS, buggery laws and homophobia in the region. Additionally, valuable funding opportunities provided by local and foreign interventions have dictated the ways that queer populations are imagined. They also fail to take into account how "numerous systems of oppression interact to regulate and police most people's lives" (Cohen 1997, 441). Or, as Caribbean academic Amar Wahab (2012, 50) emphasizes, "in Western liberal formations, dominant LGBTQ activism echoes a bourgeois brand of styling, seeking to incorporate itself into the public via the dominant discursive register of respectability (the responsible gay citizen)". Researchers, especially those who receive academic and administrative support from outside the region, must therefore be cognizant of the ways that their work can further homogenize otherwise diverse sets of realities and experiences that have been normalized by a largely white, elitist, gay, male, queer political agenda emanating from the Global North.

As a researcher, self-reflexivity is the process of constantly acknowledging one's identities and positionalities within research dynamics and one's relationship with the field. Writing on her fieldwork experience in Suriname with Creole mati women, Wekker (2006, 4) notes that "it is the person of the researcher, which serves as the most central and sensitive instrument of research, it behooves us to be transparent, accountable and reflexive about the different modalities in which the self engages with others". As researchers trained at various Canadian institutions, we are aware of our relationship to the region, as citizens and nationals, but also as diasporic subjects with the privilege of institutional support and external resources. We are also aware of how our age, gender expression, sex and sexual orientation, socioeconomic class and location mediate our interactions in the field, the relationships we create with people, the ways we define the field and the ways we conduct qualitative research.

Qualitative research has been critiqued by positivist traditions for being highly subjective in nature. However, from a transnational feminist standpoint, the opportunity for extensive self-reflexivity helps researchers of queer Caribbean sexuality produce scholarship that is attentive to the power dynamics that mediate the field. This attention to the researcher's and participant's roles as active knowledge producers works to deepen our analyses. While qualitative work like ours is not committed to quantifying experiences, our investments remain focused on "aspects of everyday physical life, the disavowed, and abject (low class, low life, low brow, low down) that are usually excluded from the 'high' political realm (high class, high politics, high minded, high and mighty)" (Sheller 2012, 24). This type of research tries to capture the voices and perspectives of the oft-excluded and near-invisible (King 2014).

This is especially important when researchers themselves share similarities with the populations and theorize from an emic perspective. As Attai shared:

> I mean I am reflecting and thinking about the respectability politics in the Caribbean, in Trinidad and how we kind of distance ourselves from "these people", and even coming into my own, as . . . I mean I don't even know what I am, or according to one of my research participants, I am LGBTO, everything other than dem, I in everything right . . . so, I mean I'm very kind of uncomfortable around this naming . . . what am I? (Roundtable)

Speaking about naming the groups being researched, Attai noted that his own sexual fluidity poses additional responsibilities for his representing the group as an insider-participant-researcher, but also for negotiating what Wekker (2006, 15) refers to as the "erotic equation in field work". Through her mati relationship with Juliette Cummings, her main research partici- pant, Wekker privileges the complex, multilayered creation of knowledge fostered by their interactions (22). These investments reveal the ways in which researchers' relationships to participants are never objective, stable and free from sexual and emotional intimacy. By acknowledging this, researchers are able to present scholarship that is relatable, involving real identities and praxes that must navigate the complexities of researcher/ participant dynamics.

Self-reflexive praxis is often a messy and disruptive process, as it forces researchers to confront their subjective positioning and the power dynamics that influence interactions in the field. Power differentials are inevitable and inherent in every research process, and researchers must address these disparities and name their own subjective positions (that is, racial, gender, sexual, class, etc.). Moore mentioned this in reference to the treatment of the working class as somehow inarticulate around issues of sexuality and gender: "[It] comes back to this idea that somehow middle-class and upper-class same gender–desiring Jamaicans would be more comfortable with themselves somehow, or would have thought about themselves more and be in an ideological space where they could actually articulate their experience, whereas people from low-income backgrounds can't because they just never thought about it and don't know enough about themselves to talk about themselves, right?" (Roundtable).

There is epistemic violence in denying that working- and lower-class sexual and gender-nonconforming individuals who have varying capaci- ties to name, understand and speak of their experiences. While they may not use academic language, they can represent themselves in in-depth and interesting ways that reflect their social experiences. There have been limited representations of female same-sex desire in Caribbean sexuality studies but when addressed (as with Wekker [2006] or Tinsley [2010]) the focus has been on working-class women. Ghisyawan and Kumar both deliberately include women of the upper working class, of the middle and upper classes, and Indo-Caribbean women who are "near invisible" in this literature.

Research also offers the researcher an opportunity to build rapport with participants by sharing their own experiences. Attai acknowledged that while conducting research with trans and gender-nonconforming people in Trinidad and Tobago in 2016, research participants were often interested in the topics being investigated and sought the chance to ask questions and share concerns. For example, after interviewing Amanda Glasscock, a research participant, about his experience in local drag queen pageants, Glasscock cautiously asked, "So I could ask you a lil questions too?", since for him it was also a learning experience. This simple exchange points to the importance of qualitative work on and for queer populations, especially when the "third world [subject] is denied voice in narratives of queer sexual encounter" (Allen 2011, 173).

In addition to these opportunities to gather thick data, these interactions constantly require researchers to openly accept how their location in the field affects the data collection process. For instance, while Kumar's subjective positions of being Guyanese, racialized Indian/East Indian, queer and young operated to situate her as an "insider" in the community in Guyana helped her establish rapport with some women, they also hindered data collection with other participants who perceived her social characteristics as differences. Her additional positions of being a diasporic Guyanese living in Toronto, having limited connections to the queer community in Guyana, and generally being perceived as being really young simultaneously marked her as an outsider and influenced the ways in which women responded to her. Sometimes these responses were dismissive as when women in Berbice and Georgetown were apprehensive about her interactions with them, while in other instances their interest was too keen.

Kumar reflected on this issue in the context of safety and meeting participants in the field: "[A] participant, after the interview invited me out to a BBQ spot and I agreed to go. However, in the car I started to realize not only was I alone with her and her driver, but I had no idea where we were going, how far out of the city it was and how safe I felt for myself" (Roundtable). This dynamic is important to note because, as Wekker (2006, 4) reminds us, "both researcher and the people involved are subject, active agents with their own emotions and agendas".

Ethical Responsibilities of Researchers Working with Same Sex–Desiring People

At moments she would touch my hand or reach out to pull me closer, but I wouldn't reciprocate with the touches. I wanted things to be clear between us, but I also knew that here I was socializing with a participant. I know that I haven't hung out with anyone to this extent. I am not attracted to her or anything, but I knew I didn't want her to think that I was interested in her. I wonder if she was intentionally flirting with me . . . or if I am reading too much into these interactions between us. (Kumar, Roundtable)

What are the ethical responsibilities of the researcher in the field? Who decides on these responsibilities? What is/are the relationship(s) that we are building with participants in the field? Where and how does the researcher define the boundaries between one's self and a participant? What are the parameters when it comes to intimacy, sex, desire, attraction and power in the field? For Caribbean researchers returning from the diaspora, issues of power loom large in considerations of ethical responsibility: How did our position[s], funding support, even the option of leaving the country if the research created complications, impact our positions in relation to our subjects? How do we navigate that safely? Beyond that, how do we mind, ignore or postpone sexual and romantic interests that arise in research with peers? How can we engage in these highly charged conversations with our participants, community members and academic communities? In this section, we turn toward these inevitable experiences that take place in our fieldwork, while recognizing and acknowledging that we are all still working through the tensions that arise.

The power exercised by research participants can also result in uncomfortable and unsafe situations, especially when participants expect additional favours beyond agreed-upon remuneration. Ghisyawan mentioned being propositioned by potential research participants who wanted to trade a date/lime for an interview. Below she describes how she negotiated attraction in the field:

> So one way I kind of negotiated that was by delaying the sexual activity and my relationship with the person, becoming friends . . . yuh know, not (kinda) let it be about the sex because I did want to remain objective – as mythical as objectivity is – but I wanted to keep the boundaries there until at least I felt like I could bring down my own walls, own boundaries. At the time when I was doing this research, I wasn't open [about my sexuality]; I was still coming out and people would ask, "How do you identify?" At that time I was still navigating my bi-curiousness, my bisexuality and my queerness so that was not something that I was ready to fall into . . . but rather I had to come to, later on around what my sexual boundaries are while doing this research. (Ghisyawan, Roundtable)

As Ghisyawan was still exploring and understanding her own sexuality, she continued to be reserved about forming sexual relationships with research participants, even if this meant not having access to those women and their stories. Instead of focusing attention on individual women, Ghisyawan felt building relationships with communities of women would be a more effective strategy to gain participants, while simultaneously building rapport, strengthening ties to the community and gaining legitimacy as an authoritative voice. An important part of this process is allowing the community to speak for itself and not imposing our own words, perceptions or assumptions.

While learning how to do ethnography we are taught that we read, research and formulate research and interview questions, planning an entire path of study before setting foot in the field. But it is important to recognize that the field is a lived space and thus subject to change, making your prior research projects outdated. We are working with groups that have barely been studied, thus limited information exists that explores the complexities of these research sites. To be able to properly learn in the field, Moore found it necessary to keep the conversation going and allow space for people to say the things they wanted to say when they wanted to say them:

> Okay I am sharing a two hour with you on Wednesday afternoon at 4:00 p.m., yuh said everything you can say in that two-hour interview between 4:00 and 6:00 p.m. . . . next week yuh send me a text message "umm yuh know actually what I remember is the following" ok, I put it in. . . . "Actually I don't want yuh to mention that I said X and Y cause it's an interview", so to keep that conversation going and to make it clear to people that "no I am not here to do a one-time interview with yuh and move on and meh done with yuh forever, I'm trying to build a relationship wid yuh here" that was something that was really important for me. This work is about trying to put the Caribbean person in Caribbean studies, is what I am trying to do. (Roundtable)

Interviews and data collection were thus more discursive and collaborative, happening over the course of several meetings and conversations, rather than just within a single interview. This building of ties within the community also allowed us to identify participants through referrals and word of mouth. This had both drawbacks and advantages. For Ghisyawan, referrals meant that the women in her group were very similar to each other in many ways (social class, level of education, spaces they inhabited), yet they differed in other ways, such as their racial or religious backgrounds. Similarly, Attai noted the tendency for "particular types of respondents [to] end up coming forward", especially when approaching the community through an organization. Attai's strategy was to

> meet people where they are, so that they are comfortable, they are in their environment and we talk and stuff. And most times, they aren't worried about saying things that would offend the referring organization, or, you know they feel that

they are speaking to themselves. So in my experience, especially in this last research project, a lot of the people that I met, where they are – especially like going to the parties, hanging out with them and then eventually gaining their trust to strike up a conversation and take it from there – I find that most times, those interactions are a bit more organic . . . so yes definitely come lime with us, spend time, mmm . . . don't necessarily feel the need to ask any questions too quick. Just become part of the community as best as possible. (Roundtable)

To maintain the integrity of our research materials, it is essential that we recognize and acknowledge how sexual behaviours and praxis function in binding the communities we work with, whether this was dancing and flirting at parties, engaging in sexual banter and humour, bringing one's partners to social events (or meeting someone there), or in other ways showing oneself to be a sexual being. Complete abstention from engaging in some form of sexual praxis could constrain how one was integrated into the community and so conveying an openness about the matters being discussed strengthens the perceptions research participants have of you, the researcher. Showing oneself as able to relate to their experiences and interests without the threat of the researcher being judgemental is part of "meeting people where they are".

Conclusion: Transforming Research Practices

In an attempt to create anticolonial narratives of gender and sexualities, Wekker (2006) has argued if colonial accounts of gender and sexuality are based on a Euro-American framework, then anticolonial narratives must expose not only the effects of such representations, but also decentre the "authoritative" voice speaking about "the Other" to allow "the Other" to actively speak of their own experiences. Informed by this line of thinking, this chapter pivots on three key concepts: the myths and preconceived notions about conducting sexuality research in the Caribbean, ethical dilemmas posed in our research and our adjustments to these myths and dilemmas through methodological negotiations. Our discussion of these issues demonstrates the ways in which these limitations and issues are interconnected, but also how they stem from epistemological oversights or omissions. Throughout this chapter we engaged questions that emerged in our research but also the collaborative work of developing the panel and this chapter. While we do not answer all our questions here, we challenge ourselves and other researchers to question standard research practice and ask how a self-reflexive, decolonial research process can produce more honest research.

Notes

1. On 12 April 2018, Justice Devindra Rampersad of the High Court of Justice in Trinidad and Tobago ruled that the sodomy laws (sections 13 and 16 of the Sexual Offences Act) were unconstitutional. On 20 September 2018, Justice Rampersad amended the laws to make consensual sex between people of the same sex legal. In Jamaica, Barbados and Guyana, the other field sites, these acts remain criminalized.

2. Terms like *buller*, *bullerman*, *battyman* (referring to men who have sex with men) and *zami* (women who have sex with women) are typically uttered in the pejorative to assert queer people's Otherness, to mobilize tropes of disease, discrimination and death that confront queers across the region. However, many queer Caribbean people have also reclaimed them as markers of endearment to embody their nonconformity, and negotiate and resist dominant gender and sexual hegemonies over time. Attai invokes the term "buller" to reclaim the sexual and gender praxes that are made to appear threatened by prevailing homophobia, and to call attention to the fact that there exists a Caribbean where queer people have actualized various forms of erotic autonomy over time, have established communities, and have made significant strides in negotiating and resisting the normativity that establishes heterosexuality as the norm. Naming and identity practices are discussed in later sections of this chapter.

References

Allen, Jafari S. 2011. ¡*Venceremos? The Erotics of Black Self-Making in Cuba.* Durham, NC: Duke University Press.

Bauman, Zygmunt. 2006. *Liquid Fear.* Cambridge: Polity Press.

Canada Research Team. 2015. "Envisioning LGBT Refugee Rights in Canada: Is Canada a Safe Haven?" Envisioning Global LGBT Human Rights. York University, Toronto. https://www.dropbox.com/s/nn9qork9zqi2da1/Is%20Canada%20A%20Safe%20Haven%20-%20Report%202015.pdf?dl=0.

Cohen, Cathy J. 1997. "Punks, Bulldaggers, and Welfare Queens: The Radical Potential of Queer Politics". *Gay and Lesbian Quarterly* 3:437–65.

Ghisyawan, Krystal Nandini. 2013. "Geographies of Sexuality: Constructions of Space and Belonging". *Journal of the Department of Behavioural Sciences* 3 (1): 28–43.

———. 2016. "Queering Cartographies of Caribbean Sexuality and Citizenship: Mapping Female Same-Sex Desire, Identity and Belonging in Trinidad". PhD diss., University of the West Indies, St Augustine, Trinidad and Tobago.

Gosine, Andil. 2004. "Stumbling into Sexualities: International Discourse Discovers Dissident Desire". *Canadian Women Studies* 4 (2–3): 59–63.

Kempadoo, Kamala. 2009. "Caribbean Sexuality: Mapping the Field". *Caribbean Review of Gender Studies* 3:1–24.

Kempadoo, Kamala, and Halimah DeShong. 2013. "Caribbean Feminist Research Methods: An Editorial Note". *Caribbean Review of Gender Studies* 7:1–6.

King, Rosamond. 2014. *Island Bodies: Transgressive Sexualities in the Caribbean Imagination*. Gainesville: University Press of Florida.

King, Rosamond, and Angelique Nixon. 2013. "Embodied Theories: Local Knowledge(s), Community Organizing, and Feminist Methodologies in Caribbean Sexuality Studies". *Caribbean Review of Gender Studies* 7:1–15.

Moore, Carla. 2012. "Wah Eye Nuh See Heart Nuh Leap: Queer Marronage in the Jamaican Dancehall". MA thesis, Queen's University, Kingston, Ontario.

Sheller, Mimi. 2012. *Citizenship from Below: Erotic Agency and Caribbean Freedom*. Durham, NC: Duke University Press.

Tinsley, Omise' eke Natasha. 2010. *Thiefing Sugar: Eroticism between Women in Caribbean Literature*. Durham, NC: Duke University Press.

Wahab, Amar. 2012. "Homophobia as a State of Reason: The Case of Postcolonial Trinidad". *Gay and Lesbian Quarterly* 18 (4): 481–505.

Walcott, Rinaldo. 2015. Foreword to *Disrupting Queer Inclusion: Canadian Homonationalisms and the Politics of Belonging*, edited by OmiSoore Y. Dryden and Suzanne Lenon, vii–ix. Vancouver: University of British Columbia Press.

Wekker, Gloria. 2006. *The Politics of Passion: Women's Sexual Culture in the Afro-Surinamese Diaspora*. New York: Columbia University Press.

2.

Inclusion of LGBTQ Students in Jamaican Teacher Education
Religiosity, Respectability and Resistance

CAROL HORDATT GENTLES AND VILEITHA DAVIS-MORRISON

Homophobic bullying is an unacceptable infringement of basic human rights. In the school setting, homophobia is a direct violation of the right to quality education. It leads to absenteeism, poorer academic performance and achievement, and sometimes to suicide. The right to quality education is not the privilege of a few. It is a universal right. All students – all of them – have the right to quality education in a safe environment.
—Irina Bokova, director general, UNESCO, on the International Day against Homophobia and Transphobia, 17 May 2012

As Jamaican educators who cherish the vision of an egalitarian, socially just education system, we are deeply concerned about students whose "differences" due to socioeconomic backgrounds, learning styles, race, religion, gender, sexual orientation or health position them in educational spaces marked by discrimination, oppression, fear and injustice. Thus, we welcome the United Nations' continued commitment to inclusivity as expressed in its Sustainable Development Goal 4, which aims to "ensure inclusive and equitable quality education and promote lifelong learning opportunities for all" (United Nations 2017). We appreciate its influence on Jamaica's education sector, in which concerns for inclusion are slowly being translated into educational policy, national curricula and practice. Unfortunately, the rights of students who identify as LGBTQ remain excluded from conversations about inclusion. This reflects the high degree of homophobia and transphobia that characterizes Jamaican society and stands in the way of those who wish to challenge the oppression of LGBTQ students in Jamaican educational institutions.

Theoretical Framework

Drawing on critical pedagogy as a theoretical frame, we believe educational institutions should be at the vanguard of social change. According to McLaren (2000, 10), "critical pedagogy is a way of thinking about, negotiating, and transforming the relationship among classroom teaching, the production of knowledge, the institutional structures of the school, and the social and material relations of the wider community, society and nation-state". It offers the view that "schools should play a central role in the ongoing struggle for democracy, by becoming public spheres for the critical transformation of Self and society" (Hordatt Gentles 2003, 5). Within this framework, teachers are asked to become and practice as "transformative intellectuals" whose "intellectual practices are necessarily grounded in moral and ethical discourse exhibiting a preferential concern for the suffering and struggles of the disadvantaged and oppressed" (Giroux and McLaren 1996, 303). As Kellner (2000, 197) explains, "critical pedagogy considers how education can provide individuals [teachers] with the tools to better themselves and strengthen democracy, to create a more egalitarian and just society, and thus to deploy education in a process of progressive social change".

Using this frame leads us to envisage a teaching profession whose members have been educated, trained and socialized to be willing and able to create safe, positive spaces for LGBTQ students "as a commitment to human rights discourse that entails the notion that no student should be discriminated against on the grounds of their race, religion, gender or sexual orientation" (Mitton-Kukner, Kerns, and Tompkins 2015, 5). Our vision includes teacher education programmes in which faculty (teacher educators) and curricula demonstrate a commitment to helping trainee teachers develop competences for anti-oppressive pedagogy (Kumashiro 2002). Trainee teachers would be encouraged to construct professional identities around becoming inclusive educators, allies and maybe even advocates for all disenfranchised students, including LGBTQ youth. Sadly, against the backdrop of what we know about the negative experiences of LGBTQ students in Jamaican schools, the lack of appropriate policy, the educational ethos surrounding the issue of homosexuality and the tendency for teacher education institutions and faculty to be conservative and conformist in their outlook, we are cognizant that realizing what we envision is currently highly unlikely.

Tolerate but Do Not Include

A Human Rights Watch report (2014) states that "Jamaica has neither comprehensive anti-discrimination legislation, nor specific legislation prohibiting discrimination on the grounds of sexual orientation or gender identity. Serious rights abuses based on sexual orientation and gender identity continue, and justice for these crimes remains elusive." A review of newspaper reports of statements from the Ministry of Education over the last few years suggests that consistent with the broader cultural context, there is no educational legislation in place with respect to LGBTQ rights. There has been some movement toward an official position of tolerance for LGBTQ students but little substantive action beyond that to meet their needs. In 2012, the then minister of education gave the keynote address at the International Day against Homophobia and Transphobia, which focused on discussing matters related to homophobic bullying in schools. He said that regardless of sexual orientation, class or colour each person must be treated equally and that "the historic discrimination that has taken place over the centuries must find no place in our educational environment" ("Groups Call for End to Homophobic Bullying", *Jamaica Observer,* 18 May 2012). In 2015, the same minister of education, in response to a report on bullying in Jamaican schools (UNICEF 2015) and lobbying by the LGBTQ community in Jamaica, announced that his ministry would be releasing safety and security guidelines "to be included in the schools' curriculum . . . to become a platform to sensitize all students on issues of security" ("No Bullying Gay Youths", *Gleaner,* 18 July 2015).

In a country often identified as one of the most homophobic in the world that upholds a buggery/sodomy law forbidding anal intercourse, these statements appeared to be a positive step for securing LGBTQ rights in Jamaican schools. Unfortunately, they have remained statements with little follow-up. The revised safety and security manual announced by the minister contains a section on bullying, but without specific mention of LGBTQ issues. The guidelines for dealing with bullying are generic, leaving the responsibility for responding to and managing the issue up to the school administrator. This speaks to a political ambivalence that, as pointed out by the chairperson of the Jamaica Civil Society Coalition, "allows persons to dance around the issue without taking a position" ("Groups Call for End", *Jamaica Observer,* 18 May 2012).

A critical consideration of the Ministry of Education's statements suggests that much of what has been said is only lip-service with little real concern for the inclusion of LGBTQ students. The ministry's position fails to acknowledge that LGBTQ students have needs beyond the right not to be physically harmed at school. This was made clear when the same minister of education announced in the same forum, "we stand for policies of fairness and of modesty. We say that exhibitionism, sexual posturing and grooming are inappropriate and should have no place in schools" ("Groups Call for End", *Jamaica Observer*, 18 May 2012). What this conveyed was that while LGBTQ students would be tolerated in schools, they should not be encouraged or allowed to exhibit their "gayness". The statement also alluded to a fear that permeates the education sector: that homosexual students, if unchecked, will lure heterosexual students into homosexual activities.

A similar message was sent a few months later amid public outcry calling for revision of a new health and family life education (HFLE) curriculum for public schools. The curriculum's unit on sexuality included questions for young adolescents (aged eleven to fifteen) about anal sex, if they had ever thought they were gay, if they knew their HIV status and if they had multiple partners. The furore over this led the minister to condemn the unit and state that

> only heterosexual relationships would be promoted in the education system, while expressing tolerance for those who chose alternative lifestyles. . . . We are not going to be promoting homosexuality in this country. We're just not going to do it. . . . We are going to promote healthy heterosexual relationships, but with a tolerance and compassion for those who adopt a different lifestyle. There is a difference between grooming and conditioning, and being tolerant; and that distinction is quite possible for us to craft. ("Thwaites Says No to Gay Lifestyle in School", *Jamaica Observer*, 1 October 2012)

The "offending" sections of the HLFE manual were subsequently removed. What this conveyed was that LGBTQ students could expect to be tolerated but should not consider themselves or their needs to be "normal". It relegated them to spaces in the education system where they would be allowed to exist but should not expect their identity to be valued or validated.

This position was made clear once again in 2016 when it was reported that many guidance counselors in Jamaican high schools refused to work with LGBTQ students on the grounds that this contravened the teachings of their Christian faith. The president of the Jamaica Teachers Association supported this position by explaining it was problematic to ask guidance counselors to be trained to respond to gay students because Jamaica's law prohibits homosexual acts. He said that while "gay students should not be shunned, counselors should not be expected to put themselves in a position to break the law and must refer the cases to the appropriate government agencies" ("Homosexual Acts Are Illegal", *Gleaner*, 12 January 2016). What this statement did was to further marginalize and oppress LGBTQ students because it publicly equated their nonheterosexual orientations with criminality.

Schools should ideally be places where LGBTQ youth can find refuge and positive spaces where they feel included, safe and where their identities are affirmed (Mitton-Kukner, Kerns, and Tompkins 2015, 5). In Jamaica, as we have suggested, this unfortunately is not the case. In a "review of literature on social factors that put LGBTI children and youth at risk for violence against them in the Jamaican context", Smith (2017, 6) asserted that "as is the case in many societies, reliable data on homophobic and transphobic violence in Jamaica are lacking". However, drawing from the few available scholarly papers and social surveys, she concludes that "Jamaican LGBTI youth are unbearably stressed and traumatized by the accumulated effects of victimization at all levels of society" (8). She cites the Human Rights Watch report (2014) delineating the lived reality of Jamaican LGBTI youth as one in which "they are taunted; threatened; fired from their jobs, thrown out of their homes; beaten, stoned, raped, and even killed" (2). In many instances, those who should be protecting them are complicit both through their actions as well as their silence. For example, a young gay man, Dervin Osbourne, bravely shared his story in the local press of being teased and bullied mercilessly throughout his high school years for being perceived as different by both students and teachers and how many teachers, including the school principal, did nothing to help him. Some even meted out verbal abuse at him ("Gay Man Tells of Tough Trials in Jamaican Schools", *Jamaica Observer*, 16 May 2015).

The picture that emerges is of schools where the rights of LGBTQ students to be valued and validated as human beings are denied and the safe spaces promised to them by the Ministry of Education are not in actuality safe. The picture implicates teachers as complicit in what appears to be a homophobic school system. This means it is characterized by homophobia/transphobia: "the fear, discomfort, intolerance, or hatred of homosexuals, transgender and other people perceived to transgress from gender norms" (UNESCO 2016, 9). If this is true of the Jamaican education system, then it suggests that little is being done to disrupt homophobia during the initial training and development of teachers. This leads to questions about the views of teacher educators on such homophobia. If the spaces in which our teachers are educated and trained are themselves hostile and oppressive toward LGBTQ youth, then the likelihood of our schools becoming safe, positive spaces is small. If Jamaican teacher educators hold homophobic views it is hard to imagine that they are addressing LGBTQ issues in positive ways with trainee teachers.

Teacher Educators' Views on LGBTQ Issues

What we know about the views of Jamaican teacher educators on LGBTQ issues is anecdotal. As university faculty (one of us works in citizenship education and HFLE; the other works in teacher education and teacher development) and external examiners for the Joint Board of Teacher Education in Jamaica, our work has afforded us opportunities to have both formal and informal discussions with teachers and teacher educators about various topics including homosexuality and homophobia. However, little formal research has been done to explore this. In our quest, therefore, to start a conversation about the possibilities of engaging teacher education to prepare teachers to be inclusive of LGBTQ students, we initiated a research project aimed at ascertaining what Jamaican teacher educators think about this. The idea was to use a survey followed by qualitative interviews with a hundred Jamaican teacher educators from eight teacher training colleges. We wanted to find out what degree of inclusion teacher educators value and enact with respect to LGBTQ students on campus and how much they agree with the idea that teacher education should play a role in preparing prospective teachers to value and practice inclusion of LGBTQ students. We also wanted to know what they thought about how LGBTQ students and issues were addressed at the institutional level.

At the time of writing this chapter, we have completed the pilot survey. While it is not the norm to report the results of a pilot study, what we learned from the initial results and the process of administering the pilot was so telling that we felt it would make a useful contribution to the conversation we are hoping our chapter will begin. The questionnaire uses a Likert scale with thirty-three items and four response choices: "strongly agree", "agree", "disagree" and "strongly disagree". We developed statements to elicit the different degrees of inclusivity for LGBTQ students in the views and practices of teacher educators. We understood inclusivity as "education [that] is not simply about making schools available for those who are already able to access them. It is about being proactive in identifying the barriers and obstacles learners encounter in attempting to access opportunities for quality education, as well as in removing those barriers and obstacles that lead to exclusion" (Forlin et al. 2013, 10). We conceptualized such inclusivity as being practised along a continuum ranging from exclusivity or intolerance on one end, to tolerance, inclusion and proaction on the other end. We conceptualized four levels of inclusivity:

1. *Intolerance:* practice and values that do not recognize diversity or student differences that are due to gender orientation. An example of

intolerance is the view that being asked to openly welcome LGBTQ students into one's classroom will cause feelings of resentment. Another example is the view that inclusion of LGBTQ students on campus is offensive to teacher educators' religious beliefs.

2. *Tolerance:* practices and values that reflect some acceptance of student diversity and differences due to gender orientation. An example of tolerance is not objecting to the presence of LGBTQ students in the classroom.

3. *Inclusion:* values and practices that uphold that all students, including LGBTQ students, have the right to recognition in terms of who they are, their culture, beliefs, experiences, interests, lifestyles and uniqueness. An example of inclusion is teacher educators recognizing the importance of practices that foster safe teaching/learning classroom environments for LGBTQ students.

4. *Proaction:* values and practices that actively support and can be used to advocate for removal of barriers to inclusive education for LGBTQ students. A teacher educator whose values and practices are proactive is one who is comfortable intervening when an LGBTQ student is being bullied.

The pilot questionnaire was distributed to fifty teacher educators at their annual professional development conference. Thirty-four completed and returned the instrument. Two questionnaires were spoiled. Fourteen of the teacher educators we approached refused to complete it. The data was analysed using a simple frequency distribution to generate percentages of responses that fell into the four categories of the inclusion continuum.

Findings

Research question 1: What degree of inclusion do teacher educators value and enact with respect to LGBTQ students on campus?

Table 2.1 suggests that practices and values that reflect intolerance were acceptable to 38 per cent of college teacher educators and not acceptable to 56 per cent. Six per cent of the respondents chose not to respond. Seventy per cent agreed with values and practices that showed tolerance, 25 per cent disagreed and 5 per cent did not respond. With respect to views and practices that value inclusion, 45 per cent agreed, 49 per cent disagreed and 65 per cent chose not to respond. Values and practices that suggest proactive views were acceptable to 31 per cent of respondents, unacceptable to 60 per cent and 9 per cent did not respond. These initial results suggest

Table 2.1. Degree of Inclusion Teacher Educators Find Acceptable to Value and Enact

	Agree	Disagree	No Response	Total
Intolerance	38%	56%	6%	100%
Tolerance	70%	26%	4%	100%
Inclusion	45%	49%	6%	100%
Proaction	31%	60%	9%	100%

that although more than a third of teacher educators were uncomfortable including LGBTQ students, about two-thirds were willing to tolerate them. However, the inclination to be inclusive declines when asked to consider enacting inclusion.

Research question 2: How much do teacher educators agree with the idea that teacher education institutions should play a role in preparing prospective teachers to value and practice inclusion of LGBTQ students and issues?

Table 2.2 suggests a similar trend with respect to the role of teacher education institutions in deliberately influencing the ways teacher trainees think about and practice inclusion. While they do not think intolerance should be taught, they are divided on their views about teaching inclusion, and only a third think teacher trainees should be taught to value advocacy for LGBTQ rights. More specifically, none agreed that teacher education institutions should prepare prospective teachers to be intolerant of LGBTQ students and issues. Sixty-nine per cent agreed teacher education institutions should play a role in preparing teachers to be tolerant, but 30 per cent disagreed, while 1 per cent did not respond. With respect to teacher education institutions preparing future teachers to be inclusive, 49 per cent agreed and 50 per cent disagreed. One per cent did not respond. In terms of preparing teachers to be proactive in supporting LGBTQ students, only 30 per cent agreed, while 67 per cent disagreed and 3 per cent did not respond.

Table 2.2. Degree to which Teacher Educators Agree that Teacher Education Should Play a Role in Preparing Prospective Teachers to be Inclusive

	Agree	Disagree	No Response	Total
Intolerance	0%	0%	0%	100%
Tolerance	69%	30%	1%	100%
Inclusion	49%	50%	1%	100%
Proaction	30%	67%	3%	100%

Table 2.3. Teacher Educators' Views on Degree of Inclusion Through Policy at the Institutional Level

	Agree	Disagree	No Response	Total
Intolerance	56%	15%	29%	100%
Tolerance	44%	34%	22%	100%
Inclusion	17%	64%	19%	100%
Proaction	17%	66%	17%	100%

Research question 3. What are teacher educators' views on the degree of inclusion in institutional policies?

Table 2.3 suggests that 56 per cent of the teacher educators surveyed did not think their institution should have policies to support intolerance of LGBTQ students. However, 15 per cent did not disagree with the idea. Twenty-nine per cent chose not to respond to this question. When asked if their teacher education institutions should have policies that support tolerance, 44 per cent agreed, but 34 per cent disagreed, while 22 per cent did not respond. When asked if their teacher education institutions should have policies that facilitate inclusion of LGBTQ students and issues, only 17 per cent of teacher educators agreed, while 64 per cent disagreed, and 19 per cent did not respond. Similarly, 17 per cent of teacher educators supported the idea of institutional policies being proactive with respect to LGBTQ students and issues. Sixty-six per cent, however, disagreed, while 17 per cent chose not to respond.

Although interpretations are speculative, it is worthwhile to note what the two male teacher educators whom we had asked to distribute the questionnaires reported about their colleagues' responses to the request to complete the survey. They spoke volumes.

- "Some people did not even want to touch it, literally. They started reading and handed it back to me."
- "One colleague said she would do it for me but then she jokingly called me 'gay boy' for the rest of the day."
- "One asked, 'Why they want to find this out for?'"
- "The lecturer from a performing arts institution remarked, 'Oh, this is no problem for me, we have so many of them at our college.'"

The general trends in the results of this pilot survey were instructive in several ways. They suggest that tolerance for LGBTQ students is valued and practised by about half the teacher educators surveyed and that there is some degree of support for valuing and enacting inclusivity of LGBTQ students in proactive ways. It is also evident that teacher educators are not comfortable with the idea of inclusion being enacted at the institutional level. This suggests that values and practices that support tolerance, inclusion and proaction for LGBTQ students and issues are not being taught by the teacher educators we surveyed. This implies that teachers graduate from teacher education institutions without the knowledge, skills and values needed to create safe, inclusive teaching/learning environments for LGBTQ students.

Our research suggests that the views and practices of the teacher educators we surveyed with respect to the rights of LGBTQ students are in keeping with the official position of the Ministry of Education: show tolerance by allowing LGBTQ students to occupy spaces in schools, but it is okay *not* to practice inclusion. It is also okay to privilege one's religious beliefs over one's professional duty as a teacher to provide inclusive and equitable education for all students. The results and our observations also show a high and worrisome degree of intolerance.

On the other hand, it is encouraging that some teacher educators do not disagree with the idea of greater inclusion for LGBTQ students. This offers a small ray of hope that positive change in Jamaican teacher education with respect to the treatment of LGBTQ students can be accomplished. But it will require a huge cultural shift precipitated and supported by steadfast advocacy and strategic professional capacity building aimed at improving teacher educators' knowledge of and attitudes toward LGBTQ issues. Work done in other countries shows that this can be accomplished through workshops (Kitchen and Bellini 2012), university courses (Heffernan and Gutierez-Schmich 2016; Mitton-Kukner, Kearns, and Tompkins 2015; Sadowski 2016a) and infusion of anti-oppressive pedagogy in curricula (Kumashiro 2002) aimed at challenging and interrupting LGBTQ oppression in schools. These methods focus on raising awareness of the oppression and violence that characterize the lives of LGBTQ students, building personal and professional outrage about the devastating impact of such oppression on LGBTQ students' ability to achieve and develop, and training teachers in skills and strategies for building safe spaces for LGBTQ students in schools (Sadowski 2016b). These capitalize on what Duke (2004) has identified as key factors in getting educators to change: building their commitment and competence. Commitment is the willingness and motivation to work at changing. Competence is the professional capacity to "undergo change . . . including the acquisition of new skills, knowledge, and beliefs" (124).

Ideologies and Intellectual Resistance to Inclusion

In the Jamaican context, building such commitment and competence will be extremely challenging for several reasons. First, given Jamaica's anti-sodomy law, it could be considered to be asking teacher educators to go against what is considered legal, valued and expected of them in the education sector. Second, it would be asking them to "disrupt ways of thinking and doing – ideologies that are deeply entrenched in their personal and professional identities" (Hordatt Gentles 2018, 14). Ideologies are "systems of belief . . . usually seen as 'the way things really are' by the groups holding them, and they become the taken-for-granted ways of making sense of their world" that influence "various types of social practices, rituals and representations that [teachers] tend to accept as natural and common sense" (McLaren 1997, 184). Giroux (1997) explains that ideologies support resistance to change when those who hold them do not recognize that knowledge is socially constructed. This makes them vulnerable to accepting the knowledge held by those in authority without question and to allow themselves to be positioned as subordinate cultures, groups who "live out social relations in subordination to the dominant culture" (McLaren 1997, 180). Such hegemony is maintained through the imposition of ideologies and forms of authority through the practice of consensual social practices in social settings like educational institutions. Both the dominant and subordinate cultures support this hegemony by accepting it as natural and inevitable because they have been socialized to do so.

Research on teacher education in Jamaica suggests it has historically been characterized by authoritarian, traditional ideologies that value conformity and adherence to the status quo. These reflect a colonial legacy of expecting those who train teachers to privilege inculcating submission to authority and Christianizing and preparing teachers to be exemplars of religious virtue and social respectability over preparing them for academic success.[1] These expectations still permeate the pedagogical and institutional cultures of our teacher education colleges (Evans and Tucker 2007; Hall and Bryan 1997; Hordatt Gentles 2003; Jennings 2001). For example, most of them are denominational with strong religious ideologies manifest in expectations like requiring students and faculty to attend religious devotions, read the Bible and uphold Christian principles. Some also have strict guidelines designed to socialize teacher trainees to acquire habits of respectability like requiring them to wear uniforms and have hairstyles that ensure modesty. There are also strict rules about social and sexual behaviour both on and off campus (Hordatt Gentles 2003).

Expectations of conformity by staff and students are reinforced by strong bureaucratic ideologies supported by the pyramidal, hierarchical organization of institutional power and authority (Hordatt Gentles 2003). These ideologies are supported for the most part by pedagogies that are teacher-centred, in keeping with what Freire (1970) called a banking style of education, in which teachers see their role as transmitters of an accepted body of knowledge to be learned by rote. Students are taught to believe in the superiority of their teachers and are expected to passively accept their philosophies and perspectives. They are not encouraged to have a voice in what happens or what is conveyed in the classroom.

This produces a kind of intellectual resistance toward anything that contradicts the established order. It is antithetical to thinking or discourse around democratizing classrooms with respect to the treatment of LGBTQ students. This is so because it does not support development of the type of critically conscious, intellectual and emotional skills needed to disrupt and transform oppressive ideologies and practices. For teacher educators to think in critically conscious ways, they would have to be open to the notion that social worlds exist because of how we perceive them and that human activity and human knowledge act as both a "product and a force in the shaping of social reality" (Giroux 1997, 43). Freire (1970) asserts that all human beings have the right to be subjects – to have ownership over how they make sense of the world. To become critically conscious thinkers, our teacher educators would have to become comfortable with the idea that "knowledge is not a fixed immutable phenomenon" and that "it can be thought about dialectically in order to critique, deconstruct and reconstruct" it (Hordatt Gentles 2006, 6).

Without such critical consciousness it will be very difficult for teacher educators to develop and enact the intellectual dispositions, confidence and capacity to see beyond the ideologies that support homophobia in Jamaica. The most pervasive of these is "cultural heterosexism", which Allyn (2012) says Jamaica uses as "one of its ideological organizing principles". She explains it as a "term used for systemic presuppositions about and discrimination against anyone who does not fit into the heterosexual binary gender system; it is the belief that everyone is, or should, be heteronormative and the social maintenance of this belief" (9). This heteronormativity fuels the hegemony of church teachings about homosexuality that depict it as ungodly and immoral (Rezvany 2016). Findings from a national study commissioned by J-FLAG in 2015 found that 93 per cent of Jamaicans agreed with the statement "homosexuality is a sin", 89 per cent regarded being gay or bisexual as wrong, 87 per cent viewed female homosexuality as wrong and 63 per cent indicated that they rejected the LGBTQ lifestyle on moral and religious grounds. Sixty-one per cent of the sample believed that with professional help (conversion therapy) LGBTQ people could become heterosexuals (Smith 2017, 3).

Without critical consciousness it will be challenging for our teacher educators to rise above such heterosexism and religiosity. Not only will it be intellectually difficult, it will also be seen by them as professionally dangerous. This is so because anything associated with homosexuality is perceived as a threat to one's social respectability. As Murray (2012, 110–11) explains, "[h]omosexuality is generally not a category associated with respectability . . . if anything, it would appear that the homosexual represents the exact opposite. He (as we have seen, the male homosexual is the focus of most public talk) is a threat to the norm of respectable citizenship; his perceived effeminate presence is an improper assemblage of sexual and gendered desires." As we have seen, in Jamaican teacher education, the acquisition and maintenance of one's respectability is a key concern. Thus, anyone, whether faculty or teacher trainee, risks loss of respectability if they appear supportive of LGBTQ issues. This is exacerbated by the myth that one can become gay by association: that doing anything in support of LGBTQ people can lead to being labelled as homosexual, immoral or not respectable. This fear even extends to the teaching of health and sexuality issues. Various studies have shown that Jamaican teachers are uncomfortable and psychologically unprepared to teach sexuality issues (Beckford 2012; Elliot-Norman 2016; Davis-Morrison and Lambert 2017; Robinson 2010). In their evaluation of the pilot of the Health and Family Life Education (HFLE) curriculum, Henry, Black, and Lewis (2010) reported that the instructors thought the course content for the theme "Sexuality and Sexual Health" was insensitive to the religious beliefs of the students because it mentioned sexual differences. Beckford (2012), who conducted interviews with twenty-five teachers in a rural shift system school and observed nine HFLE classes, reported that teachers' conservative beliefs and values impacted negatively on the teaching of the theme "sexuality and sexual health". They believed that if they followed the curriculum and taught children that differences in sexual orientation exist, it would influence them to become gay. She quoted a teacher: "The curriculum implicitly teaches the children to be tolerable [sic] of each other's sex. Miss, they are teaching the children to become homos [homosexuals]. I am not teaching those things. . . . From my religious views those aren't welcome at all and I will not teach it" (55).

Conclusion

Given what has been discussed – the lack of positive support for LGBTQ students reflected in government policies, in teacher educators' views, throughout the education sector, in churches and in society at large – realization of the vision we shared at the beginning of this chapter is challenging. Taken together, within the context of the pervasive cultural heterosexism that characterizes Jamaican society and supports its homophobia, these cultural realities help to explain how and why getting teacher educators to include LGBTQ students in conversations about inclusion is so difficult. They also help to explain how ironic it is that the Jamaica Charter of Fundamental Rights and Freedom (2011) guarantees *all* citizens the right to freedom from discrimination on the grounds of being male or female, race, place of origin, social class, colour, religion or political opinion. Yet it does not include LGBT people as a legitimate group within "all citizens". There is no mention of sexual orientation and gender identification. It is also ironic that a host of national documents like the National Task Force Report on Education Reform (2004), the National Education Strategic Plan (NESP) 2011–2020, Vision 2030, the Jamaica National Development Plan, the Health and Family Life Policy and the National Policy for HIV and AIDS Management in Schools all urge our education institutions to become more caring and supportive and to create learning communities that facilitate the needs of all students irrespective of race, class, gender, disability or intellectual capacity. Yet, LGBTQ students are continuously denied the right to be cared about or supported (Allyn 2012; Smith 2017).

It is worrisome that many of our teacher educators privilege concerns about upholding religious beliefs and retaining respectability over acknowledging the suffering of students who identify as LGBTQ. By doing this, they fail to acknowledge that "homophobic and transphobic violence in educational settings measurably impacts on students' access to quality education and achievements" (UNESCO 2016, 28). Research suggests that for students who study or suffer violence in homophobic and transphobic environments the fallout is unacceptable. They feel unsafe at school, avoid school activities, miss classes or skip school altogether, drop out of school and achieve lower academic results than their peers (UNESCO 2016).

The resistance on the part of teacher educators to valuing and enacting inclusion is cause for deep concern in several ways. First, it has negative implications for experiences of trainee teachers in teacher education programmes who identify as LGBTQ. It also increases the likelihood that teachers will graduate without the type of knowledge and professional dispositions and skills that can help improve the negative experiences of LGBTQ students and facilitate their full inclusion in Jamaican schools.

In light of our discussion, it is clear the road to inclusion of LGBTQ issues within the space of teacher education in Jamaica is obstacle-ridden, long, challenging and wrought with controversy and danger. Yet from our critical pedagogical perspective, it is incumbent on us to seek strategies that can disrupt social injustice in educational spaces for LGBTQ students.

We see several possibilities. First, we have, with this chapter, described and interrogated the cultural realities of oppression of LGBTQ students. We have theorized ideological resistance to possibilities for challenging this oppression within the space of teacher education. This, for us, is a key step for constructing cultural knowledge that supports advocacy for changes in national and educational policies on inclusion so that they treat sexual orientation explicitly, in the same manner as gender, race, class, gender, disability and intellectual capacity.

We see possibilities through our scholarship for breaking the silence about unjust educational practices and starting conversations about improving the experiences of LGBTQ students in Jamaican schools. In our work as faculty in a school of education, we work with teacher educators who are pursuing graduate degrees. Our location provides us spaces within which to enact and model inclusion and advocacy about LGBTQ issues in education. Infusing our concerns about the oppression of LGBTQ students into our dialogue with our students is a way of encouraging them to think in critically conscious ways about homophobia in schools. This could provide the impetus for them to interrogate their own beliefs and values systems about LGBTQ people.

We also see possibilities in our professional capacity in development work in the teachers' colleges as external examiners for the Joint Board of Teacher Education. Given the high degree of ideological resistance to inclusion of LGBTQ issues in teacher education, it would be useful to begin advocacy work in a more generic and thus less confrontational way. For example, we can facilitate professional development workshops on values analysis and clarification strategies that enhance critical reflection and reduce dissonant confrontations. Training lecturers to acquire and teach life skills, including cognitive, emotional, psychological and social skills, to student teachers will help to foster values and attitudes that reduce discrimination and stigmatization of marginalized students.

There is a Jamaican saying that "one one coco full basket". It means that every action, no matter how small, can contribute to achieving one's goals. What we have proposed in this chapter, given the challenges inherent in disrupting homophobia in Jamaica, are small steps toward realizing our vision of Jamaican teacher education as a space to improve inclusion of LGBTQ issues. What matters is that they are steps in the direction that is right.

Note

1. This way of viewing the world of teaching and teacher education was inculcated during the colonial era between emancipation in 1838 and independence in 1962. During this time, teacher training colleges acted as socialization agencies to ensure the emancipated masses "would accept the rigid colonial class authority of mid-nineteenth century society" (Keith 1974, 138). It was thought that even though the black masses were legally no longer slaves, it was still possible to socialize them to be obedient, hardworking, submissive, colonial citizens through education. Teacher training was, for the most part, established and funded by various religious groups, like the Wesleyans, Moravians, Baptists, Church Missionary Society and Presbyterians, who were vying for African souls to be converted to Christianity. Training teachers facilitated teaching the freed slaves the rudiments of reading, writing and arithmetic – skills to ensure they could read the Bible and support their religious missions. Thus, teacher education was a medium for producing native black teachers who would teach poor, black children in ways that inculcated respect and submission to social superiors and the church. This was valued more than the role they played in preparing them for academic achievement. As the inspector of schools intimated in 1847, for black teacher trainees, "intellectual attainment was secondary to their moral character and patient endurance: Christianizing black students was a major objective" of teacher training colleges (D'Oyley 1979, 16).

References

Allyn, Angela R. 2012. "Homophobia in Jamaica: A Study of Cultural Heterosexism in Praxis". *SSRN*. https://papers.ssrn.com/sol3/papers .cfm?abstract_id=2097180.

Beckford, L. 2012. *Teachers' Perception of the Teaching of the New Revised Health and Family Life Education Curriculum in a Rural Primary School*. MEd thesis, University of the West Indies, Mona, Jamaica.

Davis-Morrison, Vileitha, and Clement Lambert. 2017. "The State of Health and Family Life Education Programme in the Teachers' College". Ministry of Education, Guidance and Counselling Unit, Kingston, Jamaica.

D'Oyley, Vincent. 1979. "Plans and Progress in Nineteenth-Century Jamaican Teacher Education". In *Development and Disillusion in Third World Education with an Emphasis on Jamaica*, edited by Vincent D'Oyley and Reginald Murray, 5–32. Toronto: Ontario Institute for Studies in Education.

Duke, Daniel. 2004. *The Challenges of Educational Change*. New York: Pearson Education.

Elliot-Norman, Collene. 2016. "Parents' Perceptions Concerning Sex Education at an Urban Co-Educational High School in Jamaica". MEd thesis, University of the West Indies, Mona, Jamaica.

Evans, Hyacinth, and Joan Tucker. 2007. "Confronting Post-Colonial Legacies through Pre-Service Teacher Education: The Case of Jamaica". In *Urban Teacher Education and Teaching: Innovative Practices for Diversity and Social Justice,* edited by R. Patrick Solomon and Dia Sekayi, 147–64. London: Lawrence Erlbaum Associates.

Forlin, Chris, Dianne Chambers, Tim Loreman, Joanne Deppeler, and Umesh Sharma. 2013. *Inclusive Education for Students with Disability: A Review of the Best Evidence in Relation to Theory and Practice.* Canberra: ARACY (The Australian Research Alliance for Children and Youth). Accessed 21 January 2020. https://www.aracy.org.au/publications-resources/command/download_file/id/246/filename/Inclusive_education_for_students_with_disability_-_A_review_of_the_best_evidence_in_relation_to_theory_and_practice.pdf.

Freire, Paulo. 1970. *Pedagogy of the Oppressed.* Harmondsworth, UK: Penguin.

Giroux, Henry. 1997. *Pedagogy and the Politics of Hope: Theory, Culture and Schooling: A Critical Reader.* Boulder: Westview.

Giroux, Henry, and Peter McLaren. 1996. "Teacher Education and the Politics of Engagement: The Case for Democratic Schooling". In *Breaking Free: The Transformative Power of Critical Pedagogy,* edited by Pepi Leistyna, Arlie Woodrum and Stephen Sherblom, 301–31. Cambridge, MA: Harvard Educational Review.

Hall, Madge, and Beverley Bryan. 1997. "Rethinking Pathways to Excellence in Teacher Education". *Caribbean Journal of Education* 19 (2): 239–53.

Heffernan, Julie, and Tina Gutierez-Schmich. 2016. "We Recruit: A Queer Pedagogy for Teacher Education". In *LGBTQ Voices in Education: Changing the Culture of Schooling,* edited by Veronica Bloomfield and Marni Fisher, 145–60. New York: Routledge.

Henry, Martin, Joan Black, and Balford Lewis. 2010. "HFLE Curriculum Evaluation, Research Analyst Consultancy Report". GOJ/UNICEF Country Programme of Cooperation, Health and Family Life Education Curriculum Policy Research.

Hordatt Gentles, Carol. 2003. "The Pedagogical Culture of New College: A Critical Examination of Pedagogy in a Jamaican Teachers College". PhD dissertation, University of Toronto.

———. 2006. "A Rationale for the Critical Reorientation of Jamaican Teacher Education". In *Broadening the Vision for Teacher Education in the Caribbean,* edited by Rose Davies and Lorna Down, 1–22. Kingston: Institute of Education, University of the West Indies.

———. 2018. "Reorienting Jamaican Teacher Education to Address Sustainability: Challenges, Implications and Possibilities". *Caribbean Quarterly* 64 (1): 149–66. doi:10.1080/00086495.2018.143534.

Human Rights Watch. 2014. "Not Safe at Home: Violence and Discrimination against LGBT People in Jamaica". Accessed 12 October 2017. https://www.hrw

.org/report/2014/10/21/not-safe-home/violence-and-discrimination-against
-lgbt-people-jamaica.

Jennings, Zellynne. 2001. "Teacher Education in Selected Countries in the
Commonwealth Caribbean: The Ideal of Policy versus the Reality of Practice".
Comparative Education 37 (1): 107–34.

Keith, Sherry. 1974. "Socialization in the Jamaican Primary School: A Study of
Teacher Evaluation and Student Participation". In *Sociology of Education: A
Caribbean Reader*, edited by Peter Figueroa and Ganga Persaud, 118–40. Oxford:
Oxford University Press.

Kellner, Douglas. 2000. "Multiple Literacies and Critical Pedagogies". In *Revolutionary Pedagogies: Cultural Politics, Instituting Education, and the Discourse of
Theory*, edited by Peter Trifonas, 196–221. New York: Routledge.

Kitchen, Julian, and Christine Bellini. 2012. "Addressing Lesbian, Gay, Bisexual,
Transgender, and Queer (LGBTQ) Issues in Teacher Education: Teacher
Candidates' Perceptions". *Alberta Journal of Educational Research* 58 (3): 444–60.

Kumashiro, Kevin. 2002. *Troubling Education: Queer Activism and Anti-Oppressive
Pedagogy*. New York: Routledge-Falmer.

McLaren, Peter. 1997. *Life in Schools: An Introduction to Critical Pedagogy in the
Foundations of Education*. 2nd ed. Toronto: Irwin.

———. 2000. "Paulo Freire's Pedagogy of Possibility". In *Freirean Pedagogy, Praxis
and Possibilities: Projects for the New Millennium*, edited by Stanley Steiner, H.
Mark Krank, Peter McLaren, and Robert Bahruth, 1–22. New York: Falmer.

Mitton-Kukner, Jennifer, Laura-Lee Kearns, and Joanne Tompkins. 2015. "Pre-Service
Educators and Anti-Oppressive Pedagogy: Interrupting and Challenging LGBTQ
Oppression in Schools". *Asia-Pacific Journal of Teacher Education* 44 (1): 1–15.

Murray, David. 2012. *Flaming Souls: Homosexuality, Homophobia, and Social
Change in Barbados*. Toronto: University of Toronto Press. Kindle edition.

Rezvany, Roxy. 2016. "The Challenges of Running a Queer Homeless Shelter in
Jamaica". *Vice*. 22 March. Accessed 9 November 2017. https://www.vice.com
/en_se/article/the-struggle-for-queer-shelters-in-jamaica.

Robinson, Bernadette. 2010. "HIV/AIDS Education in Four Jamaican High
Schools: The Teachers' Perspective". MEd thesis, University of the West Indies,
Mona, Jamaica.

Sadowski, Michael. 2016a. "How Old Ideas Can Help New Teachers: Support for
LGBTQ Students as a Core Value". In *LGBTQ Voices in Education: Changing the
Culture of Schooling*, edited by Veronica Bloomfield and Marni Fisher, 553–771.
New York: Routledge.

———. 2016b. *Safe Is Not Enough: Better Schools for LGBTQ Students*. Cambridge,
MA: Harvard Education Press.

Smith, Delores. 2017. "Homophobic and Transphobic Violence against Youth: The
Jamaican Context". *International Journal of Adolescence and Youth* 23 (2): 250–58.
doi:10.1080/02673843.2017.1336106.

UNESCO. 2016. *Out in the Open: Education Sector Responses to Violence Based on
Sexual Orientation and Gender Identity/Expression*. Paris: UNESCO. Accessed 20
January 2020. http://unesdoc.unesco.org/images/0024/002447/244756e.pdf.

UNICEF. 2015. "Investigating the Prevalence and Impact of Peer Abuse (Bullying) on the Development of Jamaica's Children". Child Development Agency. Kingston, Jamaica. Accessed 21 January 2020. https://www.unicef.org/jamaica/media/1996/file/Investigating-the-Prevalence-and-Impact-of-Peer-Abuse-Bullying-on-The-Development-of-Jamaicas-Children.pd.

United Nations. 2017. "Sustainable Knowledge Development Platform". Accessed 20 January 2020. https://sustainabledevelopment.un.org/sdg4.

3.

Level 5

Betwixt and Between "Homophobia" in
Trinidad and Tobago

KEITH E. McNEAL

This chapter presents an important empirical finding regarding experiences
and perceptions of homophobia in Trinidad and Tobago – the majority of
homosexual men and transgender women interviewed consider the level of
homophobia in the country to be around level 5 on a scale of 1 being the lowest
and 10 being the highest – and surveys the ways the research subjects made
this assessment and understood its societal significance. These findings
complicate attempts to characterize the country in broad strokes as either
homophobic or not homophobic. They are significant for documenting the
lived experience of homophobia in Trinidad and Tobago, as well as for better
understanding the politics at stake not only among those for and against
LGBT rights, but also among queer activists and in advocacy organizations.

The discussion begins with a brief exploration of some of the ways
homophobia is invoked in local anti-homophobia awareness campaigns
and then proceeds to an examination of the ideological and behavioural
environments queer men and transgender women navigate in terms of
homophobia and transphobia in the region in order to contextualize the
level 5 findings. The chapter concludes by reconsidering the deeper history
of homophobia as a concept in relation to the politics of sexual orientation and social change and raises questions about its status as a discursive import from the Global North. I argue that "homophobia" in Trinidad
and Tobago and elsewhere be seen as a complex assemblage of discourse
and practice that manifests differentially in relation to a range of variables
contingent upon social status and personal circumstance.

#HomophobiaKills #SafeSpace #EraseHate #LitWithPride

Homophobia matters in the Caribbean. As so poignantly documented by
the short film *A Safe Space*, it can even kill.[1] The pioneering youth group

that produced this film, Trinidad and Tobago's Silver Lining Foundation (SLF), was founded in response to the tragic September 2011 suicide of George Kazanjian, an upper-class, Arab-Trinidadian sixteen-year-old who hanged himself in the utility room of his family's posh suburban Port of Spain home. Though never explicitly identified in the media as related to any struggle over his sexuality, it was nonetheless an open secret that Kazanjian was gay and ended his life in order to avoid his family finding out. A 13 September 2011 *Express* newspaper article acknowledged that "[a] suicide note was also found in George's room, which indicated that he loved his family but [that] they would not understand why he took his life". In one of his last tweets, he wrote: "Only God can judge me; that's what I'm afraid of" (15 August 2011). Inside details concerning the real story spread delicately among the more affluent communities of the capital city and quickly throughout the twin-island republic's queer networks. Not only had homophobia killed, it also seemed to be suffocating society's response to the tragedy – salt in the wound for some.

News of Kazanjian's suicide hit an especially raw nerve upon finding its way to Jeremy Steffan Edwards, a mild-mannered, twenty-year-old, Indo-Trinidadian living with his parents in their middle-class Chaguanas home. He too had been contemplating suicide for similar reasons and was devastated to hear about George's plight. Yet the senselessness of the tragedy helped Edwards attain some perspective and reach out for support, rather than kill himself. As he explains in the film: "Around the same time George Kazanjian was experiencing his struggles and that ultimately led to his demise, I would have been going through similar struggles. And I would have reached to the same point that he was at – that moment where you believe in your mind that everything is so hopeless and that you have no support and that it's so lonely and so terrifying that the only option out is suicide." Yet Edwards was moved by the officiating priest's remarks at Kazanjian's funeral: youth shouldn't have to carry their burdens alone, but they should reach out to those whom they could trust, and if they did not have anyone whom they could depend on, should say a prayer asking God to lead them to someone who cares. This last-ditch tactic bore fruit, and Jeremy subsequently met a young woman who became a source of sustenance and dear friend.

Edwards also posted to the CAISO (Coalition Advocating for the Inclusion of Sexual Orientation, Trinidad and Tobago's premier queer activist organization) Facebook group, lamenting what a tragedy it was that Kazanjian had felt so unwanted and unsafe as to conclude he had no other choice than to take his life. Edwards decried the lack of community

Figure 3.1. "HOMOPHOBIA KILLS" – sign on commemorative shrine for Matthew Shepard, a twenty-one-year-old white gay American man murdered in a torturous 1998 hate crime, reproduced in SLF TT's 2015 documentary *A Safe Space*.

resources and support networks for helping people like George (and himself), calling for progressive social change on behalf of queer young folks suffering from homophobia, discrimination, stigma and alienation. The post became a lightning rod, quickly growing into an organic call to action. And thus, a group of largely university-oriented young people formed the Silver Lining Foundation to address problems of bullying and violence in relation to sexual diversity among the nation's youth. Given the impetus for the group's formation, it initially called itself the George Kazanjian Foundation, in honour of homophobia's most recent local martyr. Yet to avoid further scandalous attention regarding the underlying reality of George's death, the family declined when asked for approval to use the name – another symptom of local homophobia, as they did not want any public association of homosexuality with their son. After considerable brainstorming, it was agreed that "Silver Lining" captured the spirit of their message, echoing North America's "It Gets Better" campaign, which so many of SLF's founding members applauded and embraced.

The Silver Lining Foundation emphasizes consciousness-raising and the building of support networks as responses to societal homophobia and bullying of nonheteronormative youth. In order to educate the public about discrimination and violence directed against LGBT youth, the nongovernmental organization's debut consisted of establishing an annual observance of the International Day of Silence on the St Augustine, Trinidad, campus of the University of the West Indies. This event was synchronized with like-minded efforts all over the world that raise awareness and educate the public about discrimination and violence directed against LGBT youth. The SLF's first online intervention documented their Day of Silence efforts in a series of brief, media-savvy videos.[2] *A Safe Space* (2015) was their first short film, making its debut to great acclaim at the Trinidad and Tobago Film Festival in 2016. It chronicles the Kazanjian tragedy, including surprisingly candid interview footage from George's mother in light of the family's initial reticence about any public spotlight concerning the real story, then weaves that plotline into an overview of SLF's mission and praxis. Central to the film's narrative is an interview with Edwards, who effectively "outs" Kazanjian in relation to his own personal struggle and offers a message of hope and support for youth as an antidote to suffering and suicide. The SLF mission has been operationalized in various efforts to bring critically honest awareness to the grim realities of sexuality- and gender-based discrimination and bullying, to build information and support networks, and to advocate for change, all of which are briefly documented by the film.[3]

Figure 3.2. SLF "Day of Silence" Facebook image. Courtesy of Silver Lining Foundation.

One of the SLF's most substantive transformative efforts is a support group for young adults on the University of West Indies campus called "Safe Space", begun in collaboration with the university's Counselling and Psychological Services (CAPS) and facilitated by clinical psychologist Dr Sarah Chin Yuen Kee. Participants, mostly but not entirely university students, meet privately weekly for ten weeks, during which time they share their stories and discuss and debate issues, all the while supporting each other and establishing solidarity. The programme has been such a success that the collaboration has inspired the founding of the Yellow Pebble Foundation, a similar organization focused on youth mental health and well-being which has created similar "safe spaces" elsewhere in the twin-island nation. Homophobia may kill, but it does not have to. It does get better. This important psychotherapeutic initiative is also chronicled in *A Safe Space*: a young Afro-Trinbagonian man reflects on its transformative potential, observing that "acceptance is a very long and hard road, and unless you're willing to go through that kind of trial and tribulation to get to the brighter side, it could be very lonely inside".

It must be noted that funding for the film was granted by the US embassy in Trinidad and Tobago, which co-produced *A Safe Space*. As part of its effort to raise awareness and foster acceptance of LGBT rights, the embassy hosted Matthew Shepard's parents in Trinidad in order to raise awareness and foster acceptance of LGBT rights.[4] Matthew Wayne Shepard was a twenty-two-year-old gay student at the University of Wyoming who was beaten, tortured, and left to die near Laramie, Wyoming, on the night of 6 October 1998. During their visit, the Shepards were interviewed for the film and had the opportunity to meet the Kazanjian family. *A Safe Space* includes touching footage of George's mother Katherine hugging and speaking with the Shepards while Jeremy Edwards lingers in the background. Judy Shepard calls for parents to become "crusaders" for their children's safety and well-being, while Dennis Shepard emphasizes the value of youth as a vital resource for national development. The film then cuts to Edwards's commentary, interspersed with images of news media reporting on Father Reginald Hezekiah, the priest who presided at George's funeral, calling out to the nation's youth and telling them "you are not alone". The film then cuts back to George's mother lamenting the lack of community resources and social services regarding suicide, bullying and stigma – a call to which the SLF has responded. These Trinbagonian and American morality tales concerning homophobia – one a torturous hate-murder, the other a tragic suicide – are thereby linked by the film's narrative structure.

Teenagers warned, 'You are not alone', after classmate's suicide

By —Gyasi Gonzales

Story Created: Sep 20, 2011 at 12:51 AM ECT
(Story Updated: Sep 20, 2011 at 12:51 AM ECT)

FR Reginald Hezekiah yesterday pleaded with the young people gathered for the funeral of 16-year-old George Kazanjian to talk about their issues because, "You are not alone. Your parents and relatives are here for you and they love you."

Kazanjian, a pupil of St Mary's College, was laid to rest yesterday afternoon following an hour-and-a-half-long ceremony at the Church of the Assumption in Maraval.

Difficult time: Relatives of George Kazanjian, inset, carry his casket out of the Church of the Assumption in Maraval yesterday following the funeral service. —Photo: CURTIS CHASE

TOOLS

Like 23   SHARE

PRINT THIS ARTICLE

Last week Monday he was found hanging in the washroom of his family's Nutmeg Avenue, Haleland Park, home from a rope that was tied to the room's burglar-proofing.

He left a note telling his family he loved them but he never said why he took his own life.

None of his relatives or friends wanted to say anything about the suicide yesterday as this was a "difficult time".

The teenager's funeral was well attended and scores of people had to remain outside the church. Just under half of the mourners were pupils in school uniform with their watery, glazed eyes remaining fixed on Kazanjian's light-coloured wooden casket.

"With so many of you here let's try to ease our pain and our grief because life and death has an effect on all of us," said Fr Hezekiah.

As he continued his lecture to the young people he reminded them, "There is no need for

Figure 3.3. Image of Kazanjian funeral news article "You Are Not Alone".

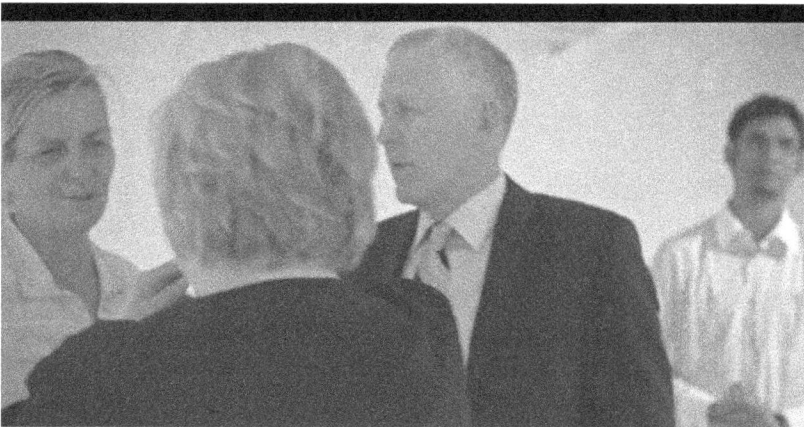

Figure 3.4. Katherine Kazanjian with the Shepards with Jeremy Steffan Edwards in background.

A series of cinematic frames then notes the betrayal by the former United National Congress government under Prime Minister Kamla Persad-Bissessar who initially promised to push for progressive change between 2010 and 2012 regarding LGBT rights but then by 2014 had fully backed down. The film ends with a frame stating that "Silver Lining Foundation resolve remains firm in seeking the protection of the LGBT community and ensuring that they are afforded equal rights. They continue to spread their message of 'Acceptance over Tolerance.'" Imagery of purple rubber awareness wristbands inscribed with "Matthew Shepard" and "Erase Hate" flows across the screen and then becomes the background for the superimposition of information regarding the Silver Lining and Matthew Shepard Foundations, as well as the phone number for a new local suicide hotline, accompanied by the hashtags #SafeSpace and #EraseHate.

The Politics of Homophobia in the Caribbean

Some measure of the ideological environment LGBT people and activists face in the region can be gleaned from the recent study "Homophobia and Transphobia in Caribbean Media" (IGLHRC 2015). It was conducted by the International Gay and Lesbian Human Rights Commission in partnership with United and Strong, St Lucia's premier queer advocacy organization, and with assistance from Groundation Grenada, Guyana Rainbow Foundation, J-FLAG (Jamaica Forum for Lesbians, All-Sexuals and Gays), PETAL (a Belizean organization whose acronym stands for Promoting Empowerment Through Awareness for Les/Bi Women) and the United Belize Advocacy Movement. These Caribbean queer advocacy organizations monitored print and online media in Belize, Grenada, Guyana, Jamaica and St Lucia in July 2014, identifying regional anglophone patterns and trends. In the report's executive summary, they wrote, "The results show that many media outlets reinforce negative stereotypes that can lead to violence against LGBTI people. The media largely ignored stories of importance about this community – policy issues and concerns about exclusion, or those depicting them engaged in positive activities. Overall, media coverage created an unbalanced, inaccurate and largely unflattering picture of the community" (2).[5]

Although Caribbean folk continue to cope with media patterns that consistently marginalize their experiences, reinforce stigma and perpetuate homophobia, betwixt and between these homophobic manifestations of public culture, people adapt and craft lives characterized by complex and dynamic experiences and perspectives. The Caribbean Men's Internet Survey (CARIMIS) provides a more nuanced understanding of the lived experience of stigma and discrimination across the region among men who have sex with men (MSM). The Caribbean's largest study of homosexual and bisexual males, this inquiry was conducted online from November 2011 through June 2012 by the Joint UN Programme on HIV and AIDS, in partnership with the London School of Hygiene and Tropical Medicine. The sample comprised 3,567 men from the Dutch-, English-, French- and Spanish-speaking countries and territories in the Caribbean.[6]

Regarding stigma, discrimination and homophobia, the study disclosed complex patterns and poignant paradoxes. One-third of the sample reported having been antagonistically stared at or intimidated, a quarter experienced verbal insult or name-calling and one-tenth reported having been physically assaulted within the last five years as a result of their sexuality. Generally speaking, vulnerability to homophobic intimidation and abuse correlates with being younger as well as with being out. According to UNAIDS Caribbean director Dr Ernest Massiah, these dynamics produce a troubling "paradox of stigma", in which visibility is associated with a greater likelihood of engaging in safer sex on the one hand, yet also correlates with experiencing higher levels of homophobic discrimination and abuse on the other. Many respondents harboured negative feelings and self-perceptions derived from internalized social attitudes linked with stress, increased rates of risky sexual behaviour and worse sexual-health outcomes. This profile is not only more likely for younger MSMs, but also for those who have never tested for HIV and those who also have sexual relations with women. The majority of the sample expressed feelings of loneliness and social isolation in relation to their sexuality, experiences inflected and refracted by age, level of education, degree of outness, seropositivity and bisexuality. Interestingly, respondents from anglophone areas were more likely to express loneliness (72 per cent) than those from hispanophone (66 per cent), neerlandophone (63 per cent) and francophone (51 per cent) areas. Likewise, subjects from Dutch-speaking territories had a significantly lower average internalized homonegativity score than respondents from the other areas.

This study depicts oppressive societal trends and disconcerting patterns of personal experience, but it also clearly points to a diverse and complex spectrum of experience. More than half the sample (58 per cent) self-identified as gay or homosexual, 24 per cent bisexual, 2 per cent straight and 15 per cent indicated that they do not use any term to describe their sexual orientation or identity. In the year prior to being surveyed, the majority of the sample (91 per cent) had had sex with at least one man, and 23 per cent reported having had sex with both men and women. Yet despite this variability, the majority of respondents, regardless of identification or praxis, expressed a desire for stable relationships, emotional connection, freedom from psychological and social barriers, and safer sex.

This material not only brings to light the complexity of MSM experience, but also helps us better grasp the ambivalence, challenges and trade-offs of negotiating the Trinbagonian closet, both from within and without. Indeed, being safely "out" is a privilege only some queer folk – certainly not all – pursue as their ideal, much less attain. So, while the CARIMIS study evinces extensive societal heterosexism and internalized homophobia, it also indexes a significant degree of openness about sexuality correlated with empowered health behaviour among Caribbean MSM. It therefore compels recognition of substantial diversity in patterns of behaviour and identification among homosexually behaving men in the Caribbean, including in their experience of homophobia. Some are out and some are not, many are somewhere in-between, some experience homophobia more than others and homophobia is itself a complex and contested assemblage. The study also informs questions of social change with its recommendations for more nuanced and informed policies and programming targeting MSM in the region.

While some queer activist organizations, such as the SLF, emphasize the terrible existential and societal tolls of homophobia in Trinidad and Tobago, the sociological complexity of "homophobia" and the reality of progressive change are two important reasons that CAISO does not generally support queer asylum-seeking abroad by Trinbagonian nationals. It is their view as Trinidad and Tobago's highest-profile, longest-running LGBT rights advocacy group that it is possible to be gay and live your life in Trinidad and Tobago, that homophobia far from necessarily kills, that things have indeed been getting better, that LGBT asylum-seeking encourages a queer brain drain and depletes the local movement of energy and resources, and that rhetorical substantiation of queer asylum claims in Europe and North America are premised upon quasi-racist, neocolonial imagery of the Caribbean as pathologically backward in its level of homophobia. Of course, CAISO advances many of the same cultural criticisms and political orientations as the SLF and other like-minded organizations, yet only CAISO has staked out an explicit principle *against* queer asylum-seeking premised upon an argument about homophobia.[7] "Homophobia", therefore, emerges as an essentially political concept, not only in relation to identifying prejudice and responding to discrimination and violence against LGBT Trinbagonians as discussed above, but also as a deeply contested construct among queer rights advocates themselves. Homophobia matters in more ways than many realize.

Another area of contention implicating the politics of homophobia concerns strategies for change in relation to anti-homosexual legislation enshrined in Trinidad and Tobago's national law. Most overt is the 1969 Immigration Act, which bars the entry of homosexuals into the country, and the anti-sodomy, or "buggery" clause, of the updated Sexual Offences Act (2000), which criminalizes anal sex and raises the maximum penalty for consensual adult homosex from ten to twenty-five years in jail. Meanwhile, the nation's own antidiscrimination legislation (the Equal Opportunity Act of 1999) that outlaws discrimination based on the usual roster of categories of experience such as race, sex, religion, and so on, and obliges the state to protect victims of such discrimination, explicitly excludes sexuality from its purview. In other words, Trinidad and Tobago's premier antidiscrimination law itself actively discriminates.[8] While CAISO emphasizes that criminal charges are practically never brought against anyone based on these laws and has chosen not to directly challenge them in court, instead focusing its energies on building interorganizational coalitions and fostering more organic patterns of social change through messaging campaigns, lobbying efforts and so forth, others see challenging the law as the single-most important route for driving progressive social change in Trinidad and Tobago.

Legal action was taken in February 2017 by a Trinidad-born, Trinidad and Tobago–UK binational, London-resident Jason Jones, suing the Government of Trinidad and Tobago over its discriminatory legal statutes. Jones made an initial local foray into LGBT activism when he returned to the country for a time in 2011–12 and began openly lobbying for the decriminalization of homosexuality, starting a new queer activist group, I am ONE TnT,[9] which has subsequently become more lesbian in leadership and membership after Jones returned to the United Kingdom. He re-emerged on the scene dramatically in early 2016, making headlines for having come back to mount a legal challenge to the state and seeking to have existing laws criminalizing homosexuality declared null and void. Though the laws are rarely enforced, he argues, they nonetheless encourage and rationalize a "culture of homophobia". As he states in an early 2017 interview:

After going full time into human rights, I thought that – alongside the advocacy that we do around visibility – the legal situation had to be addressed. Most of the homophobic religious organisations and other organisations, even the man on the street, if they believe that it [homosexuality] is illegal, they feel that they are entitled to discriminate against us. They think the law protects them. The death threats and other negative messages that I have been receiving on social media prove that fact. People are showing their faces and names on Facebook and making death threats, and they feel entitled. That is because of this law; this law entitles them to discriminate. So, for me, changing the law is where every-thing has to begin. The community response has been incredibly powerful and positive. I've had hundreds and hundreds of messages from LGBTIQ people in Trinidad and Tobago, and people who are from Trinidad and Tobago who live overseas, who have been excited and incentivised by this lawsuit.[10]

Jones's case also contends that Trinidad and Tobago's anti-homosexual laws not only infringe upon his right to privacy and freedom, but also contradict the country's obligations under international law and human rights conventions as member of the United Nations, the Organization of American States, signatory to the Inter-American Commission on Human Rights, and so forth. Jones moved to the United Kingdom as a young man after growing up in Trinidad, where he experienced stigma and discrimina-tion and was disowned by his family for his sexuality. Now he has returned on a mission to right wrongs.

This historic legal case has recently been adjudicated and promises to radically transform the landscape of lesbian and gay rights in Trinidad and Tobago. In late January 2018, the case of Jones against the attorney general of Trinidad and Tobago (Claim No. CV2017-00720) was heard in the High Court of Justice challenging sections 13 and 16 of the Sexual Offences Act, which criminalize male homosexuality with penalties up to a maximum of twenty-five years in jail if convicted. On 12 April 2018, the presiding judge, the Honourable Mr Justice Devindra Rampersad, ruled that these sections of the act were "unconstitutional, illegal, null, void, invalid and are no effect to the extent that these laws criminalize any acts constituting consensual sexual conduct between adults". On 20 September 2018, Justice Rampersad confirmed and clarified the earlier decision, affirming that consensual adult homosex remains legal and that it is also legal for minors who are sixteen or seventeen years of age to have consensual non-penetrative sexual intimacy. The case has been appealed by the Government of Trinidad and Tobago and will be heard at an as-yet-unknown date by Trinidad and Tobago's Court of Appeal. Regardless of the outcome, the case is likely to eventually make its way to the Privy Council in London, which is the highest appellate court for Trinidad and Tobago. The case will, therefore, take several more years before being finally adjudicated and have sociopolitical implications for queer Trinbagonian citizens. In the meantime, the sections of the law in question cannot be enforced.

We cannot ignore homophobia's viciousness. While it may not necessarily kill, it nonetheless victimizes in many ways. It stigmatizes and marginalizes. It prompts some to hate themselves or their families to disown them. It causes others to flee home and migrate elsewhere. It enshrines prejudice in law, in turn rationalizing societal bigotry and discrimination, from school to workplace. Yet not everyone experiences homophobia in the same way or to the same degree. Indeed, some queer Trinbagonians are able to be relatively "out" among friends and family, perhaps even sometimes at work or in school. And many believe things are changing for the better, including the country's premier advocacy group, which claims that homophobia is not generally bad enough to warrant support for queer asylum-seeking abroad, aside from the rare exceptional case.[11] Lately the SLF is #LitWithPride.

As we've seen, "homophobia" is not a singular or homogenous phenomenon, but a complex assemblage of personal sentiment and political practice that is never static. The CARIMIS study clarifies that neither visibility nor invisibility is an easy road and that each involves deeply poignant

Figure 3.5. SLF #LitWithPride image. Courtesy of Silver Lining Foundation.

challenges and trade-offs experienced by everyone along the entire spectrum of queer sexual orientations. Homophobia is, therefore, not only individually variable at the level of personal experience but also sociologically complex in public discourse, political culture and institutional life. All of which adds up to a political concept invoked by both defenders and critics of LGBT rights alike, as well as being deeply contested among queers themselves and their advocates. One's experience of, or perspective on, homophobia influences one's positions on domestic politics, national strategies for change and the international right to seek asylum.

In order to get a deeper, more nuanced view of how homophobia is experienced in Trinidad and Tobago, I turn to an important and fascinating finding that has emerged in the course of my research among homosexual men and transgender women living in and out of the country. It helps better account for the multifaceted complexity of homophobia as a lived phenomenon, which facilitates differing personal perspectives and ideological positions. These materials also invite further scrutiny concerning the queer Caribbean's past and possible futures.

Level 5 in Trinidad and Tobago

The finding to which I refer may be simply put, but not so easily understood. My research on queer Trinidad and Tobago has included many years of participant observation, more than a decade informally since 1997 then in a formal capacity since 2011. It has also entailed semi-structured life-history interviews with approximately seventy-five Trinbagonians. This interview sample consists predominantly of homosexually behaving men of varied orientations and identifications complemented by a smaller subset of transgender women, either living in Trinidad and Tobago (the majority) or abroad. Toward the end of my interviews exploring their life histories, I inquired about people's perceptions and assessment of homophobia and asked them to rate Trinidad and Tobago on a scale from 1 to 10, with 10 being the highest possible level. This is an admittedly contrived, subjective question, yet it is productive of rich commentary and revealing conversation.

By far and away the preponderance of my interlocutors claimed that Trinidad and Tobago's level of homophobia was 5. At first I didn't know what to expect, but over time, 5 became so common a response, I almost came to expect it and was surprised when other levels were mentioned. Overall, responses ranged from 3 to 8, with 5 the clear median. The few who rated a level under 5 did not go below 3, citing one or more of the following:

the fact that Trinidad and Tobago still has discriminatory laws on the books, that it does not have state human rights protections based on sexual orientation or gender expression, that it was not possible to be fully "out", accepted, and live a life on par with heterosexuals, or that pockets of prejudice still fester, especially among conservative religious communities. Responses above 5 were more prevalent than those below it and were generally stronger versions of the rationale offered for the most common rating of 5.

So how and why did so many people explain their L5 assessments? Here are the main reasons and characterizations, separated for analytical purposes, but variously held in intertwined configurations by different subjects:

- Homophobia in Trinidad and Tobago is not as bad as Jamaica, which is clearly the worst in the region; therefore Trinidad and Tobago is around level 5. (In this regard, Trinbagonians share a dominant global perception of Jamaica as extraordinarily homophobic.)
- In reality, Trinbagonians are generally tolerant, including of LGBT people; it's just that they do not fully accept them, invoking a crucial distinction between tolerance and acceptance. (This is precisely why the SLF rhetoric promotes acceptance over tolerance, as described above.)
- Most Trinbagonians do not really care what same sex–loving people do, so long as they do it in private. If one does not have to witness it, it doesn't matter.
- The problem of "homophobia" does not concern sexuality per se, but transgressive gender behaviour: you can do what you want as long as you more or less adhere to heteronormative public behaviour. (This idea connects with the one before, as well as to the problem of transphobia below.)
- Homophobia in Trinidad and Tobago is more verbal than physical, so yes, it's there and isn't nice; indeed, it can be quite unpleasant and even vicious, but one doesn't have to generally fear for one's life or physical well-being in response to anti-homosexual prejudice in society. A few L5ers further commented on this idea by saying that Trinbagonians are either too "selfish" or "lazy" to go out of their way to physically harass or interfere with others, even when they disapprove of or have a problem with homosexuality.
- Gay men have it worse than lesbians, so it's a mixed bag when it comes to homophobia in Trinidad and Tobago (higher for males, but lower for females), generating a national average of level 5.

- It's the conservative religious people who are the problem and chiefly responsible for homophobia in Trinidad and Tobago. If they would back down and get with the programme, the country's level of homophobia would decrease considerably.
- Homophobia in Trinidad and Tobago depends on how much money you have: if you have it, you can be gay and no one bothers you; but if you do not, it is another ugly story altogether. However, a counter-view held by a smaller number of people states that the more money and status you have, the more you have to lose, therefore the more incentive to remain "closeted", a trope explicitly used by many of my interviewees. Therefore, while many agree that socioeconomic status matters, they disagree about how and why it matters. The majority of my respondents saw a correlation between being privileged and the ability to be gay and even relatively visible about it, however.

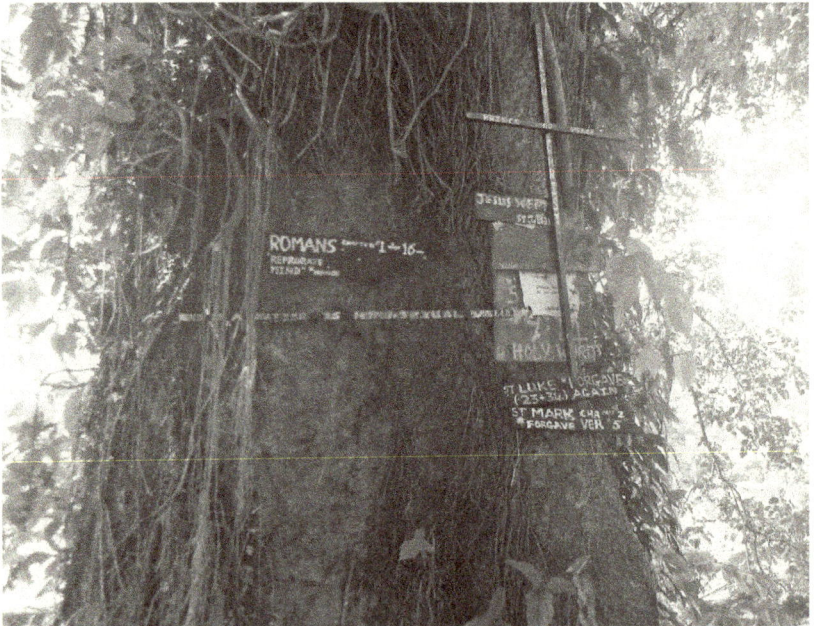

Figure 3.6. Image of anti-gay Christian signage along Saddle Road in upper Maraval heading toward Maracas Beach. In addition to some Biblical quotations and a cross on which is written "Jesus Christ – Prince of Peace", there is also signage referencing Romans 1:16 saying "REPROBATE MIND: HOMOS" and another just below it stating "END OF A NATION IS HOMOSEXUAL YOU!" This photograph was taken by the author in July 2016, but the signage no longer exists as a result of infrastructural efforts to widen the road, which led to the trees in that area being removed.

Figure 3.7. Image of the front public wall of an Afro-religious Orisha Shrine in Laventille on which is painted the admonition "NO GAYS" as well as the instructions "NO SHORT PANT", "NO VESTS", "NO BEERS" and "WOMEN PROPERLY ATTIRED". Photograph taken by the author in March 2012.

- Things are, or have been, getting better, a belief that further breaks down into two divergent expectations about the future: things are getting better and will continue getting better as a result of national development and the progressive social change associated with continuing globalization and the like; versus the idea that things have recently gotten better, but they are as good as it gets at this point and one cannot expect much more. In other words, queers have, by now, maxed out their partial space for tolerance in society, with some fearing or predicting the tide will turn regressive again, fostering a backlash that will push Trinidad and Tobago's level of homophobia higher than 5, returning to levels thought to be characteristic of the nation's past.
- Everyone agrees that homophobia is nowhere near as severe as transphobia. Indeed, there is considerably less optimism about positive or progressive change regarding transphobic sentiments and attitudes in society, including among queers too. This is partly why so many transgender folks have been seeking asylum abroad.

What to make of this varied set of ideas, perceptions and expectations, and what are the implications for thinking about the politics of homophobia and queer advocacy in Trinidad and Tobago? We must take seriously the fact that the majority of my interlocutors rated Trinidad and Tobago's level of homophobia in the mid-range of societal intensity, somewhere between the best and worst of all possible worlds. This means that the twin-island nation cannot be easily depicted as either homophobic or, contrariwise, nonhomophobic. We must be wary of simplistic generalizations and essentializing typifications, especially when lives and politics are at stake.

I am arguing here that "homophobia" in Trinidad and Tobago be seen as a complex assemblage of discourse and practice that manifests differentially in relation to a range of variables contingent upon social status and personal circumstance. Some queer folks are relatively open about their sexuality and able to craft satisfying lives for themselves somewhat free of stigma or persecution, including maintaining stable same-sex relationships known to family and friends and possibly even co-workers. Yet others experience discrimination and harassment in ways that seriously endanger their physical and psychological well-being. However, most find themselves somewhere in-between these opposite poles of experience, navigating the complex and ambivalent realities of life in a daily effort to actualize themselves while saving face in ways they deem personally comfortable or socially appropriate. This sociological landscape produces a hall-of-mirrors effect in which the line between what is actual and what is not in terms of homophobia is murky and ambiguous. This means that it is not always clear how one can behave or should comport oneself, how much one should or should not camouflage one's sexuality, whom one may trust, what boundaries are firm versus those that are open and malleable, and so forth. In some cases, this means that hiding one's sexuality is prudent and, in fact, necessary for survival. But in other cases, it means that one may be more fearful or paranoid than necessary, perpetuating vicious cycles of self-stigma and homophobia from within. There is no clear formula for living under such circumstances in which the privileges of self-actualization and visibility cannot be taken for granted.

This complex sociological reality and variable spectrum of personal experience generates differing and sometimes highly contested positions and perspectives regarding strategies for fostering progressive change and achieving social justice for queer folks. Some believe that changing the mostly unenforced laws against homosexuality matters gravely whereas others do not. Some emphasize transforming social and political institutions whereas others prioritize fostering more organic forms of change from below in everyday life. Some migrate for school or work to another country if they have the means or connections to do so, whereas others prefer or have no choice but to cope with and adapt to life as they know it at home. Seeing the differential experience and reality of homophobia in this light helps us better understand why some think it gets better and actively oppose the efforts of some queer Trinbagonians to seek asylum abroad while others make an international exit, or at least fantasize about doing so while lying low at home. For these reasons, I find myself sympathetic both to those who suffer genuine persecution that leads them to seek asylum in Europe or North America, as well as to CAISO, whose progressive nationalist vision leads it to oppose asylum-seeking by nationals in an effort to squelch the queer brain drain that might otherwise fuel a more robust movement at home (see McNeal 2019b).

The phenomenon of Trinbagonian asylum-seeking brings me to a final cautionary point about the interrelated politics of homophobia and transphobia. Over the last decade or so, a growing number of queer and transgender Trinbagonians have sought asylum in the United States, Canada and Europe, citing legally sanctioned discrimination and persecution in Trinidad and Tobago, the absence of state protections and the difficulty in crafting a satisfying life on par with heterosexuals. As indicated, this is a complex, contested issue, in relation to which different legitimate perspectives and positions coexist. What I want to address here are the ways various forms of "progressive" social change are, however partial, creating new pressures for homonormativity and "respectable" forms of lesbigay visibility as a sort of compromise with the prevailing postcolonial heteronationalist dispensation that dominates institutional life and political culture in Trinidad and Tobago. By "homonormative" I mean ways of being gay that are not *too* transgressive, whether in terms of gendered comportment (that is, being "straight-acting", or not too "real", to invoke the local vernacular) or in not being too politically radical, demanding or "in your face". This is a moral and cultural politics that privileges normality and respectability, as if to say, "we're just like you, we just happen to be gay". This may work well for some, but these developments spawn an intensification of transphobia, including within the queer "community" itself, contributing to upregulated patterns of specifically transgender asylum-seeking abroad in Europe and North America.

The point here is that battling "homophobia" by seeking social justice and cultural space for cisgender gay men or lesbians at the expensive of transgender folks is a limited and short-sighted form of queer politics. It trades homophobia for transphobia by scapegoating and sacrificing trans folk. It is ultimately a shallow and misbegotten strategy, given that homophobia and transphobia are both the ugly stepchildren of modern heteronormativity. For both political and intellectual reasons, we cannot concern ourselves with homophobia in Trinidad and Tobago – or anywhere else – without also concerning ourselves centrally with transphobia. They stem from the same source. We must learn to think more intersectionally about the entire complex spectrum of queer and transgender experience.

Betwixt and Between "Homophobia"

Homophobia is a fraught topic in Trinidad and Tobago. It kills, compels, contorts and constricts. It is also complex, contested, partial and changing. For these reasons, combined with the fact that the only on-the-ground consensus on homophobia in Trinidad and Tobago is that it is neither total-izing nor insignificant, we must employ caution and care when thinking about "homophobia" there, or anywhere else for that matter. Placing scare quotes around the term reminds us what a delicate and vexatious matter we are dealing with. Yet there is a further layer of underlying ideological complexity that must now be addressed before concluding this consider-ation of homophobia in Trinidad and Tobago.

"Homophobia" is an imported term that has experienced relatively quick adoption in Trinbagonian society over the last few decades. This is clearly evidenced in my life-history interviews with folks from several generations, who came of age spanning the last quarter of the twentieth and first quarter of the twenty-first centuries. But my quarrel with "homophobia" as a discur-sive import from the Global North does not stem solely from the fact that it hails from elsewhere. Indeed, Caribbean societies are deeply globalized formations, and whether forcibly, voluntarily or somewhere in-between, much of their material and symbolic life has arrived from abroad. Once imported, it is subsequently recontextualized, modified, adapted, cross-fertilized, played with and reinvented in a complex improvisational dance with the changing sociocultural, geopolitical and colonial contingencies of the period. Indeed, the concept of "creolization" developed as an attempt to grapple with the dynamic complexities of transculturation in the region (see McNeal 2011, 323–26). To dismiss imported cultural materials solely on the basis of having been introduced from outside is simplistic and naïve. But awareness of foreign provenance necessarily raises the stakes of importation and of the adoption of concepts and terms in a globalized world of intensifying circulations of people, goods and ideas.

I therefore want to briefly consider the emergence of "homophobia" in Global Northern sociopolitical discourse, along with its assumptions and meanings, and query the ways it does not entirely fit the Caribbean situ-ation, encouraging misrecognition and friction in local queer culture and politics. Because I do not consider the Caribbean to be non-"Western", I also want to be clear that I am not arguing that "homophobia" is discur-sively irrelevant or entirely misguided, either. We must exercise caution and care when invoking "homophobia" in relation to the complexities of life and nuances of personal experience in Trinidad and Tobago and the rest of the region. Perhaps the best way to capture my take on "homophobia" is to consider it a starting point, rather than an endpoint, for discussion, analysis and debate, a heuristic concept at best, and certainly not the final word.

Psychologist George Weinberg (1972) first proposed the term "homophobia" around the same time that the American Psychiatric Association was officially depathologizing homosexuality and removing it from the *Diagnostic and Statistical Manual of Mental Disorders* (see Herek 2004 for an overview). This new concept relocated the "problem" of homosexuality from gay people themselves to the heterosexuals who were intolerant of them, whether or not it might return to them, as it often did, in the form of internalized homophobic stigma. These developments must be understood as having arisen in relation to gains made by earlier homophile and gay rights movements in Western Europe and North America, which sought to legitimate the reality of homoerotic desire and same-sex sexualities. Yet these advances were themselves premised on the modern scientific notion of sexual orientation that posited diametrically opposed notions of exclusive "heterosexuality" and "homosexuality", which had emerged by the late nineteenth century in the North Atlantic. Of course, in their original conceptualization, these polarized orientations saw heterosexuality as the legitimate, "natural" norm and homosexuality as its pathological alter ego. Yet this formulation posited what was, in fact, a radically new idea in the cultural history of human sexuality: people had relatively stable sexual "orientations" determining whether they were attracted to men or women.

Though the struggle to validate homosexuality and gay rights has been long, complex and contested, it can, nevertheless, be understood as having inverted the moral valence ascribed to homosexuality as an orientation from negative to positive. It is only within this context that we can grasp the ideological significance of "homophobia's" emergence onto the scene, consolidating the view of homosexuality as a moral good and placing the blame for its irrational denigration squarely upon the shoulders of heterosexist society. It is also only within the context of further developments in the so-called West, such as the decriminalization of "sodomy" and attaining the rights to same-sex marriage, gay adoption, serving openly in the military, and so forth in the late twentieth and early twenty-first centuries, that LGBT rights have become fully incorporated within the gamut of established human rights on the international scene. And now that western European and North American countries have gotten with the programme of LGBT rights, a discourse has emerged castigating postcolonial nations throughout the Global South that have inherited and reproduced colonial laws discriminating against homosexuality as problematically "homophobic". I see this as one of the newest iterations of what the late Michel-Rolph Trouillot (2003) called the "Savage slot": ideological ways of carving up the world between an ostensibly civilized West and the primitive Rest. Global Northern countries enshrining LGBT rights as sacred espouse a form of politics that Jasbir Puar (2007) has dubbed "homonationalism", enabling them to feel morally and politically superior to the "homophobic" Global South.[12] This is precisely the sort of quasi-racist, neocolonial imagery that CAISO resists as part of its rationale for opposing queer asylum-seeking by Trinbagonian nationals abroad.

To invoke "homophobia", then, is to activate the meanings and assumptions embedded in the history of the term. The dominant notion of homophobia assumes an exclusive homosexual orientation and presupposes an "epistemology of the closet" (Sedgwick 1990) that privileges outness and visibility as the ideal forms of self-actualization and freedom. Any "developed" nation or person should strive to be "out" and "proud" about its gayness within this paradigm. Choosing to remain "in the closet" or on the "downlow" is considered a form of arrested development (McCune 2014; Ross 2005; Snorton 2014). With this in mind, it becomes clear how the dominant Western terminology of "homophobia" does not perfectly fit in relation to Caribbean realities characterized by the relative commonness of bisexuality and the nowhere-near-any-consensus about the ostensible ideals of being out, proud and visible. "Homophobia" applied to the Caribbean involves all sorts of slippages and friction that we must not sweep under the carpet. Many queer Trinbagonian men speak of the alternative freedoms made possible by "secrecy" and discretion in living and pursuing their sexuality, especially on a small island in which everyone tends to know everyone else's business. And if "outness" and visibility are privileges afforded by socioeconomic status and resources, then we need to be careful not to let implicit classist assumptions and aspersions slip in the backdoor in our deliberations about homophobia.

Which leads me to one further complicating point. In referring above to the dominant Western terminology of "homophobia", I am not implying that Trinidad and Tobago is a non-Western society. Indeed, an important and profound school of thought inaugurated by C.L.R. James (1963) has taught us to think of the Caribbean as precociously modern and deeply global, what the late Sidney Mintz (1977, 1989, 1996) called the First World's First World (also see Scott 2004). Trouillot (2003) extended this line of analysis by showing how Caribbean societies are not in fact non-Western, but alternatively Western from within, arguing that we not only need to learn how to de-idealize the "West", but that the study of the Caribbean is one of the most effective ways to go about this empirically. What this means for this discussion is that we simultaneously interrogate the genealogy and meanings of "homophobia" in the Caribbean while also remaining alive to the ways it is being lived, deployed and debated on the ground. Indeed, the term has become common and important among queer youth and those who have come of age since the late twentieth century, with no signs of losing salience, especially within the context of ongoing globalization in media, travel, migration and so forth. What we need are more nuanced understandings of the ways people live and love, as well as dialogue and debate, betwixt and between "homophobia" in Trinidad and Tobago.

Notes

1. Available online at https://www.youtube.com/watch?v=UKhtQXxRyzY.

2. See, for example, https://www.youtube.com/watch?v=5RGxD788DlM; https://www.youtube.com/watch?v=u8EWSizYwWI. For an entire archive of the SLF's videography, see https://www.youtube.com/user/thesilverliningfound, which includes their recent #LitWithPride campaign.

3. More recently, the SLF has embarked on a data-collection project regarding the prevalence and dynamics of homophobia among students in the national school system, to be used in the development of sensitivity and reconciliation training for teachers and administrators, as well as foster innovative pedagogical policies and programmes.

4. See https://trinidadexpress.com/news/local/a-need-for-understanding/article_fb235582-74ee-5b19-92f2-adb9b91190d5.html.

5. See https://unitedandstrongstlucia.files.wordpress.com/2015/08/final-baseline august102015-2.pdf.

6. See http://sigmaresearch.org.uk/files/report2014d.pdf.

7. I address the politics of queer asylum-seeking from Trinidad and Tobago to the United Kingdom from a different and more rigorously theorized perspective in McNeal (2019).

8. See McNeal (2012, n.d.) for an overview of Trinidad and Tobago law relating to sexuality.

9. See https://www.facebook.com/iamonetnt/.

10. Coverage of the case can be found at https://outrightinternational.org/content/interview-jason-jones-activist-challenging-trinidad-and-tobago%E2%80%99s-anti-gay-law. For news coverage of the case, see http://www.trinidadexpress.com/20170223/news/gay-rights-advocate-challenges-tts-homosexuality-laws; http://www.guardian.co.tt/news/2017-02-24/gay-activist-challenges-tt%E2%80%99s-homophobic-laws; http://www.jamaicaobserver.com/news/Gay-activist-files-lawsuit-challenging-Sexual-Offences-Act-in-T-T; http://www.washingtonblade.com/2017/03/14/activist-threatened-challenging-trinidad-tobago-sodomy-law/.

11. On the politics of queer and transgender asylum-seeking to the United Kingdom and Netherlands, see McNeal (2019a) and McNeal and Brennan (forthcoming), respectively.

12. Of course, there is a profound historical irony here in that the homonationalist countries that look down upon those occupying the new homophobic Savage slot are the very same ones that, in a former high colonial-Christian-modernist-nationalist dispensation that privileged heterosexuality and pathologized homosexuality, used to castigate their colonial Others as racially inferior and sexually licentious for condoning homosexuality and other forms of ostensible perversion. The timetable of this twentieth-century rhetorical transformation correlates precisely with the post–World War II emergence and eventual success of the modern gay rights movement, with tropes of Global Southern nations morphing from "queer" to "homophobic" as Global Northern nations incorporated a mainstreamed and commodified form of homosexuality and LGBT rights (that is, homonationalism) into their political culture and institutions (see Eleys 1996; Drucker 2015).

References

Drucker, Peter. 2015. *Warped: Gay Normality and Queer Anti-Capitalism*. Leiden: Brill.

Eleys, Rudi C. 1996. *The Geography of Perversion: Male-to-Male Sexual Behaviour outside the West and the Ethnographic Imagination, 1750–1918*. New York: New York University Press.

Herek, Gregory M. 2004. "Beyond 'Homophobia': Thinking about Sexual Prejudice and Stigma in the Twenty-First Century". *Sexuality Research and Social Policy* 1 (2): 6–24.

International Gay and Lesbian Human Rights Commission (IGLHRC) and United and Strong. 2015. "Homophobia and Transphobia in Caribbean Media: A Baseline Study in Belize, Grenada, Guyana, Jamaica and St Lucia". New York. Accessed 22 January 2020. https://unitedandstrongstlucia.files.wordpress.com /2015/08/final-baselineaugust102015-2.pdf.

James, C.L.R. 1963. "Appendix: From Toussaint L'Ouverture to Fidel Castro". *The Black Jacobins: Toussaint L'Ouverture and the San Domingo Revolution*. 2nd rev. ed. New York: Vintage.

McCune Jr, Jeffrey Q. 2014. *Sexual Discretion: Black Masculinity and the Politics of Passing*. Chicago: University of Chicago Press.

McNeal, Keith E. 2011. *Trance and Modernity in the Southern Caribbean: African and Hindu Popular Religions in Trinidad and Tobago*. Gainesville: University Press of Florida.

———. 2012. "Heteronationalism, Homonormativity, and the Problem of Sexual Citizenship in Trinidad and Tobago". Institute for Gender and Development Studies (University of the West Indies) lecture. https://www.youtube .com/watch?v=9wNuhG7MI1g.

———. 2019a. "Confessions of an Ambivalent Country Expert: Queer Refugeeism and the Politics of Queer (Im)Mobility in and out of Trinidad and Tobago". *Anthropological Theory* 19 (1): 191–215.

———. 2019b "Queering the Citizen in the Shadows of Globalisation: Dispatches from Trinidad and Tobago". Manuscript.

McNeal, Keith E., and Sarah French Brennan. Forthcoming. "Between Homonationalism and Islamophobia: Comparing Queer Caribbean and Muslim Asylum-Seeking in/to the Netherlands". In *Queer Migration, Diaspora and Asylum*, edited by R. Mole. London: University College of London Press.

Mintz, Sidney W. 1977. "The So-Called World System: Local Initiative and Local Response". *Dialectical Anthropology* 2 (2): 253–70.

———. 1989. *Caribbean Transformations*. New York: Columbia University Press.

———. 1996. "Enduring Substances, Trying Theories: The Caribbean as Oikoumene". *Journal of the Royal Anthropological Institute* 2 (2): 289–311.

Puar, Jasbir. 2007. *Terrorist Assemblages: Homonationalism in Queer Times*. Durham, NC: Duke University Press.

Ross, Marlon. 2005. "Beyond the Closet as Raceless Paradigm". In *Black Queer Studies: A Critical Anthology*, edited by E.P. Johnson and M.G. Henderson, 161–89. Durham, NC: Duke University Press.

Scott, David. 2004. "Modernity that Predated the Modern: Sidney Mintz's Caribbean". *History Workshop Journal* 58:191–210.

Sedgwick, Eve Kosofsky. 1990. *Epistemology of the Closet*. Berkeley: University of California Press.

Snorton, C. Riley. 2014. *Nobody Is Supposed to Know: Black Sexuality on the Down Low*. Minneapolis: University of Minnesota Press.

Trouillot, Michel-Rolph. 2003. *Global Transformations: Anthropology and the Modern World*. New York: Palgrave.

Weinberg, George. 1972. *Society and the Healthy Homosexual*. New York: St Martin's.

Part 2.

Queering the Spiritual,
Queering the Artistic

4.

I Am a Messenger
Spiritual Baptism and the Queer Afterlife of Faith

LYNDON K. GILL

By now, same sex–desirous and gender-nonconforming devotees are a gloriously unavoidable presence even in the most resistant candle-bearing corners of the kindred first-generation creole religions of the Americas – Candomblé, Vodoun and Santería certainly figuring most prominently among these queer faith traditions.[1] An ancient social phenomenon rooted as deeply in the not-so-New World as it is in the Old World (African and Asian as well as European), queerness of various denominations has travelled for centuries across ocean and desert, mountain and plain, up through the Caribbean archipelago and back down the mighty Mississippi. Routed through the ebb and flow of bodies – native, pirate, missionary, colonist, enslaved, indentured, immigrant, tourist – and desires, black religious institutions throughout the African diaspora are as multiple as the relationships people in this hemisphere have long had to each other, to their genders and to a host of spiritual traditions rooted, brought and created here.

And yet – intently focusing the conversation about the continuum of black religiosity, gender identity and sexuality in the Americas on Christianity is hardly arbitrary, given the disproportionate influence of a range of Christian traditions throughout North and South America. However, even in the Americas, the persistent faithfulness of African-descended worshipers to the fellowship fostered in their mosques, synagogues, sanghas or temples is far from negligible. And these non-Christian traditions are as important for any conversation about religion, gender and sexuality in the African Americas as the influential syncretic faiths that convene black peoples in terreiros, hounfours, houses, groundations, tabernacles or conjure circles. Broadening the spectrum of what comes to light as recognizably Christian, the creole faiths cultivated in these worship spaces are at the very least symbolic supplications to consider spiritual worlds beyond straightforward US American Christian denominations, which in many instances are themselves not-so-straightforward – and thus, queer – syncretic paths.

Previously published in *Small Axe* 22, no. 1 (2018), pp. 71–84. Reprinted by permission of Duke University Press, © Duke University Press 2018.

Still largely overlooked in scholarly conversations about "New World" spiritual traditions, the Spiritual Baptist faith is what I am calling a second-generation creole religion that serves at once as a geo-conceptual crossroads where the North American South and the Southern Caribbean, the Christian and the non-Christian, and the African, Asian and European worlds of ritual and iconography meet and merge. Although like most syncretic faiths, Spiritual Baptism resists definitive, singular or linear origin narratives, one of its most convincing genesis stories, corroborated by much of the available historical evidence, identifies in its constitution a strong African American Southern Baptist tradition deeply accented in the Caribbean with West African and Catholic aural aesthetics, ritual objects, adornment practices, initiation rites and spirit-possession precepts.

Like a current or a breeze, the Spiritual Baptist faith emerges from, transforms through and calls attention to movement across space and time. The peregrinations that created the religion are a testament to the mobility of the sacred – across various physical and metaphysical sites – that parallels a temporal mobility by which the faith passes fluidly between the past and the present (Duncan 2008, x, xi, 4).[2] Through marking the journey and development of this creole spiritual tradition in what follows, one comes to recognize its history as not mere background, but rather as a vital interpretive framework for the present and potential future iterations of the faith (68). The grounding trope of journeying – (meta)physically and temporally – in the Spiritual Baptist tradition is attributable in no small part to the long history of border crossings that constitute the faith. This process of *journeying into being* also insists metaphorically on the kind of boundary crossing that calls queerness as a classic norm (or limit) contesting posture into being as a theory. This broadly conceived spatial, temporal and conceptual queerness *of* Spiritual Baptism opens a more respectful path by which to approach LGBT practitioners who manifest queerness *in* the faith. These queer Spiritual Baptists are a crossroads that is also a bridge.

Still, while the proliferation of same-sex desiring and gender-nonconforming practitioners from new initiates to revered religious elders has been for some time garnering popular, artistic and scholarly attention in the classic "New World" spiritual traditions, the Spiritual Baptist faith has received very little attention with respect to its equally prominent queer believers (Conner and Sparks 2004).[3] Ignored in much of the scholarly literature on the faith, the intimacy between Caribbean queer communities and various Spiritual Baptist churches remains nonetheless experientially ever present. In fact, the faith first captured my attention as a seemingly pervasive referent during the course of my fieldwork on lesbian and gay communities in the Republic of Trinidad and Tobago (Gill 2018).[4] I had not gone to Trinidad or Tobago searching for queerness in the Spiritual Baptist faith; I went looking for queer artistry and activism. But I was quickly made to understand that I could not fully comprehend either without some attention to this religious tradition that was seemingly secret only to me – a black, queer Trinidadian-American raised with as much Trinbagonian culture as New York City would allow.[5]

Coming face to face again and again with Spiritual Baptist practitioners within communities of LGBT Trinbagonians over the course of the near decade and a half that I have been travelling to Trinidad and Tobago as an out adult has slowly begun to seem less and less coincidental and more and more pointedly consequential. As I consider my next book project, *Love Jumbie: Spiritual Baptism and the Queer Sacred Arts*, these initial notes toward a new research agenda have begun to chart a cartography of interest (Allen 2010).[6] Still, this potential map (like all maps) must come to terms – terms that Trinidadian-Canadian lesbian poet, novelist, essayist and activist Dionne Brand (1999, 52–53) gives to us – with its inevitable inadequacies in the face of geographies of experience:

> This map cannot note the great fluidity of maps, which is like the fluidity of air. Paper rarely contains – even its latitudinal and longitudinal lines gesture continuations. Paper does not halt land any more than it can halt thoughts. Or rain showers, for that matter. The best cartographer is only trying to hold water, to draw approximations of rocks, inclines, bays, depths, plains. . . . That is where a map succumbs to anarchy. Maps' inadequacies give out here.

However, to begin this journey, one requires a map, even if that map is a kind of topographical intervention designed to quake the boundaries of a region. Providing yet another interpretive bridge between the two sites in the Americas (outside of Brazil) that boast the largest concentration of black peoples, this work bridges the US South and the Caribbean precisely because they not so coincidentally share the stigma of a popularly presumed irrational and violent homophobia too often attributed to the ostensible blinding religiosity of both regions (Glave 2008; Johnson 2008).[7] What might it mean to buttress the bridge that has long connected these demonized sites of religious fervour and homophobic excess in an effort to unmask ancient racist assumptions of black incivility, irrationality, savagery and superstitious abandon? Are there a few queer lessons writ large about spirituality, but also about religious institutions in particular that the black bodies shared between the southern Caribbean and the US South have to teach us?

These are lessons in the afterlife of faith – the vitality of belief among the queer faithful when so much of queer studies has buried spirituality in general, but especially Christianity, in tombs of homophobic irrationality. This is the queer afterlife of faith when so much of queer theory, unable to see beyond the presumption of death's finality, has laid faith to rot in sarcophaguses of fear and loathing. The quotidian resolution of a presumed religious crusade against LGBT livelihood that certainly has its vituperative and violent frontlines, but also its irreverent and intimate fault lines, is fought for in the contextual specificities of queer living and believing. So, this analysis focuses on the spiritual moorings of one particularly prominent queer Afro-Caribbean calypso singer and religious elder whose life and career have long shuttled her between the scared and the profane, the feminine and the masculine, and the United States and the Caribbean (Gill 2018, 139–64).[8] This lauded Tobagonian lesbian artist Linda McCartha Sandy Lewis (known affectionately worldwide by her sobriquet "Calypso Rose") is but one – though undoubtedly one of the most charismatic – of various same sex–desiring Spiritual Baptists I encountered without looking. But before I formally introduce the calypso queen and spiritual mother, I must first introduce her faith.

Spiritual Baptists: A Second-Generation Creole Faith

Although there are various origin narratives scattered throughout the scholarly literature on the Spiritual Baptist faith, the available historical evidence points suggestively toward a particular genesis of the religion as one of the first begotten spiritual children of the syncretizing contact between black religious communities of the US South and the Southern Caribbean (Duncan 2008, 68–69, 91, 113; Glazier 1983; Henry 2003, 32; Houk 1995; Lum 2000, 29–35; Zane 1999).[9] Cousin cultural regions bridged by the common origins of various West and Central African peoples planted on the shores of the Gulf of Mexico and the Caribbean Sea in the fertile belly of the Americas, the American South and the southern Caribbean also share a later history of interconnection that is certainly less forcefully imposed and continues up to the present moment. The inauguration of the Spiritual Baptist faith is but one early indicator that contact among common peoples separated and acculturated in different souths was bearing fruit that would draw these centuries-separated African peoples together again in worship. A bridge faith gifted through the bridge regions of the Americas, the Spiritual Baptist communion ironically owes much to the Anglo-American War of 1812.

Waged in an effort to resolve many of the disagreements still lingering from the American Revolutionary War – an eight-year conflict that finally came to an end in 1783 – this Second War of Independence provided the British an opportunity to recruit enslaved Americans of African descent into their Corps of Colonial Marines under the promise of freedom and land (Wood 1968, 38).[10] Hardly an altruistic gesture, the deployment of these African American marines fighting on behalf of the British crown undoubtedly served the dual purposes of undermining American authority in its touchy southern underbelly and saving British troops from having to fight two wars simultaneously in the tropics – one against the Americans and the other, perhaps just as severe, against the environment. By 1815, the war had come to an end and the British made good on their promise to grant the African American marines their freedom, which could only be guaranteed in the British-protected areas of the Americas. So, in the early nineteenth century, a sizable group of black Americans resettled on crown-granted lands in Trinidad – one of the most sparsely populated of the various remaining English colonies in the Caribbean (Henry 2003, 31; Houk 1995; Lum 2000, 32). In 1816, more than seventy years before the British officially linked Trinidad and Tobago administratively, nearly eight hundred formerly enslaved black American Southerners settled in six "Company Villages", named for the regimental lines (or "companies") in which they served, in the south-west of Trinidad (Brereton 1981, 68; De-Light and Thomas, 2001, 228; Duncan 2008, 71; Lum 2000, 33).[11] These colonial marines brought with them the Baptist faith of America's nineteenth-century Protestant revivalist movement (the Second Great Awakening) with its emphasis on rejoicing, handclapping, dancing and shouting in the service of worship.[12] Although William Hamilton quickly established the first black Baptist church in Trinidad the same year of the companies' arrival, the Baptist faith in Trinidad very early began to develop a particular character.[13]

If the black Southern Baptists who first arrived in Trinidad were already deeply influenced by the West and Central African theological grammars and surreptitious ritual practices that Americans of African descent were able to actively and unconsciously preserve despite their forced embrace of Christianity, then this influence was both deepened and expanded as they settled into their new southern Caribbean context. The early influence of Yoruba cosmology and spiritual practice would be combined with elements of Kabbalism, Roman Catholicism, Anglicanism, Spiritism, Hinduism and Islam at various moments in the development of this new Baptist communion (Glazier 1983, 3; Lum 2000, 17, 40). Yet, what would come to be known as the *Spiritual* Baptist faith in Trinidad, Tobago and throughout the larger Caribbean region presents itself as a philosophically Christian religion even if it allows for a wide range of borrowing in the expression of that Christian philosophy (Zane 1999, 4). After all, the *spirit* emphasized in this iteration of Baptist faith is irrefutably the Holy Spirit of the Christian Trinity. Although that spirit may manifest in Spiritual Baptist worshippers, there remains for them a marked distinction between that manifestation of the presumed one truly holy spirit and all other spirit possession possibilities permissible in other – especially Yoruba-based – traditions (Lum 2000, 6). The vocal exuberance of both these spiritual manifestations in particular and the worship service in general early on earned the followers of this faith the uneasy appellation "Shouter Baptists" (or simply "Shouters").[14] Beyond this identificatory aural cue, an emphasis on Holy Spirit manifestation, and an insistence on total adult immersion baptismal rites, this distinctly Afro-Caribbean-accented African American spiritual tradition incorporates an intensely mission-driven evangelism, dream divination, individual-centred repentance and spiritual regeneration, shaking, dancing, speaking in tongues, bell ringing, altar construction and most centrally a particular type of mourning ritual (Henry 2003, 36, 37; Lum 2000, 33).

If one of the most distinguishing characteristics of the Spiritual Baptist faith is an emphasis on spiritual travel, then the mourning ritual is perhaps the richest representation of that travel in the faith (Duncan 2008, 55; Zane 1999, 4). Modelled in the biblical book of Daniel, this elaborate ascetic process clears a space for spiritual revelations through an intensely humbling course of isolated fasting and meditation that can last from one to three weeks and proves essential both as an initiation rite and as a means by which to ascend in the hierarchy of any given church.[15] This journey into a new, or perhaps deeper, spiritual awareness is decidedly the most significant travel metaphor in the faith, but others certainly abound; the most prominent of these being the common symbolic transmutation of the church structure itself into a ship with its leader as captain, its identifying flags, its map and compass in the Bible, its sacred central mast (or centre pole) from which a symbolic steering wheel hangs and its crew of congregants charged with keeping the ship afloat (Lum 2000, 41–47). It is unsurprising that this emphasis on metaphorical and metaphysical travel should be symbolically prominent for an already itinerant religion adopted and adapted by two displaced and re-rooted cousin cultures of the African diaspora. The literal waterborne journeys foregrounded in the collective memory of the African American and Caribbean midwives of the Spiritual Baptist faith provide a tropic master referent for the transformative spiritual travel required in perpetuity of the devotee.

In Thy Midst: Spiritual Baptists and One Resounding Queer Presence

One such devotee – Linda McCartha Monica Sandy – was born on 27 April 1940 in the hilltop village of Bethel on the island of Tobago. She is the fourth of eleven children the Spiritual Baptist minister Altino Sandy and his wife Dorchea Sandy (née Ford) were to bring into and keep in the world. In what follows, I refer to Mrs McCartha Sandy Lewis by her unhyphenated married name according to her personal preference.[16] Lewis spent the first decade of her life in rocky Bethel village, named for a prophetic biblical city that Jacob anoints and names in Genesis, before she was taken to live with her uncle and his common-law wife in Barataria, Trinidad, at the age of nine.[17] Lewis wrote her first calypso in 1955 and began her professional career in Trinidad's capital Port of Spain in 1963, where she was christened with the delicate (though thorny) sobriquet "Calypso Rose". Although quick to acknowledge that she is not the first woman to sing calypso in the tents, Lewis was the first female calypsonian to win the nation's most prestigious calypso monarch title in 1978. Despite some explicit references to her same-sex desire in song or in conversation over the course of her fifty-year professional career, Lewis's highly visible presence as a calypso icon has ironically rendered her largely invisible as a same sex–desiring Caribbean woman. Or perhaps it is more a public refusal to recognize or openly discuss Lewis's sexuality – part of a lingering Victorian legacy of sexual conservatism overlaid onto a (stereo)typically sexually fecund region – that renders her invisible as a lesbian. This silence about her sexual self is as loud as it is because she is a popular figure in a performance genre that is hardly shy about sex.

More often than not, the surreal insistence on the invisibility of Caribbean female same-sex desire in the popular imagination remains unconvincing even given the materiality of flesh, palms pressed, thighs touched, chests breathing in unison or the flutter of kisses on her body's tender seams.[18] Yet nearly drowned in a swirling silence that swallows like the sea, desire still speaks its name with tongues on fire.[19] Speak still this tongue even when the words are not there:

> I am a . . . how you call the word? How you call the word? I have a friend or a lover and she always says, "Your work – because this is what you love – your work comes first." But I still divide [my time between] my work [and] my lover and we are domestic partners. This year will make it eleven years I've been married. . . . September will make it eleven years. We were married in a church in California – a Catholic Church.

I say, look, this is my life. I was raped when I was eighteen, so I have never had a man in my life. I was raped by three men when I was eighteen years of age. So, I never had any man in my life [and because of that] all the Calypsonians [would taunt me by saying,] "She's a lesbian", [only] because I never slept with any of them. Thank the Lord for that!

So, I made it final [by deciding to "marry" my long-term partner] because this is my life. My family accepts me – my whole family knew . . . my aunt had known. . . . [That same] aunt – the lady who raised me – accepted me. Everybody accepts me. And who can't accept me, chew them!

[People in Trinidad and Tobago] do talk about me, but I don't care. [They may talk] but not in a negative way. Not in a negative way at all. If they saying negative, it's probably in their mind. But they still hug me, they still kiss me, they still bow to me. Oh yes! Every time I arrive home [to Trinidad and Tobago], they bow to me, man! (Lewis, interview with author, 18 January 2007, Queens, New York; hereafter cited as "interview")

Lewis finds a way around using any particular language to describe her sexual identity. During the course of my interview with her, I hesitated to offer "lesbian", "homosexual" or "queer" to fill the space that Lewis left unfilled.[20] Instead of attempting a word to describe what she *is*, Lewis shifted quickly instead to describe whom she *has*. Her now more than two-decade domestic partnership with a woman – consecrated by a California Catholic church more than a decade before any official legal inroads had been made for gay marriage in the state – is a testament to Lewis's comfort with her same-sex desire, so her hesitance to name that desire comes from somewhere other than self-denial. Perhaps for her, the available terms are not sufficient.[21]

A rape survivor who is also a breast cancer survivor, Lewis holds as tightly to the love of her partner as she does to her love of life – a life she lives her way to the tune of her own happiness, uncluttered by any necessary referent for her affections.[22] The fact that her family acknowledges and accepts her bold resolve to live and love in a manner that brings her joy can only be a boon to Lewis. Later in the interview, upon asking her explicitly if she would describe herself as a "lesbian", Lewis quickly smiled at me and with all the ease of a breath said, "I am happy."[23] And as best as I can tell, she is happy; she is calypso royalty. She must have a sense of the rumours circulating always just out of ear shot – the pests of all royals, it seems – but she is comforted by knowing that her subjects still bow lovingly before her.[24] She must be comforted too by the reassurance that rumour feeds on secrecy and shame; this over-seventy-year-old woman, who has found love with another woman, suffers neither.[25]

Healing, Mourning and Prophecy in a Queer Spiritual Baptist Ascension

In fact, Lewis's same-sex desire has seldom come into conflict with a reverence for the unseen sown deeply in her consciousness at an early age. From those earliest days in the Tobagonian villages named for biblical cities, it appeared unavoidably true that Lewis had been touched to serve God:

> Before I could have comprehended [it completely], my father tells me that I born with a gift. Because when I was small – before I went to Trinidad – many times they [would] miss me [not knowing where to find me]; and when they miss me, they [would] have to go hunting the whole of Bethel and Bethlehem looking for me. . . . Some spirit used to come into me and lead me away.

> One time when they found me, they found me in a house in Bethlehem – the whole yard was full of people. I was healing people. . . . I know that I have a sort of a spiritual gift within me. (Interview)

Whether a true child prophet laying hands on the people of a village aptly named or a precocious young girl anxious to minister like her father in a village destined to hope for the birth of a Caribbean Christ, Lewis had been led by a compulsion beyond her reckoning to the faith of her father. It would not be until adulthood that Lewis could be formally baptized a Spiritual Baptist and begin her spiritual trials on a quest to deepen that faith:

> We – the Spiritual Baptists – when we go into the inner chamber to gain higher wisdom, we go into a room and [are] locked away for certain number of days – it depends – five days, seven days, two weeks or whatever. . . . I did it five times. I was mourned five times. We call it "mourning", when you seclude yourself from the carnal world and you go to the spiritual world. And all you do is pray – all you do is drink water and pray. You are fasting. There is light, but your eyes are banned. And the reason why your eyes are banned is as a symbol that you are banning yourself from the sight of the world.

> So, I mourned five times. The first time I mourned, I was a healer. The second time I mourned I was a Diver and Searching Warrior [spiritual roles in faith]. The third time I mourned, I'm a Mother. The fourth, I'm a Mother; the fifth time, I'm a Mother. [I ask for clarification.] A "Mother" is at the head . . . which means to say that I can put bands on my children [offer sacred protection and guidance to her own circle of followers]. I can baptize children, put seals and signs on them, and mourn them [initiate and offer spiritual counsel to newcomers in the faith]. I am very high up there. (Interview)

Having mourned the death of her carnal self five times, and each time experiencing a transfiguration of spirit, Mother McCartha cherishes her role as a religious leader.

Lewis believes she has been called to the position of divine leadership through various phases of metaphysical (and theological) enlightenment.[26] These phases are revealed to the fasting suppliant during the earlier described mourning ritual; devotees come to see themselves – their spiritual selves – more clearly as they journey toward higher planes in the religious tradition. First seeing herself as a Healer, Lewis believes she has been given the ability to soothe pain with her touch, as precociously prophesized by her childhood healing practice. As a Diver and Searching Warrior, revealed in her second journey into her sacred self, Lewis believes she was chosen to be a spiritual warrior tasked with scouring the sea floor in search of lost spirits in order to guide them home. One cannot help but imagine these diving warriors of this syncretic religion having been given the task of walking the watery underbelly of the Middle Passage looking for those unsettled souls, presumed to be roaming the fathoms of the Atlantic, yearning for a way home. In her final three crosses into the realm of the otherworldly, Lewis is thrice called a spiritual Mother, and though she has had no child of her own flesh, she has reached such a rarefied height in the Spiritual Baptist tradition that the mandate for her to guide and nurture metaphysically echoes through her.

There is hardly a discordant note in Lewis's song of self; her full-throated queerness has not silenced, and perhaps cannot silence, what she believes to be her resounding religious foundation:

> [A strong Spiritual Baptist rhythm is] in me, I born with it. [She laughs.] As I told you, I born a Baptist. . . . I am a Baptist from birth. I grew up with it and no matter what I do, it's within me. And there is something that one has to know, you cannot hide from that fact – you may try to take me out of the religion – [but] . . . the spiritual aspect, they can't take that out of me because no matter what, it is here in my singing, in my speaking . . . my spiritual background and who I am spiritually also help me to create. . . . I believe my music does something for people. That's why I feel that I am a messenger. (Ottley 1992, 11–12)

Suspicious of essentialist presumptions about an ontological spiritual self or perhaps, following Caribbean transnational lesbian feminist M. Jacqui Alexander's (2005, 327) graceful lead, aspiring toward a more sophisticated understanding of the "permanent impermanence" of an ever-changing sacred essence, we nevertheless hear in Lewis's testament a firm belief in her spiritual mandate. If sexuality – or sensual intimacy more broadly – is popularly positioned far from conventional religious terrain, it is in her music as spiritual *and* sensual sermon that Lewis aborts this false dichotomy that black lesbian feminists have insisted we relinquish for decades (Alexander 2005, 298, 320, 329; Lorde [1978] 1984, 56). If this prophetic lesbian messenger offers her gift in song, then she does so with what is perhaps the most miraculous and sensuous (not to mention ancient) instruments yet known: the human voice. Voice acquires a mysterious sensuality here not merely because of its relationship to the mouth but also because its very production is an intimate vibration that comes from flesh and air resisting or giving way, muscles tightening or relaxing, in the soft folds of the vocal tract (Wood 1994, 27).[27] Lewis's voice carries within it – in speech or in song – the echoes of a harmonized sensual-spiritual whose resonance bridges the presumed divide between the sexual and the religious. In her flesh, Lewis holds these truths together simultaneously; her same-sex desire, calypso poetics and Spiritual Baptist leadership cannot exist as separate spheres of experience precisely because a unified consciousness reaches across them. The longest reigning queen of the calypso kingdom unites two distant territories of our collective misconception, calling forth sensuality and spirituality in a single breath.

We Have Come This Far by Faith: A Conclusion That Is Not One . . .

Although Calypso Rose is one of the most prominent same sex–desiring elders in the transnational Spiritual Baptist faith – which has travelled as believers have travelled both within and beyond the Caribbean region – she is hardly a singular queer presence in the large body of Baptist congregants in Trinidad, Tobago and beyond.[28] These shouting and singing apertures of queer possibility await their cartography. As the Spiritual Baptist landscape shifts and broadens with each successive wave of baptized initiates throughout the Caribbean diaspora, this map of same sex–desiring and gender-nonconforming leaders and practitioners in the faith must also shift and broaden. Calypso Rose and her queer Baptist kin encourage us to ask other kinds of questions of Christianity in the African diaspora. They implore us to explore various queer possibilities in the fertile palimpsestic religious traditions of the Americas. What might it mean to begin our investigatory journeys into black diasporic religiosity eager to find flourishing queer presence instead of prohibiting queer absence? Which sites – both metaphysical and material – of black queer spiritual possibility draw our attention on that journey? Home to the largest population of black peoples outside of the African continent, the Americas – from Canada through the Caribbean and Central America and down to Chile – are an unavoidable initiation ground.

The predominance of a range of Christian traditions (from Catholicism to Pentecostalism) and Christian-influenced creole faiths (from Spiritual Baptist to Vodou) throughout the Americas makes it both convenient and necessary to begin the conversation about black same-sex desire, gender nonconformity and religiosity writ large in the widest possible Christian frame. Within this frame, special concerted attention to the US South and the Caribbean – precisely because these sites hold the largest concentration of black peoples in the Americas outside of Brazil – may reveal black queer sacred potential in these bridged regions, long linked by the movement (forced and voluntary) of black bodies between them and contemporarily presumed to categorically exclude LGBTQ life. But by the grace of God, these lives persist. Not simply tolerated in various religious spaces, but divinely ordained, black queer believers in the Spiritual Baptist faith and other Christian and non-Christian spiritual traditions have a larger lesson to teach us about the seemingly impossible made flesh again and again in a multiplicity of black places of worship – be they churches, mosques, hounfours, sanghas or clearings in the woods or perhaps in the heart.

An initiatory testimony, this admittedly limited investigation is the beginning of a concerted search for black queer presence in the sites where it is presumed that black same-sex desire, gender nonconformity or (more broadly) any type of antinormative posture even among heterosexuals should not or cannot exist. It is precisely among the black queer individuals and communities that inhabit and flourish within these seemingly disavowing geographical and ideological hinterlands that we will find the resilient strength and steady grounding that is as necessary for the preservation and cultivation of black queer life in Bon Accord, Tobago or Savannah, Georgia, as it is in New York City or Toronto. As both a theorist and a priest of Vodou and Santería, Jacqui Alexander has offered one of the most poetically compelling and intellectually rigorous invitations into recognizing the vital importance of sacred knowledge and the communities that preserve it in "Pedagogies of the Sacred: Making the Invisible Tangible", the final chapter of her tour de force text *Pedagogies of the Crossing: Meditations on Feminism, Sexual Politics, Memory and the Sacred* (2005, 287–332). Following Alexander's lead, I ask that we turn our attention to the black queer spiritual workers who are harnessing the power of the sacred here in the very womb of the Americas where North America, Central America and the Antilles all expose their tender bellies to the Caribbean Sea.

If indeed black queer diaspora is in part a spiritual, sensual and political project about the sharing of sacred, intimate and material resources transnationally and locally, then one of the richest, though overlooked territories of black queer experience – not nearly as keenly surveyed as intimate liveli-hoods or political rallying throughout the diaspora – has been our spiritual grounding. A shared resource that provides many of us who are black queer believers and spiritual practitioners with the moorings for our understanding of self inextricably linked to the social and the sacred, our spirituality is in harmony with our same-sex desire, at peace with our gender nonconformity and embattled with even the subtlest fetishization of faithlessness in queer life (Alexander 2005, 295). We are unwilling to relinquish our faith even in the midst of a chorus of dismissals determined to heal the wounds of various homophobic and transphobic exclusions with the salt of secularization in large part because a fertile, potent and expansive spiritual landscape is one of the most important heirlooms in our collective inheritance as queers of African descent. We hold tightly to spirit because we are convinced that an adequately compelling or even remotely comparable alternative does not exist. What could we possibly exchange for the workings of spirit in our lives? While this belief cannot mean that we stand arrogantly beyond the shadows of doubt, we are faithful pilgrims travelling a long ancient road. Many of the black queer children of Africa's diaspora have made of this journey a blessing, using the trials of its sharp peaks and steep valleys to draw us closer in fellow-ship with each other and with the sacred. We stride on – black, queer, vulner-able and faithful still – confident that if no other truth holds promise for us, we know for sure in our open hearts and across divisions of denomination or even religious traditions that we have come this far by faith and faith alone.

Notes

1. My gratitude to religious historian Vaughn A. Booker for alerting me in a personal communication (21 February 2018) to the recent emergence of the phrase "African heritage religions", which respected religious studies elders Dianne M. Stewart and Tracey Hucks have coined to describe what I refer to here as "creole religions". And while I do not use this appealing neologism in what follows, I have an affinity for the cultural and historical politics it discursively represents. My use of "creole" embraces an African heritage at the same time that it attends to new reli-gious creativity (a gesture toward the still uncertain etymology of the term "creole", perhaps from the verb "to create") in the influencing contexts of the Americas.

2. Duncan provides the most insightful, respectful and grounded participant observation-based engagements with the Spiritual Baptist faith in a diasporic Caribbean community second to none in the region.

3. Connor and Sparks's oft-looked-to compilation still provides one of the most wide-reaching treatments of queerness in the various syncretic faiths of the Amer-icas even though they do not engage Spiritual Baptism directly.

4. From 2003 to 2009, I conducted field research in the Republic of Trinidad and Tobago for what has become my first book. During the course of those seven years, I regularly shifted back and forth between the two largest eponymous islands of this archipelagic nation-state for various lengths of time culminating in a sixteen-month research trip funded by a Fulbright Fellowship. And I have continued returning to Trinidad and Tobago since 2009 for research follow-up trips and – most important – to visit my grandmother, who lives in Lowlands, Tobago. The southernmost island nation of the Caribbean, Trinidad and Tobago lies northeast of Venezuela and right outside the chain of islands known as the Lesser Antilles (though it is informally considered to be part of this chain).

5. The tragic death by fire of Judith Jennifer Ollivierre (neé Brown), the eldest daughter of my grandmother's eldest sister, Theodora Brown-Cooper (neé Gill), on 6 July 2007 during a Spiritual Baptist ritual, revealed to me that the Spiritual Baptist faith had long been a part of my family, even if the faith was seldom discussed in my presence. Both my dearly departed Aunty Judith and her deceased mother (known affectionately as "Aunty Ivy") were practising Spiritual Baptists.

6. Allen both models and inspires the open intention behind sharing the direction my research may take in hopes of welcoming other scholars to join me in walking a path through largely unattended specificities of black queer lives throughout the African diaspora.

7. Glave's compilation and Johnson's monograph have both been watershed texts in shifting the current against the racialized stigmatization of these two blackest regions of the Americas as summarily the most homophobic. Many eagerly anticipate that Johnson's follow-up oral history of black lesbian life in the US South, *Black. Queer. Southern. Women*, and its companion work of creative nonfiction, *Honey Pot: Black Southern Women Who Love Women*, will broaden and deepen this resistant flow.

8. Calypso is a quintessentially Trinbagonian music genre whose origins date back to the early eighteenth century. I provide a deeper engagement with calypso's various origin narratives in my book; however, it suffices to say here that this musical form has long been and continues to be arguably *the* most important in Trinidad and Tobago and one of the most important Caribbean music genres overall.

9. In his comparative study of the Spiritual Baptist faith, Lum resists offering one definitive history of the religion and instead opts to include the various "ethno-histories" he gathered while conducting ethnographic fieldwork in Trinidad in the mid-to-late 1980s. In her more contemporary ethnography of the faith in diaspora, Duncan also holds space for various simultaneous origin narratives that she suggests ultimately say more about those recounting that history than about the actual birth and development of the religion itself. Glazier, Houk, Zane and Duncan nod toward one of the two most reasonable origin narratives that argues that the faith may have originated in St Vincent and was later brought to Trinidad sometime in the nineteenth century. In what follows, I outline the second, following Henry's lead, more convinced of its persuasiveness in no small part by the available historical evidence.

10. Wood indicates that the British army had been, from as early as 1795, recruiting these enslaved Americans into what was initially the West Indies Regiment and

later became the Corp of Colonial Marines. So intent were they on these African Americans as soldiers that the British army purchased a significant number of these men out of slavery.

11. Contemporarily the villages officially named "First Company", "Third Company", "Fourth Company" and "Fifth Company" still mark, according to Brereton, Lum and Duncan, the legacy of freed African American soldiers resettled just east of Princes Town. One notices immediately the absence of a "Second Company" village; De-Light and Thomas propose that this entire unit was tragically lost at sea on the way to Trinidad. Trinbagonians refer to the region of the country in which we find these company villages simply as "South". And it is not unusual to hear a Trinidadian or Tobagonian say they are going "down South" meaning usually a trip to San Fernando, Trinidad's principal southern city, or any of the towns and villages in this part of the country closest to South America. The resonance here with the US South is a whisper that is also a bridge.

12. The Second Great Awakening follows the Christian revitalization movement of Protestant Europe and colonial America in the 1730s and 1740s (the First Great Awakening) and precedes the postmillennial Protestant activism movement (the Third Great Awakening) in early America from the late 1850s to the early twentieth century.

13. For more comprehensive treatments of these black American Baptists in Trinidad, see Glazier (1983), Hackshaw (1992), Weiss (2002) and Henry (2003). These studies inform and guide my own.

14. Shared Yoruba-based influences and the overlapping of both worship practices and practitioners have resulted in a discursive false marriage between Shango (as Orisha worship is known in Trinidad and Tobago, indicating the influence of that deity over and above the others of the elaborate Yoruba pantheon) and Spiritual Baptism. Although popular, the deceptive misnomer "Shango Baptist" is more often than not a flippant or inattentive referent that ignores the important distinctions between these two cousin religions. Hardly mutually exclusive, Shango and Spiritual Baptist devotees are often one in the same, but this congruence does not erase the still substantial differences between the faiths. The fact remains that the theological and ritual infrastructure of Shango is much more Yoruba than Christian while the opposite is true of Spiritual Baptism.

15. Providing one of the most attentive descriptions of the mourning ritual as customarily undertaken on the island of Tobago, but with wider resonance certainly, Maarit Laitinen (2002, 23) outlines the process thus: "*Mourning* is a ritual of self-denial and sensory deprivation during which a *pilgrim*, the initiate, travels in the Spiritual world . . . through prayers and meditation. The ritual starts with a special *pointing* ceremony, after which the pilgrims are taken into a small room in the church compound, the *Mourn[ing] room*, where they lie on their backs for at least seven . . . days. During this time, they are blindfolded, not allowed to speak, bathe, eat or drink, save three sips of water twice a day and a cup of aloes or bush tea in the morning. . . . After their journey is complete, their return to the world is embedded in a Sunday service in the church, where they finally recount their *tracks*, important features and events of their journey, to the rest of the Spiritual family. Mourning is essential in

unfolding the mysteries of the faith. . . . Baptists also receive personal advice during the ritual, such as medication for illness or direction and comfort in problematic situations in life. . . . Also, the gift of *healing*, doing Spiritual work, is acquired or fortified in mourning." And for a detailed ethnographic engagement with the mourning ritual on the island of Trinidad, see Lum's (2008, 72–79) experientially driven descriptions.

16. Ms Sandy married Aubrey Lewis in 1966 as a strategic attempt to avoid deportation for performing illegally in a US territory. This marriage of convenience, initiated plainly as such by her American band member, ought not to distract us from the reality of Lewis's uncompromising same-sex desire.

17. The consummate Trinbagonian for having lived significant portions of her life on both islands, Lewis is quick nevertheless to sing the praises of her Tobagonian roots as a figurative battle cry against the too frequent elision of Tobago and Tobagonian cultural specificities in the popular and official discourses about Trinbagonian culture.

18. Silvera's now classic text (1996) that indirectly brings this invisibility to light receives a lyrical postscript in King's meditation (2008/2005).

19. Elwin's 1997 book is the only full-length compilation that I am familiar with that directly addresses Caribbean female same-sex desire. Combining the oral histories and fiction of twenty-seven queer Caribbean women living in the region and in the diaspora, *Tongues on Fire* serves as a peppery testament to the invisible made real.

20. I hardly hesitate now, though, to call Lewis a "lesbian" in part as a discursive means by which to push back against the overwhelming heterosexist insistence (through silence) that she must be straight, but also as a way to insist on a broadening of the category "lesbian" to encompass a wider world of possible experiences following the opening of the term as lived by black lesbian feminists such as Audre Lorde, Cheryl Clarke and Barbara Smith, among many others.

21. Lewis's statement about having been married in a "Catholic church" is ambiguous at best. There are several California churches that then as now use the moniker "Catholic", but should not be confused with Roman Catholic churches. It is most likely in one of these other kinds of gay-affirming Catholic churches that Lewis was married, but one must understand the undeniable symbolic import for two Trinbagonian women (Lewis's wife is a Trinidadian, who currently lives in California) raised in a nation where Roman Catholicism remains an exceedingly prominent faith marrying each other in a church that is far from Roman Catholicism in its official tenets but still remained irrefutably Catholic even if in name alone. I must thank the Reverend Dr D. Maurice Charles for his careful and generous assistance working through this seeming impossibility specifically and for his guidance with this essay in general.

22. In 1996, Lewis underwent invasive surgery for breast cancer.

23. During an interview for the programme *Ginger Tea*, as part of a 2012 Chutney Pride *HalloQueen* event in New York City, Lewis, who attended as a featured performer, deploys much more specific sexual identity language while affirming her role as an icon for the queer community. In what is likely the most easily accessible and public declaration of her same-sex desire and LGBTQ political solidarity to date, Calypso Rose comfortably declares: "I am gay. And I'm supportive of gays. I've been married to a woman for the past seventeen years. . . . And I'm not ashamed or

afraid to say it right now. And that's the reason I am here tonight: to give my sons, my daughters, my brothers, my sisters, the support they need in the community. . . . For years, our people have been clamouring and living in [a] silence that is so painful. Now, we are here surviving and alive!" Chutney Pride, *Ginger Tea* interview with Calypso Rose, 2012, https://www.youtube.com/watch?v=JkRIMcP4nGU&t=4s.

24. Although singled out for this analysis, Lewis is part of a long history – as Carol Duncan reminded the author in a personal communication (12 July 2017) – of singing women in Caribbean expressive cultures whose sexual and gender propriety has been at best called into question or at worst maligned simply because they are women who dare to sing in public.

25. Lewis's bold defiance of secrecy and shame has been repeatedly compromised recently by her European manager Jean Michel Gibert. Gibert threatened legal action to force *Caribbean Beat* writer Joshua Surtees to remove any mention of Lewis and the LGBTQ community from his 2016 cover story "Ever-Blooming Rose". Surtees reluctantly complied out of respect for what he was led to believe were Lewis's wishes (Joshua Surtees, "Ever-Blooming Rose" unpublished draft shared with the author, and final edited version in *Caribbean Beat*, November/December; Joshua Surtees, personal communication with the author, 15 January 2017). Similarly, Gibert threatened the publication of my manuscript *Erotic Islands* if Lewis was discussed at all in this queer text (Jean Michel Gibert, personal communication with the author, 16 July 2017). However, I stand firmly behind her inclusion, despite her manager's weak faith in the power of integrity, and I remain inspired by Lewis's own deleted declaration to Surtees about defying discrimination and ignorance: "Why discriminate? Why castigate? God says, 'I make you in my own image and likeness', so who are you to condemn me? I am a child of God. I did not create myself. I was created by the Heavenly Master. So, why condemn? Learn!" (quoted in Surtees, "Ever-Blooming Rose", unpublished draft; deleted from published version). Indeed, we all have so much to learn from the Calypso Queen of the World.

26. In 1987, while still performing widely as a calypsonian, Lewis became an ordained minister (Guilbault 2007, 109).

27. For a more elaborate discussion of Lewis's voice and its queer potentiality, see chapter 4, "Calypso Rose's 'Palet' and the Sweet Treat of Erotic Aurality", in Gill (2018).

28. For an extended engagement with a Trinidadian lesbian not only involved in the Spiritual Baptist faith but also committed to fostering the spiritual consciousness of other Trinbagonian lesbians, see Gill (2012).

References

Alexander, M. Jacqui. 2005. *Pedagogies of Crossing: Meditations on Feminism, Sexual Politics, Memory and the Sacred*. Durham, NC: Duke University Press.

Allen, Jafari. 2010. "Blackness, Sexuality, and Desire: Initial Notes toward a New Research Agenda". In *Black Sexualities: Probing Powers, Passions, Practices, and Policies*, edited by Juan Battle and Sandra L. Barnes, 82–96. Piscataway, NJ: Rutgers University Press.

Brand, Dionne. 1999. *At the Full and Change of the Moon*. New York: Grove Press.

Brereton, Bridget. 1981. *A History of Modern Trinidad, 1783–1962*. Kingston, Jamaica: Heinemann.

Conner, Randy, and David Sparks. 2004. *Queering Creole Spiritual Traditions: Lesbian, Gay, Bisexual, and Transgender Participation in African-Inspired Traditions in the Americas*. New York: Harrington Park Press.

De-Light, Dominique, and Polly Thomas. 2001. *The Rough Guide to Trinidad and Tobago*. London: Penguin.

Duncan, Carol B. 2008. *This Spot of Ground: Spiritual Baptists in Toronto*. Waterloo, ON: Wilfrid Laurier University Press.

Elwin, Rosamond. 1997. *Tongues on Fire: Caribbean Lesbian Lives and Stories*. Toronto: Women's Press.

Gill, Lyndon K. 2012. "Situating Black, Situating Queer: Black Queer Diaspora Studies and the Art of Embodied Listening". *Transforming Anthropology* 20 (1): 32–44.

———. 2018. *Erotic Islands: Art and Activism in the Queer Caribbean*. Durham, NC: Duke University Press.

Glave, Thomas. 2008. *Our Caribbean: A Gathering of Lesbian and Gay Writing from the Antilles*. Durham, NC: Duke University Press.

Glazier, Stephen. 1983. *Marchin' the Pilgrims Home: Leadership and Decision-Making in an Afro-Caribbean Faith*. London: Greenwood Press.

Guilbault, Jocelyn. 2007. *Governing Sound: The Cultural Politics of Trinidad's Carnival Musics*. Chicago: University of Chicago Press.

Hackshaw, John. 1992. *The Baptist Denomination: A Concise History Commemorating One Hundred Seventy-Five Years (1816–1991) of the Establishment of the "Company Villages" and the Baptist Faith in Trinidad and Tobago*. Diego Martin, Trinidad: Jackson Memorial Society.

Henry, Frances. 2003. *Reclaiming African Religions in Trinidad: The Socio-political Legitimation of the Orisha and Spiritual Baptist Faiths*. Kingston: University of the West Indies Press.

Houk, James. 1995. *Spirits, Blood, and Drums*. Philadelphia: Temple University Press.

Johnson, E. Patrick. 2008. *Sweet Tea: Black Gay Men of the South*. Chapel Hill: University of North Carolina Press.

King, Rosamond. (2005) 2008. "More Notes on the Invisibility of Caribbean Lesbians". In *Our Caribbean: A Gathering of Lesbian and Gay Writing from the Antilles*, edited by Thomas Glave, 191–96. Durham, NC: Duke University Press.

Laitinen, Maarit. 2002. "Aspects of Gender in the Spiritual Baptist Religion in Tobago: Notes from the Field", Working Paper #6. St Augustine, Trinidad: University of the West Indies.

Lorde, Audre. (1978) 1984. "Uses of the Erotic: The Erotic as Power". In *Sister Outsider: Essays and Speeches*, 53–59. Berkeley, CA: Crossing Press.

Lum, Kenneth. 2000. *Praising His Name in the Dance: Spirit Possession in the Spiritual Baptist Faith and Orisha Work in Trinidad, West Indies*. Amsterdam: Harwood.

Ottley, Rudolph. 1992. "Calypso Rose". In *Women in Calypso: Part 1*, 11–12. Airma, Trinidad: Author.

Silvera, Makeda. 1996. "Man Royals and Sodomites: Some Thoughts on the Invisibility of Afro-Caribbean Lesbians". In *Lesbian Subjects: A Feminist Studies Reader*, edited by Martha Vicinus, 157–77. Bloomington: Indiana University Press.

Weiss, John. (1995) 2002. *The Merikens: Free Black American Settlers in Trinidad 1815–16*. London: McNish and Weiss.

Wood, Donald. 1968. *Trinidad in Transition: The Years after Slavery*. Oxford: Oxford University Press.

Wood, Elizabeth. 1994. "Sapphonics". In *Queering the Pitch: The New Gay and Lesbian Musicology*, edited by Philip Brett, Elizabeth Wood and Gary C. Thomas, 27–66. New York: Routledge.

Zane, Wallace W. 1999. *Journeys to the Spiritual Lands: The Natural History of a West Indian Religion*. Oxford: Oxford University Press.

5.

A Symphony in Four Movements

Religion, Syphilis and Homosexuality in Marlon James's
John Crow's Devil

ANNA KASAFI PERKINS

Eventually it is revealed that the "Apostle" is both syphilitic and homosexual. Is
this a value judgement? Indeed, by tearing down the kingdom of Satan, we are left
to wonder if "Apostle" is not himself Satan. That, at any rate, is the impression
left by this Salkey-inspired parable of sin and redemption.
—Ian Thomson, "God and Rum", *Independent*, 27 October 2005

And while fundamentalist religion is devoutly religious, it has the intellectual certi-
tude of a housefly. This is because thinking is anathema to religion and any form
of intellectual discourse is tantamount to having kids with Satan.
—Marlon James, blog post, 27 July 2006

As a contemporary writer, Marlon James has not been subject to much
literary analysis. This may well change with him having received the Man
Booker Prize in 2015 for his *A Brief History of Seven Killings* (2014). Furthermore, having come out as a gay man from Jamaica, he has entered the
rather narrow canon of Jamaican gay writers, or better yet, a Jamaican writer
who happens to be gay, and as such catalogues the experiences of gay men
in the fraught Jamaican context (marlon-james.blogspot.com). However,
before there was *A Brief History* there was *John Crow's Devil*, his 2005 debut
novel, which only saw the light of day on the seventy-ninth time of submission. *John Crow's Devil* is a Caribbean Gothic tale in which James treats
with Freudian tropes of religion and madness and sexuality and madness.
A key antagonist, Apostle Lucas York, is driven insane by tertiary syphilis
or, at the very least, his insanity is expressed through religious mania and
a dabbling in the dark arts. *John Crow's Devil* maintains that religion is

akin to syphilis as it too progresses in four phases ("a symphony of four movements"): "The fourth movement comes with madness and blindness, consumption and illness of the breath" (James 2010, 213–14; hereafter, only pages numbers are given). Through York's progressive deterioration and its catastrophic consequences, James makes a trenchant critique of religion that mirrors his own distancing from dogmatic Christianity, which he characterizes in his 14 November 2006 blog post entitled "Losing My Religion" as being religion without questioning ("dogma") and faith without reasoning ("a holy witchcraft"). He is particularly concerned about "Jamaican churches that insist on their pastors being a final authority" in spite to the unspeakable harm this causes to the innocent.

According to James, these kinds of religion "leave [bloodshed] in their wake [and] convinces me that there is no God in them" (27 July 2006 blog post). This description mirrors James's image of syphilis as it traverses through the body leaving a bloody trail of a disease that has no being in itself, rather existing in the bodies it infects. As such, James makes clear his singular intent in writing *John Crow's Devil*: "I wrote a novel about this [kind of religion], set in the past because I refused to believe that I was telling a contemporary story. Boy was I wrong" (14 November 2006 blog post).

This chapter examines James's singular and peculiar use of the image of syphilis to describe religious experience, particularly dogmatic, or fundamentalist, Christianity, and the impact that has on the overall depiction of homosexuality or "nasty nastiness" as it is called by Lucinda, the key female antagonist, in the novel. *John Crow's Devil* critiques intertextually the madness expressed in the Christian beliefs and actions of inhabitants of Gibbeah – Gibbeahnites as I call them – including Lucinda, Apostle York and Clarence. It causes the reader to question the value and purpose of dogmatic religion that corrupts the individual believer and the larger communal body such that sexual identities like that of the homosexual can become warped by lust or paedophilia. Therefore, the exploration is a partial response to Bethany Louise Grimm's call in her 2016 thesis, "'Nasty Nastiness': The Critical Body in Marlon James's *John Crow's Devil*", for further examination of the description of Apostle York's syphilitic body and Lucinda's transgressive female body. At the same time, the critique in this chapter pushes beyond Grimm by taking seriously the role of dogmatic religion in shaping perceptions of less acceptable gender identities in Jamaica. In so doing, this critique demonstrates the contemporary relevance of the novel as social critique.

Reading John Crow's Devil

John Crow's Devil does not make easy reading. It belongs to the genre of Caribbean Gothic in which the grotesque and hyperbolic generate horror and even some terror. Yet it is a funny book, laced with satire, irony and telling little asides like "Nothing was the only thing you could cut by half and still have too much". Still, *John Crow's Devil* is not for the faint of heart, especially those who take their Christian faith overly seriously. As Sheri-Marie Harrison (2014) testifies in *Jamaica's Difficult Subjects*, when she first read the book, she threw it across the room and left it there; she was frustrated at what she saw as its uncritical presentation of paedophilia, incest and bestiality as norms of rural life in Jamaica. She reports being confused by York's use of "Christian rhetoric to incite an entire community to horrific acts of violence against each other" (2). Worse yet, she was even more perplexed by "the novel['s use of] a literal bout of syphilis to symbolically pathologize homosexuality and cast it as a predatory disease" (2). Harrison is wrong in this initial reading. I suspect her initial sensibilities lay in the same place of concern about the violated body and the diseased body of the queer subject as was heard about in the Beyond Homophobia conference plenary and explored by Grimm (2016). However, it is not homosexuality that is cast as a predatory disease but religion! Furthermore, there are predatory homosexuals aplenty in *John Crow's Devil*, but as Harrison (2014, 162) later admits, it is sexuality generally that is the issue: "Sexuality – heterosexuality included – in Gibbeah is consistently prefigured as perverse and violent." At the same time, James leaves little doubt that colonialism has contributed to the perversion of sexuality in the Caribbean region. Indeed, James pokes at the sleeping beast of colonialism time and again.

As a Catholic theologian, I enjoyed reading the book, especially with regard to the earthy, Jamaican flavour of the imagery and the language – "Lawd Puppa Jesus!" – but also for the knowledge displayed of Caribbean Charismatic Christian worship forms such as getting in the Spirit and speaking in tongues, "Oh bababa-lekim-shakam!", and Pentecostal preaching ("I can only minister against the sinister", "Can I get a witness, Clarence?" [44]). The book is littered with biblical references ("Some people say Second Book of John, verse one to eleven, say that Jesus turn water into wine, so him [the Rum Preacher] must drink wine too" [7]) and allusions ("The cup had passed, and sliding toward him [the Rum Preacher] was another, wet, golden, and tinkling with ice" [42]) that add flavour to the story.

One further example in which James sneakily thumbs his nose at the reader who does not know while demonstrating some familiarity with biblical scholarship is the scene with Lucinda and the Apostle: Lucinda is struggling with desire for the Apostle who is at her mercy, unconscious after a battle with the Rum Preacher. "His crotch seems to have risen like a new mountain" so she is confronted with "a huge black hill between the huge ridges of his thighs" (134). She tries everything, including prayer and leaving the room, but her night persona, "Night Lucinda", takes over. The narrator tells us, "Far below grief was lust, and like any other sin, it came with opportunity" (135). Her night persona urges her to "touch where life come from", and she ignores the warning from her day persona that "God will punish you for your wickedness". And so "She sat down on the side of the Apostle's bed and *touched his feet*" (135; emphasis added).

The uninitiated reader would be unaware of what Lucinda is doing. She is groping the unconscious Apostle, who has become tumescent. At this point, James is perhaps alluding to the story of Ruth and Boaz in the book of Ruth, where Ruth uncovers Boaz's feet and lies down beside him (Ruth 3:3–4). In other words, the scene with Apostle and Lucinda only makes sense when it is understood that "feet" are used as a euphemism in Scripture for the genitals of either sex. So when Lucinda "touched his feet" after being urged to "touch where life comes from" (135), we know what she did that night!

John Crow's Devil: The Story

So let me tell you the story about a story and that story is Marlon James's *John Crow's Devil*. Bear in mind that, unlike the usual pattern of a story, "The End" is "The Beginning" connected by a "Reckoning". The story centres around a fictional free village named Gibbeah, thirty miles from the Astor sugar plantation, somewhere in rural Jamaica, about one hundred years after emancipation. Its revival church, the Holy Sepulchral Full Gospel Church of St Thomas Apostolic, is served by a guilt-ridden alcoholic pastor, Hector Bligh, "the Rum Preacher", a laughing stock in the village. Ash Wednesday 1957, Bligh is unceremoniously ejected from his church by the mysterious Apostle Lucas York, who rides in one night on a motor bike, seen only by the moon, Satan and an owl. His coming is presaged by the appearance of a murder of turkey vultures or john crows – hundreds! It is conveniently ironic that the collective noun for a group of crows is "murder" and murder they do! As the story declares, "John Crows were messengers of the Devil – everybody knew it" (17). Similarly, in Jamaican folk culture, the owl is known as a patoo, and it is also considered an avian emissary of the Devil.

In the unfolding of the story, each man is served by a female sidekick: York's willing acolyte is the church-going, obeah-working, lustful Sunday school teacher Lucinda, whose mother had early on beaten her into two people, Day Lucinda and Night Lucinda. The defenestrated Bligh's accidental helpmeet is the embittered, non-church-going, childhood rival of Lucinda, the widowed-too-soon Mary Greenfield. Then there is Clarence, "the Apostle's man". He literally and figuratively maintains a competing presence against Lucinda, whose love for the Apostle leads her to betray the Rum Preacher, handing him over, like a female Judas, to his death. Both men of God become locked in an epic battle in the spiritual and physical realms for the souls of the people of Gibbeah. In the process, the syphilitic York leads the Gibbeahnites on a path of deadly destruction that eventually ends with the death of many, including, of course, Bligh, York, Clarence and Lucinda. Bligh or "Blight", as the Apostle calls him, is stoned to death, and there is a Reckoning at the hand, or rather, claws and beaks of a cloud of doves, who appear to be anything but emissaries of peace. In The End, which is The Beginning, the Widow emerges as a symbol of "judgment and redemption, rescue and damnation, despair and hope" (218). Mary Greenfield, whose names spell hope, fecundity and new life, is Redemptrix unwitting.

Gibbeah

The fictional Gibbeah in *John Crow's Devil* channels a biblical city of the same name Gibeah, found in the Book of Judges, chapter 19. Gibeah in the Bible is in the territory of the tribe of Benjamin. One night, the men of the city descend on the home of an elderly man demanding that he give them his Levite guest – a stranger – so they may "know him". In biblical language to "know" someone refers to having sexual relations with that person. In this case, forcible sexual relations – homosexual gang rape – is desired. The old man begs the men not to undertake such an outrage against hospitality and even offers his virgin daughter as well as the Levite's concubine to slake their rapacious lust for his male guest. The men refuse. In the end, the Levite throws his concubine out to them and they rape and abuse her till morning. The next morning the Levite finds her battered body with hand clinging to the doorstep. (We are unclear whether she is alive or dead.). He takes her home to the tribal land of Ephraim, cuts her body into twelve pieces, which he sends around to the other tribes of Israel as a call to arms against the Benjaminites. "An attempted rape of the Levite by the Benjaminites, followed by the actual rape of the Levite's Israelite property, his concubine, ultimately led to civil war" (Wright Knust 2011,

170). The bodily integrity of the woman is sacrificed to save the man. When the codes of hospitality are violated so terribly, violence and chaos follow (Wright Knust 2011). Gibbeah, like the biblical Gibeah, violates many rules of hospitality, including the injunction to welcome the stranger, whom they eventually wall out or stone to death.

Contemporary Relevance

The issues raised in this novel are of immediate contemporary relevance in Jamaica with the recent allegations of sexual abuse of girls by pastors and the reactions and responses of some religious people (Public Theology Forum, 19 February 2017). Sexual abuse of girls and boys, including by men of the Cloth – the Five Deacons, for example – is a horrifying theme in *John Crow's Devil* but seems unremarked by many in the village. James criticizes a similar real-life case of the gang rape of a girl organized by a church deacon (14 November 2006 blog post). Indeed, many of the villagers seemed to prefer the status quo as the narrator says: "Maybe is fi we fault cause country people take things as them be, as if white man goin beat we if we change them" (7). Allusions to the impact of colonialism on the mindset of the people of Gibbeah occur frequently.

A Preying Pastor

Interestingly, the description of a Christian pastor given by Jamaican journalist George Davis (2017) evokes the description of Apostle York, again unwittingly pointing to the contemporary relevance of the concerns in *John Crow's Devil*. According to the *Gleaner*, this handsome unnamed pastor set up shop in Davis's St Catherine village and ended up impregnating a thirteen-year-old girl with seeming impunity. This unnamed pastor in many ways sounds like the model for Apostle Lucas York, as is demonstrated in table 5.1.

Of course, Davis's unnamed pastor was not the source of James's York, but he reinforces some of the elements present in clergy, who may be abusers and exploiters of the youth: handsome features, dogmatic certainty, charisma, self-centredness.

Significantly, York himself was a victim of sexual abuse at the hands of a minister, the incumbent before Bligh, Pastor Palmer, who gave him syphilis. In this regard, Harrison (2014, 162) laments, as so many do in Jamaica today, that "[r]epresentatives of God like Pastor Palmer exploit their perceived moral authority in the service of victimizing the vulnerable". York represents this exploitation of moral authority. By the time York realizes that he is afflicted with "the Pox", it is too late. He returns to Gibbeah,

Table 5.1. Comparison of Apostle York and Unnamed Pastor

York	Pastor X
"He was ruddy and handsome, mixed black and white, or maybe light Indian or Creole Chinaman. His long curly hair was unruly" (21). "Jesus looked like him" (25).	He was young, tall, strapping, handsome and brown enough to earn extra ratings from the country folk as a "brown man".
"He grinned. Laugh lines interlocked with each other and weakened her [Lucinda's] knees" (27).	All the women fancied him . . . many had visions of being the queen that this hunk of a clergyman would give pride of place beside him as he watched over the flock of his church.
"He came like a thief on a night coloured silver" (10). "She had helped the Apostle move. . . . Yet there was not much to move as the Apostle had taken next to nothing for his journey" (25).	[H]e came to the community without a wife . . . and seemingly without a past.
"Church was so full that Lucinda had The Five set up stacking chairs at the front and side doors. Some came to praise and worship, but most came to see. They sat and spoke and gossiped and laughed like penny stinkers" (30).	This man's popularity soared in quick time, and his Zionist Church was all the rage in the community, drawing not just congregants but large crowds, who stood cheek to jowl at every available window to see this most wonderful man at work during service on a Sunday afternoon.
"The man who made the Holy Ghost thunder" (26). "Maybe it was the coolie blood coursing through him that made his hair seem always wet. Unruly. Moreso, they were caught up in his dance. When the Apostle gave a word, a sweet word, chased by a blast of organ and a chorus of Amens, he would jump and spread his arms wide, shouting, *Hallelujahs!*" (53).	Of course, no clergyman is worth anything if he cannot speak. And not only was this man a pretty boy, he could talk the rust off a piece of steel in a way that made even those who despised his version of Christianity acknowledge that he was indeed blessed with significant gifts by God.

Sources: James 2010; Davis 2017.

bearing the yoke his name signals – the burden of his abuse, sickness, madness and hatred – to wreak vengeance on the community, including Bligh, for their wilful blindness that allowed decades of unthinkable abuse of young boys even as they indulged in incest, adultery, domestic violence, obeah, prostitution, abortion and murder. This is the moral hypocrisy that James laments is the outcome of the perversion of dogmatic Christianity and its authoritarian leaders (14 November 2006 blog post). York rejected the perverse authority of the man of God who afflicted him with that terrible disease and created for himself a religion in which he becomes God. Apotheosis! The religious sensibilities of the Gibbeahnites make them easy prey for his entreaties to violence for the Bible already demands that anything that offends should be cut off in order to gain heaven: "If your right hand causes you to sin, cut it off" (Matthew 5:30; Matthew 18:8; Mark 9:43). "Cut it out", the Apostle says literally and colloquially, requesting that sinful behaviour cease. The Gibbeahnites respond with violence against the sinners, cutting them out of and off from the church body, usually by beating, rape or death. York stands on a strong foundation with his call to violence as the Bible sanctions violence against those that do not belong to God's chosen people, the Children of Israel, as happened with the Canaanites inhabiting the Promised Land (Deuteronomy 20:17; Perkins 2005). No wonder York could entreat, "[c]ome now, Church, who is ready to be violent for the Lord?" (87).

A Symphony in Four Movements

In the 2010 edition of *John Crow's Devil*, the narrator delivers this startling commentary:

> Syphilis, the great imitator, is a symphony in four movements. Like religion, it has *no being* in itself, but *lives* in *the lives* it touches. Like a *God or a Devil*. There are four movements. The first exists mostly in darkness, hiding more than showing. A spot on the anus, a lesion in the vagina, a corpuscle in the mouth that vanishes as quickly as a *miracle*. The third movement hides deeper than the first, waiting low in *the flesh* until time to *rise* again. The fourth movement comes with madness and blindness, consumption and illness of the *breath*. This is the *trinity*. One with *soul* and *body* after *mind* has been rotted. But the second movement is the one that leaves a trail. (213–14; emphases added)

This is where James deploys the image of syphilis to describe religion. However, this brief but powerful paragraph is all there is as the book ends shortly after. Indeed, two and a half pages later (218), the book ends with the Widow standing outside the fence surrounding the village with her right hand raised and two fingers pointing, imitating the gesture of power and demand for obedience adopted by the now dead Apostle, perhaps adopted from images of Christ as Pantokrator (Ruler of All) in Christian iconography. But conceivably no further discussion is necessary as the story that had previously unfolded was the epitome of the warped religion that elicits the comparison with syphilis.

Syphilis

Syphilis is a highly infectious disease caused by a bacterium similar to the one that causes yaws; it is mainly transmitted through sexual contact. Human beings have no natural immunity to syphilis. James rightly describes syphilis as "the great imitator" as it mimics other diseases and is therefore difficult to diagnose. The sores caused by syphilis have been mistaken for abscesses, haemorrhoids and even cancer. In fact, there was a resurgence of syphilis in the United States in the 1990s, which was said to "fool a new generation" since they had no experience with it (Altman 1990). As recently as 2017, Barbados released a report on an outbreak of syphilis among its population. There was a resurgence of infections in Barbados between 2011 and 2013, with most of the cases affecting men between fifteen and forty-nine ("Syphilis Causes a Concern for Barbados Health Authorities", *Jamaica Observer*, 14 March 2017).

In the case of Jamaica, in 1934, two decades before the events in *John Crow's Devil*, a naval report was released stating that Jamaica was rife with venereal disease, especially syphilis. Briggs (2016) describes this report as causing a moral panic that resulted in misdirected public policy and spending for the next ten years. The writer of the report, one Colonel Stevenson, suggested that up to 80 per cent of the population was affected, including children as young as eight years old. The reason for this epidemic, according to the report, was "the almost complete absence of morals existing among a large class of Jamaicans", especially "female descendants of the slave days" (Briggs 2016). The Stevenson report greatly exaggerated the prevalence of syphilis and raised alarm among the upper and middle classes about "the diseased bodies and immorality of the Afro-Jamaican masses". The "calls for a campaign against venereal disease drowned out competing voices pleading for further investment in public health infrastructure and diverted scarce public health resources". Yet, the primary disease was yaws.

In his visceral description of syphilis, James takes literary licence to allow him to fit his disease metaphor to his religious imagery and its stark critique of dogmatic Christianity. In medical epidemiology, syphilis is categorized as a disease that progresses in three stages: primary, secondary and tertiary. Other descriptions of syphilis include a latent stage, which follows the secondary stage, making it a disease in four parts. James uses this latter descriptive model and so includes a quaternary movement, allowing him to compare the disease paradoxically or redundantly to a symphony. James's third movement is mapped unto the latent stage of the disease where, while there are no signs and symptoms, fundamental damage is being done to internal organs. His fourth movement therefore maps unto tertiary, or late-stage, syphilis, which rises again even more deadly than before. (See table 5.2.)

A symphony is a musical composition in four parts so the idea of four is already present therein. James probably positions "symphony" ironically given that the expected beauty of a symphony is not present in the syphilitic symphony, or perhaps there is a tragic beauty to its movements. He does not narrate the stages and their symptoms in order but places the most important and deadly stages (3 and 4) in the middle. In so doing, he separates out a particular set of symptoms of late-stage syphilis and gives them a terrible singular place in the progress of the disease. In a way, this is unsurprising as late-stage syphilis is disabling and can lead to death.

Table 5.2 juxtaposes medical descriptions of syphilis, syphilis as it afflicts York and Clarence, and the religious imagery that imbues their suffering from the disease. The four movements in Gibbeah's religious symphony are not as clearly delineated as they appear. Rather, they merge, overlap and even presage each other. Nonetheless, roughly, they are:

- The coming of the charismatic and authoritarian York who infects a susceptible village with his powerful but blasphemous message while banishing their ineffective pastor and calling them to deeper commitment. This looks like real religion yet manifests violence, unstable emotionalism and blind obedience hidden in a darkness that presages latency.
- A bloody fest of cleansing and cutting off, leaving a trail of blood in the death of Bligh, Mr Garvey and his nephews, and the disciplining of insiders such as Clarence and Mrs Johnson.
- A hidden festering as the socioculturally supported violence against women and girls is ritualized and even the name of Jesus is banned, fundamentally undermining true Christian faith. Significant damage is done to the individual villager but the village itself rots to the core and is the stomping ground of carrion crows, the defamed john crows.

Table 5.2. Medical Syphilis, Syphilis in *John Crow's Devil* and Allusions to the Christian Scriptures and Dogma

Stage/ Movement	Medical Syphilis	Syphilis in *John Crow's Devil*	Allusions to Christian Scriptures and Dogma
1 – Primary/ First Movement	Small, painless sores, primary chancre on genitals, tongue, anus, cervix "[P]atient becomes a biological bomb waiting to develop tertiary syphilis" (Schaffner in Altmann 1990). Bacterium spreads through the blood to cause stage 2. Mild symptoms, infectious, but easily treated.	"The first exists mostly in darkness, hiding more than showing. A spot on the anus, a lesion on the vagina, a corpuscle in the mouth that vanishes as quickly as a miracle" (214). About the Apostle: "The beard hid the healed sore below his lip, but there were others above and below his belt" (84).	"Miracle" (143). "Miraculous healing, Clarence. Miraculous healing. . . . His back was healing itself through the grooves of his wound. The cuts closed like zippers and disappeared in the smoothness of his skin" (143). "Most came because of the miracle. The Rum Preacher had killed the Apostle, they said. He was dead, but then he came back on the third day, Lucinda would testify" (145). (The crowds followed Jesus because of the miracles he performed such as healing, exorcism and feeding of the multitudes [Mark 3:8; John 6:2, 10:41]).
2 – Secondary/ Second Movement	Skin rash, usually on the palms of the hand and soles of the feet. Sores in or around the mouth, vagina, penis . . . swollen lymph nodes. Mild, untreated will worsen.	"But the second movement is the one that leaves a trail" (214). "As he bent to pick it up, she saw them. Spots, scars, red circles on his buttocks that looked like the red scar below his lip and on his chest and thighs" (138). "A trail of blood and slime oozed from the puss-filled [*sic*] sores on Clarence's legs and feet" (214).	"But his own blood brought the word back, sparking memory of another's blood, pricked from the rib with a spear" (226). (Alludes to Jesus's side being pierced by a spear on the Cross after he died [John 19:34].)

(*Continued*)

Table 5.2. (*continued*)

Stage/ Movement	Medical Syphilis	Syphilis in *John Crow's Devil*	Allusions to Christian Scriptures and Dogma
Latent/ Third Movement	No symptoms. Not contagious. Not everyone enters this phase; some go directly to tertiary. Can last for years. Damage caused to the eyes, liver, kidneys and other organs	"The third movement hides deeper than the first, waiting low in the flesh until time to rise again" (214).	Alludes to Jesus's time in the tomb before his Resurrection ("rise again") on the third day (Luke 24:7).
3 – Tertiary/ Quarternary Movement	Symptoms depend on which organs have been affected. Vary widely and are difficult to diagnose. Include damage to the heart, central nervous system disorders, tumours of skin, bone and liver, vision problems leading to blindness, paralysis and dementia. "Late syphilis" may be permanently disabling and lead to death.	"The fourth movement comes with madness and blindness, consumption and illness of the breath" (214). Lucinda: "Is demon him have? Me see it one time, you know. Me see the demon attack him in the office and him run me out cause him head take him" (186). "The Apostle grunted, his eyes rolled back, and his head jerked. . . . The Apostle was yelling now and he shuddered and swayed as if having a drunken fit" (167).	"Rise again" (214). "The Rum Preacher strike and kill the Apostle. But the Apostle rise after three days. Evil get beat by good, black get beat by white. The Apostle is the way, the truth and the light" (150). (John 14:6) "Any man who believes in me shall never die"! (226) (The use of the term "man" in translations of the Bible is the generic man, representing all of humanity. However, given James's oeuvre it is possible to see that York, who is quoted here, literally means a male person such as Clarence rather than a human person, male or female. The gendered discrimination against women and girls in Gibbeah as the village descends into madness bears this out as well as the Apostle's homosexual activities. Alludes to John 5:30).

Sources: Altman 1990; James 2010; New York City 2019; https://www.webmd.com/sexual-conditions/syphilis#1.

- Blind faith that leads to violence against strangers and outsiders and the walling in of the village against contaminating influences and ideas such people bring in.

The idea of stages and progressive deterioration (movements) is fundamental to the juxtaposition. Interestingly, syphilis and religion are not the only matters described in stages in James's story. There is, for example, the description of widowhood, which came "too soon" for Mary Greenfield. The death that is widowhood occurs in seven stages, beginning with "the first death", which is "the chill of sexual heat" (39), and ends with "the seventh death" "when his lungs collapse, his eyes go white, and the flies know first" (39). The Widow Greenfield carries the memory of her husband's death like Sisyphus, for he died too young. Much of James's reality is about progressive deterioration and destruction, it seems.

In the passage on syphilis and religion quoted previously, several terms are present that identify dogmatic Christianity as the target. These are highlighted in the quotation – lives/lives, Devil, God, breath, miracle, soul, mind, body, being, Trinity and rise again (Resurrection). Such dogmatic Christianity, like disease, has no being in and of itself; rather, it lives in the lives and bodies of those it infects. God or a Devil, important dramatis personae in Christianity, is identified clearly as non-beings parasitically living through the lives of their unreasoning devotees. Unsurprisingly, perhaps, James places God and a Devil on the same level, as he makes them proper nouns. Yet God is God singular and the Devil one of many ("a Devil"). At the same time, James questions the reality of God when he causes Clarence to reflect that "God was something learned, never felt" (212). The presence of God or a Devil was alive and well in the lives of the Gibbeahnites, who were ultimately driven to religiously inspired violence (killing of outsiders) on top of the socioculturally sanctioned violence they routinely perpetuated (domestic abuse, adultery, fornication, paedophilia). The death and destruction wreaked by blind religion is climactic and akin to the fourth and final deadly stage of syphilis, as *John Crow's Devil* describes it. The image of the crucified Christ entombed is strong as well as an expectation of "ris(ing) again" from the darkness. The flesh, in which the spiritual/transcendent is present, is corrupt(ed). Breath, which is akin to life/spirit, is the means by which human beings become en-livened/"living beings" (Genesis 2:7). Indeed, life is God-breathed (in-spired) yet the syphilitic breath is ill, perhaps unto death. The statement "This is the trinity" is peculiar. Its immediate referent is not clear. Especially as it follows a description of *four* movements – not three. The best suggestion seems to be that it points to the sentence that follows: "One with soul and body after mind has been rotted." The trinity (common t) is one in three that has a soul and a body along with a mind that has rotted (soul + mind + body). The presence of a colon would have made it clearer. But clarity may not have been James's intent. Of course, the religious referent is the Christian belief in a God that is Triune – three individuals in one – Father + Son + Holy Spirit.

Religion, the Great Imitator

As mentioned previously, James quotes liberally from the Bible, and uses strong Christian language, symbolism and allusions throughout the novel. Biblical quotations and references are aplenty. Harrison (2014) describes the biblical allusions as "compound allusions", "which are often contradictory and thus designed to complicate whether or not a character or situation is good or evil, right or wrong" (158). York, for example, portrays himself as one come to clean out the temple – the Holy Sepulchral Full Gospel Church of St Thomas Apostolic – yet can be seen to bring sin into the Temple. His actions allude to Luke 19:45–48 where Jesus whips the money changers from the vestibule of the temple. York is further described paradoxically in terms that are overlain by images of Christ's second coming (cf Matthew 24:4–5, 11, 23–27) and the Devil coming like a thief to kill and destroy (John 10:10).

The Christian symbolism is particularly stark in the "four movements" description and can be shown to be imitation as well as compound allusions. Imitation may well be parody as the copying is incomplete, ridiculous, terrible, demonic. Like syphilis in *John Crow's Devil*, "imagery may be parody" (Laws 1988, 13). So, the Apostle is both Christ and anti-Christ; Lucinda is both pious church sister and lustful, murderous obeah woman. This may be part of the first movement where the signs and symptoms mimic or imitate other diseases. The telltale trail of blood and slime soon become evident. The Apostle goes beyond what Christians believe as he explicitly calls himself the Messiah, which Jesus never did (Mark 14:61; Matthew 26:63). He calls for righteous violence; Jesus seems to have been mainly pacifistic (Matthew 8).

Like the disease, York "rises again" on the third day, but was never really dead. Syphilis, like the Apostle, hides deep only to rise again more terrible than before – the third movement. The Christian Messiah is believed to have truly died, buried in a tomb and resurrected on the third day. York's very appearance is parody and the omniscient narrator claims, "Jesus looked like him"! (25). Furthering the idea of blasphemy, the Apostle demands worship. He tells Clarence, "Any man who believes in me shall never die!" (226), a parody of Jesus's comforting words to Martha and Mary in John 11:25–26. A perverse trinity – three in one – is created by syphilis of a body and soul united after a mind has rotted away. Dogmatic Christianity, similarly, creates a trinity as it unites body and soul after a mind has been rotted away by the delusion of unreasoning faith and its corrupting effects on the conscience. Harrison (2014), therefore, rightly compares the impact of the Apostle on Gibbeah to the effects of the disease from which he suffers.

The best way to distinguish between syphilis and another illness, which it mimics, is testing the blood. It is not enough to say, "by their fruits you shall know them"! (84, quoting Matthew 7:20). Ironically, the evil of "the man in black" is overcome symbolically by the blood of Jesus and literally the name of Jesus. Clarence finds himself infected by a bloody pox and recognizes the Apostle as the cause. Clarence's bleeding, slimy sores recall for him the blood of another whose name had been banished from Gibbeah, "erased with ease" (226), in fact. The Apostle had forbidden the people to speak Jesus's name. "But his own blood brought the word back, sparking memory of another's blood, *pricked* from the rib with a spear" (226; emphasis added). By invoking the name of Jesus, Clarence overpowers York and is able to bludgeon him brutally with a lamp (a source of light) before immolating them both beneath the bloody bathwater three days later. The Apostle's blood that splatters Clarence in the bludgeoning "was a new baptism" for a man who killed "the only living thing he ever loved" (217). Movement four has found its denouement.

Homosexuality: A New Form of Worship

There is no redeeming portrayal of the gay male subject in *John Crow's Devil*; he is a sodomite, that perpetrator of "nasty nastiness". Mr Garvey, the main paedophile and "rape-mate" of Pastor Palmer, is referred to in most uncomplimentary terms as "a sodomite who was on his way to hell" (15). Interestingly, when we first meet Hector Bligh, we are told that he is also on his way to hell. Yet Bligh's sin was adultery with his brother's wife. In his remorse, Bligh was drinking himself to death and on the road to hell until the Apostle came.

John Crow's Devil is replete with "Voices", including the narrator's, that comment on all the happenings in Gibbeah. Voices also haunt Lucinda and eventually drive her mad; demonic voices issue from the abused Lilamae Perkins before she commits suicide. Joel Madore (2011) refers to the novel as "multi-narrated"; he identifies a principal third-person, limited, omniscient narrator, who, unlike the others, consistently uses standard Jamaican English (and never uses Jamaican bad words). This final commentator may well be the author as he summarizes and presents his views on the events in Gibbeah and their deeper meaning in a fashion that sounds a lot like James in his blog. The Voices comment on those in the village to be judged, two by two, directly quoting the Jamaican work song "Go Down a Manuel Road".

They voice the imaginings of the Gibbeahnites. Using language reminiscent of the Book of Leviticus and the dancehall artistes of today, they declare:

> The one them call Mr Garvey
> Fire pon him cause him fuck batty
> Fire pon him cause him think him better than we
> Fire pon him because it is easier for a camel to go through the eye of a needle . . .
> Him have six nephew who don't look like him . . .
> Him sin like Onan and throw way him seed.
> (151)

Garvey is indicted for many things, being wealthy and aloof are among them. In the biblically shaped world of Gibbeah, Mr Garvey is more to be condemned for anal sex ("fucking batty") and Onanism (throwing away his seed in unproductive sexual acts), the very acts that the Apostle indulges in.

The Apostle had taught Clarence a new form of worship that is in itself a parody, a perverse imitation. This worship is "at the altar of the human body, communion with sweat and semen" (214). Even as he murders York for having infected him with syphilis (it is not clear whether Clarence knew what disease he had), he loves him for "York had known him for who he truly was, and there was nothing to go back to but lies" (217). Shortly after he takes over the village, the Apostle has Clarence publicly whipped for adultery/fornication with Mrs Johnson. Later, the Apostle heals him miraculously and then "outs him" to himself:

> Follow me and I can lead you beyond pain, beyond sin, beyond miracles. I am the way, Clarence. I am the way. Beyond every single thing you thought about yourself. Beyond normal, beyond real. Every time you use this, this snake in your pants, you think you're killing the Devil inside you. You know of which Devil I speak. The Devil you've been trying to kill since you were twelve. The Devil in you that was stealing looks between my legs just now when I was sitting in front of you. You'll never kill it. Not through pain, not through sin. No matter how many times you come inside a woman, you'll never kill your heart's real desire.
> (144)

The Apostle has revealed to Clarence that his constant fornication with women – Mrs Johnson and Lucinda – was a means of running away from his true self. Thus Clarence becomes "the Apostle's man" and comes face to face with his illness. There may be a subtle lesson in there for gay men to be true to themselves. However, the idea of homosexuality and homosexual identity is complicated by the homosexual paedophilia, which is a recurring theme in the background until York's disclosure forces the reader to deal with it. Victim becoming victimizer is a clear trope. York's "special interest in children", that is, *boy* children, in his "School of Boy Prophets" suggests that even as he was victimized, York was on his way to becoming a victimizer himself. Women and girls are further disenfranchised by his governance; they are prevented from attending school, and their ritual rape by his crew of Five Deacons is normalized. The murderous judgement that is brought against the village through the doves, which are symbols of peace, adds another layer to the question of religion and violence, redemptive violence.

In Conclusion? Mad Religion?

James is highly critical of religion as blind unreasoning faith. For him, "[t]here is something essentially backward and pagan about blind faith, something unintelligent in such thinking that runs contrary to a God who seemed intent on establishing a kingdom of reason and justice on Earth" (14 November 2006 blog post). He, therefore, finds no solace in the stance of fellow Jamaican novelist Kei Miller: "Religion is superstition, and superstition is an authentic way of knowing" (Armitstead 2014). Indeed, James's critique is aimed at the kind of peasant religious experience that does not change behaviour and lifestyle. Apostle York famously declares, "Cut it out! Cut it out" at all manner of evil and sinfulness such as adultery or domestic violence, but progresses to banning even speaking the name of Jesus or the association of members of one family. Behind the constant declaration to "cut it out" is heard the biblical admonition to cut off any body part, even the right hand, if it offends (Matthew 5:30). Not only are behaviours cut away, but people who are blamed as the source of degenerate behaviour are cut out of the body politic through violent death, the key one being Pastor Bligh, who refuses to leave when given the chance. Bligh is burdened by his own sinfulness that had him covet and possess his brother's wife leading to his brother's death in circumstances that were unclear but caused him much guilt and anguish. The church becomes Bligh's salvation but also his condemnation.

At the heart of York's religion is a rejection of belief in a God/god who allows innocent suffering unleashed by a minister of the religion, a rich "religious" man (Garvey) and the Christian people of Gibbeah, who stood by and let the young York be cruelly violated and inflicted with the disease that eventually destroys him.

The omniscient narrator in *John Crow's Devil* tells us that the moral of the story is that dogmatic religion is akin to a progressively contagious sexually transmitted disease that destroys the body politic through inducing in the individual believer religious mania, blind obedience/wilful blindness, consuming preoccupations with the sins of others (especially sexual transgressions) and corrupting speech. Perhaps dogmatic religion, which James describes in his blog as having the intellectual capacity of a housefly, is the real "nasty nastiness!" (27 July 2006 blog post).

At the same time, the myth of redemptive violence is played out as Clarence frees himself by murdering the mad syphilitic York and then taking his own life. James alerts us in a gripping and singular fashion to the potentially monstrous in the religious perspective that eschews deep intellectual engagement and has an overdependence on misguided charismatic leadership. In the end, all faith is not ruled out as it is the power of the name of Jesus that is the Apostle's undoing and a widowed childless Redemptrix Mary of the Green field stands ready to fill the breach.

References

Altman, Lawrence K. 1990. "Syphilis Fools a New Generation". *New York Times.* 13 November. Accessed 22 January 2020. http://www.nytimes.com/1990/11/13 /science/the-doctor-s-world-syphilis-fools-a-new-generation.html.

Briggs, Jill. 2016. "Moral Panic and Syphilis in Jamaica: Medicine and Sexuality". *Notches.* 1 March. Accessed 20 January 2020. http://notchesblog.com/2016/03 /01/moral-panic-and-syphilis-sexuality-in-jamaica/.

Armitstead, Claire. 2014. "Kei Miller: 'My Productivity Is Linked to What Could Be Called a Disability'". *Guardian.* 28 September. Accessed 22 January 2020. https://www.theguardian.com/books/2014/sep/28/kei-miller-productivity -linked-to-what-could-be-called-disability-adhd-forward-prize#img-1.

Davis, George. 2017. "Forget the Wolves, Flee the Shepherds". *Gleaner.* 17 January. http://jamaica-gleaner.com/article/commentary/20170117/george-davis-forget -wolves-flee-shepherds.

Grimm, Bethany Louise. 2016. "'Nasty Nastiness': The Critical Body in Marlon James's *John Crow's Devil*". MA thesis, Dalarna University, Sweden.

Harrison, Sheri-Marie. 2014. *Jamaica's Difficult Subjects: Negotiating Sovereignty in Anglophone Caribbean Literature and Criticism.* Columbus: Ohio State University Press.

James, Marlon. 2010 (2005). *John Crow's Devil*. New York: One World.

Laws, Sophie. 1988. *In the Light of the Lamb: Imagery, Parody and Theology in the Apocalypse of John*. Eugene, OR: Wipf and Stock.

Madore, Joel. 2011. "Jamaican Signatures: An Archetypal Analysis of Marlon James' *John Crow's Devil*". *Journal of Caribbean Literatures* 7 (1): 69–75.

New York City Department of Health and Mental Hygiene Bureau of Sexually Transmitted Infections and the New York City STD Prevention Training Center. 2019. *The Diagnosis, Management and Prevention of Syphilis: An Update and Review*. New York: NYC Health.

Perkins, Anna Kasafi. 2005. "Resisting Definitive Interpretation: Reading the Exodus with Caribbean(ite) Eyes". *Caribbean Quarterly* 51:53–66.

Public Theology Forum. 2017. "Is It Just a Little Sex? Church, Sex and Power". *Sunday Gleaner*. 19 February. Accessed 22 January 2020. http://jamaica-gleaner .com/article/commentary/20170219/public-theology-forum-it-just-little-sex -church-sex-and-power.

Wright Knust, Jennifer. 2011. *Unprotected Texts: The Bible's Surprising Contradictions about Sex and Desire*. New York: HarperOne.

6.

The Sodom of the New World
A Queer Claim to Historical Belonging

NICK MARSELLAS

Christopher John Farley's *Kingston by Starlight* retells the story of pirates Anne Bonny, Calico Jack Rackham and Mary Read, highlighting cross-dressing, gender ambiguity, sexual fluidity and border crossing as part of a historical Jamaican identity. Originally from Ireland, Bonny (Bonn in the novel) has an African immigrant father and has spent most of his[1] life at sea, complicating the narrative of Jamaica's history as multiple, fully formed cultures (African, Indigenous, Asian, European) mixing and clashing only once they set foot on the island. Bonn's multiple heritages signal Farley's desire for a history that acknowledges constellations of identity in those who arrived on Jamaica's shores. Additionally, Bonn is still very much being formed when he sets out with Calico Jack to sail the Caribbean and, indeed, until the very end of the novel. Setting Bonn at sea while maintaining strong ties to a Jamaican setting further emphasizes the work Farley is undertaking: suggesting something Jamaican about these pirates' gender and sexual malleability and using that Jamaican-ness to respond to projects of national history that rewrite Jamaican history as more straight, more rigid and less complicated than its citizens know it to be.

By the 1660s, Jamaica's Port Royal had gained a reputation as the Sodom of the New World. While it is a provocative epithet because of queer valences that may not have been intended at the time of the naming, it also brings to mind Jamaican history's complicated relationship to the law, both governmental and religious.[2] Jamaica's recent strain of queerphobic Christianity, often attributed to evangelical preachers from the Global North, certainly does not recall Jamaica's history before the eighteenth century; a national history is created in which Jamaica is "natural" (meaning filled with people who are straight and who uphold rigid understandings of gender) until the imposition of Western queerness (Fink 2013).[3] This is not to say that Jamaica is a country of outlaws, but to say that there is room to claim some out-of-law-ness as resistance (think Nanny of the maroons), to acknowledge the limits of legal or religious doctrine, in the foundation of Jamaica. At the very least, it unsettles the story that some evangelicals tell about Western queerness tainting the cisgender heterosexual purity of the island.

Likewise, Farley's (2005) work prevents a simplistic version of Jamaican history that sees creolization as the gathering and mixing of previously foreign identities. The Bonn who arrives in Jamaica is certainly not the same Bonn who left Ireland as a child, nor is he the same Bonn who boarded Captain Jack Rackham's ship. With this novel acting as a catalogue of change, Farley suggests that the first Jamaicans did not come to the island fully formed, but that they were being constituted in relations with the sea before they set foot on the island. For Farley, the role of the historical novel is not to say, "we queers were here as early as everyone else" (though he does that work as well), but to claim the inadequacy of any concept of originary Jamaican identity that does not also acknowledge the transformative work that happens on the ocean as well as on land.

Paul Gilroy (2004) takes up nationalism's claim to land in his work on the crossings involved in the black Atlantic. A black Atlantic epistemology, according to Gilroy, "directs us not to the land, where we find that special soil in which we are told national culture takes root, but towards the sea and the maritime life that ringed and crossed the Atlantic ocean bringing more fluid and less fixed 'hybrid' cultures to life" (5). Farley appears to be working from this framework in which the sea disrupts Jamaica's formation as a "fixed" nation-state, especially the fixed nation-state that has been articulated to exclude queerness from its origins. Farley looks away from tidy heterosexual histories toward a national project that places more emphasis on the messiness of identity and locating that messiness in the ocean.

Parahuman Agency

Bonn's transformation would be impossible without the sea's intervention. Though we are typically comfortable recognizing the agency of cultural forms like courts, schools and churches, which are often hostile to queer formations of life, Farley asks us to recognize agency in nature, positioned as much more hospitable to queerness. Not the artificially orderly "nature" of "homosexuality is unnatural" rhetoric, but a more basic sense of the natural world is presented as profoundly complicated, resisting categorization, and accommodating toward various sexual orientations and iterations of gender. Farley suggests that nature, the ocean particularly, strips cultural significations and replaces them with an affirming ordinariness.

Monique Allewaert (2013) presents a similar view to nature's agency in her book *Ariel's Ecology*. In it, she suggests the importance of nature for subverting unnatural cultural oppressions like plantation slavery. Allewaert often uses the example of maroon communities as examples of subjects finding agency through relationships with ecologies/natural settings. We might see Bonn's agency in deciding to abandon his relationship to society and instead take up the sea as home. Bonn chooses the sea and invites it to act upon him. Regarding this more expansive view of relationality, Allewaert (2013, 10) says the following: "[E]verything including that which is conventionally understood as a medium – for instance, the sea – is bound up in processes of touching and proximity. Here, one entity touches upon and intensifies or exhausts or even decomposes another: this first entity's relation to the second is that of touching, of constituting, of perhaps in turn being constituted by it."

We might better understand the agency in Bonn's interaction with the ocean following Allewaert's (2013) analysis of what she calls "para-humanity". Allewaert describes this as a "category opened up by colonials attempting to manage black persons, particularly their capacity for collective resistance, the *parahuman* is distinguishable from other bodies produced in emerging biopolitical regimes because her body was broken in parts" (85). Allewaert shows great scepticism toward "the desirability of the category of human" and, instead, goes on to say that the parahuman is uniquely positioned for resistance because of her brokenness and the relationality that brokenness invites (86). In this move, she highlights strategies of resistance that were produced in the liminal space of para-humanity, being thought of between animals and nature in hierarchical relation (though Allewaert eschews this hierarchy) but also as a perversion of the named category (*para*human like *para*normal). Bonn could be said to be embodying this parahumanity on land in his resistance against "womanly professions", namely prostitution (where he would be valued for his vagina) or marriage (where he would be valued for his uterus), and in his disidentification with those parts of his body once at sea.

When drawing parallels to slave resistance, we would do well to acknowledge Bonn's privilege. Bonn's ability to pass as white in most circumstances allows Farley to write more agency into the character than would be afforded a black character (for example, Bonn's journey from Ireland to America on a slave ship is as passenger, not as cargo). Nevertheless, this invocation of parahumanity provides useful (though not congruent) because of the space for relationality that it opens up. "Freed from cultural boundaries associated with land and cities," Bonn exclaims,

> I never felt my womanhood so intensely as when I became a man of the sea. In that pampered other world, tho' you'll never hear it said aloud, a woman feels all the lust and rude emotions as are experienced by men, a woman yearns, in her secret heart, to experience all the adventures and challenges that men embrace – and yet it is all denied, and all that desire is hidden in smiles and dimples. Let that world be damn'd! (91)

The term "pampered" here indicates the irony and pain of this unwanted scrutiny – though Bonn's bombastic optimism makes him reluctant to position himself as a victim.

Travelling toward Blackness and Queerness

Farley counters the narrative that queerness is inherently white and thus un-Jamaican. As Bonn spends more time in the Jamaican waters, becoming more comfortable in his gender and sexuality, he clings less rigidly to his whiteness. Aligning queerness as well as blackness with the ocean ties Bonn's growing comfort with his gender and sexuality to his growing acceptance of his African ancestry. As Bonn becomes more comfortable embodying masculinity at sea, he becomes less hostile toward his black crewmates.

Omise'eke Tinsley (2010, 164) uses Bonn's moments of education by black pirates to suggest a different way of thinking of how cultural mores move across boundaries: "Bonn's gender/piracy finally emerges not as something that a European imports to the Caribbean but as a set of masculine 'dreams' that Bonn learns from an African traveller [later revealed to be his father] – a product of Southern histories of travel and transgression rather than Northern sexual exceptionalism." This move by Tinsley also adds layers to the ocean as a space of blackness. It is not just a site of black suffering but also a site of black possibility. When cultural structures on land reinforce slavery and oppression, Farley looks to pirates of colour like his characters Zayd, Xbalanque, Hunahpu and Laurens De Graff to imagine a history of black success made possible by the lawlessness of Jamaican waters.

Tinsley (2010) suggests that Bonn "immediately embraces" his African identity, but this is perhaps too generous a reading of the character.[4] Bonn initially rejects black crewmates' attempts at camaraderie. When gathering on shore for recruitment by Rackham, Bonn rejects an attempt at friendship from a black crewmate: "I am from Ireland", he says, "your tone [of voice] seems to suggest there is some connection between us, when no such bond exists" (73).[5] This initial rejection highlights the ocean's agency, as the harsh sun at sea kindles self-knowledge of Bonn's race that he would not have found on land, and rejection turns to acceptance. In the Caribbean sun, Bonn has a much harder time passing as white and must face the interpellations this new, darker skin brings. Bonn's interaction with his black crewmate described above also illustrates a common theme in the novel: Bonn is approached by sailors who recognize something of themselves in him (either with regard to race, gender or sexuality), but he fears transgression and so is reluctant to enter into conspiratorial comradery with them.

After some time at sea, however, Bonn is less defensive in these encounters. Tying Bonn's knowing his queerness to his blackness, Bonn's sexual and racial awakening happen almost immediately upon one another. Sequentially, Bonn is intimate with fellow gender-bending pirate Read (historically Mary Read) for the first time (178), is caught naked by Captain Rackham (178), finally takes seriously Zayd's claim to African kinship (184) and has his first sexual experience with the homosexual Rackham (184).

Drawn to the surgeon Zayd's song from his homeland, his pimento incense and his beautiful black torso (seen naked for the first time), Bonn is temporarily disoriented out of his usual confrontational attitude toward the black sailor. Zayd shares information with Bonn about the black pirate De Graff, who Caribbean authorities portrayed as white to prevent slaves from imagining themselves as pirates. Zayd uses the interaction to suggest a shared racial freedom on the ocean: "Surely I need not explain such things to you. Surely you, too, once saw liberty in the sails of every ship you spied from the shore. . . . *De Griff* is an old term for a person of three-quarters African ancestry. Is there not some of *De Griff* in you as well?" (184). Bonn's argumentative reaction to Zayd's extension of black solidarity is finally broken through: Bonn's "why do you say such things" becomes "how do you know such things?" (184). Still reeling from Zayd's music and this new perspective of his own race, Bonn is filled with queer erotic energy. Bonn narrates the scene:

> His muscles were lean and black – a blackness so dark, he seemed to be cut out of the night sky and poured into human form. Indeed the lights of the sky were reflected on his shiny, smooth muscles, as if his very being was a map of the constellations. . . . Gazing upon Zayd's form, I was filled with the most curious sensations and emotions. Although I had not exerted myself, I felt my breathing grow labored, as if I had been in the midst of a long sprint. Next, I felt a warmth spread from my bosom throughout my body, as if I had drunk a pot of warm tea spiked with Jamaican rum. My body felt buoyant, as if it was ready to cut its tether to the earth and ascend to the celestial realm. (181)

After this erotic setup, Bonn cuts their conversation short. Instead of sleeping with Zayd, he goes climactically to bed with Rackham – an interesting narrative decision on Farley's part. One might speculate about Bonn's admiration of Rackham, the voyeuristic encounter they just shared (184) or perhaps about Bonn's reluctance to sleep with someone of his own race. Farley gives us little in the way of explanation for Bonn's decision to sleep with Rackham rather than Zayd during these scenes where much is left unsaid.

Though Bonn's blackness could be said to be with him even in Ireland, the hidden status of his biological father, coupled with the perpetually cloudy climate, allows him to pass as white. He faces his first tan in South Carolina, as well as his first interpellation as being of African descent. Bonn's race inhabits the ocean as much as his gender and sexuality does. Paired in this way, Bonn makes three circuitous journeys simultaneously: he makes his way toward blackness, toward queerness and toward Jamaica. This parallelism positions Jamaica as in some ways inherently queer and black, disrupting the pairings of queer–white and straight–black that have been used to position Jamaica's black identity against any expressions of queerness.

Bonn's journeys as written by Farley help to revise narratives of queer travel. In Farley's work, water is inhabited, not crossed as one might imagine would appear in a diasporic writer's novels. As mentioned before, the direction of travel is also essential to Farley's queering of Jamaica's history. Jasbir Puar's (2007) *Terrorist Assemblages,* among other texts, points out false notions that the United States and other Global North countries lead the march toward sexual freedom, with regions like the Caribbean lagging behind (see also Tinsley 2010). Within this framework lies a more specific image of the queer diaspora from Global South to Global North as a journey from daily violence to salvation and sexual freedom. Queerphobia becomes tied to an identity of resisting the Global North. If a country like Jamaica becomes less queerphobic, those who believe in this narrative see it as acquiescing to the powers of the Global North. Not only are the people from the Global North imposing neoliberal economic policies that shape daily life in Jamaica, but they are now imposing their morality as well. Farley directly challenges this concept of Global Northern sexual exceptionalism and the corollary assumption that to be anticolonial is to be anti-queer.

In Farley's work, traversing the ocean is still essential to a queer identity, but, if it has a trajectory at all, it runs home toward the Global South, not away from it. Bonn finds greater sexual and gender freedom as he leaves the Global North and travels toward Jamaica, not the other way around. He knows that his desire to sail the seas will be impossible as a woman and so begins his career as a pirate by cross-dressing. But the performative line is blurred by characterizations of Bonn as what we might understand as transgender. Farley further complicates this by making Bonn's gender into *work*. It is not an inborn trait, but something that must be learned. About the sea, Bonn says:

> [L]arge bodies of water, to me, seemed to be churning cauldrons of manhood, stirred at the bottom by long-bearded Poseidon with his scepter; oceans, lakes, and rivers, in my mind, contain'd in their white-flecked crests the very sum of the rages and storms and swells of the [male] sex. If I could just learn the ways of the water, of ships and the sea, then, by my faith, I would have something of real value in my life. (47)

Farley disrupts common conceptions of the sea as female, and in doing so, also disrupts scholars' usual writing off of the sea as passive. The sea is not an obstacle to be crossed; it sees to Bonn's growth and teaches him masculinity. Tinsley (2010, 163) in her "Gender Pirates of the Caribbean", suggests a connection between the above passage and Bonn's performance of masculinity: "fluid masculinity now surfaces as something whose 'ways' [Bonn] can learn like the work of fishermen and boatswains". Tinsley discusses Bonn's complicated attraction to masculinity as his desire "not to find a man at sea but to become one, to train [his] body to masculinity like and along with seafaring" (163). Through emphasis on the learnability of the ways of the water, Bonn comes to an understanding of gender as essentially performative. Bonn remarks with surprise that Read "was so forthright about what he wanted that he had convinced the world to take him for who he wanted to be" (177). Read, who serves as Bonn's ideal performance of seafaring bravado and masculinity, reassures a previously self-conscious Bonn that it is one's experience, not anatomy, that decides their gender.

Desubjectification, Queering, Erosion of Boundaries

Bonn also explicitly acknowledges the ocean's ability to disrupt culturally constructed boundaries. He sees the ocean as an accomplice in asserting his full personhood, breaking down the category of woman that he found so restrictive: "Just as the surf erodes the shore, so, too, does the sea erase boundaries. The ever-crashing waves and the shifting winds make a mockery of maps and lines drawn by diplomats, kings, and queens. . . . So, following suit, the other lines to which we are so accustom'd on land, fall away while shipboard" (96). While Bonn learns masculinity from the labour of the sea, heavily masculinized in the novel, he also learns to feel more comfortable in his masculinity as gazing at the sea brings him to an epiphany at the constructedness of cultural conventions. This may be a more recuperative reading of the queering that can happen at sea, but it is certainly one of many iterations of cultural constructs falling away as one sails farther away from port.

This discussion of the ocean exemplifies the complicated task of naming agency. Bonn desires change but cannot enact that change without being in relation to the water. What is normally thought of as an uncomplicated interaction of human agent and nonhuman object is disrupted by the metaphorical (yet also material) information Bonn learns from the sea. One of the first lessons Bonn learns from the sea is a realistic reflection of how he is perceived by the world. Though he has not yet learned the masculinity that comes with working at/with the sea, he still has some measure of gender difference. He talks of looking into the ocean from the shore, saying, "When I walk quayside and see my reflection in the water I invariably carry in my mind's eye a picture of myself that stands in sharp contrast to the visage I see before me in real life" (50). This reflection, both literal and figurative, pushes Bonn to recognize his own agency in gender presentation; shortly after, he begins dressing as a man and seeking employment at sea.

Interesting here is the materiality of the sea. Of course there are metaphorical nods to water throughout the book. In dressing as a man for the first time, Bonn keeps his voice "calm and low as water without wind" (54). Likewise, marvelling at Read's masculinity, Bonn says, "his movements were decisive but flowing, like a strong river" (152). However, Bonn is very much affected by the materiality of the ocean as well as its metaphorical role in the novel. He speaks of his attraction to the sea as it issues from the docks: "As other women breathe in the scent of periwinkle or Easter lilies given to them by some gentleman caller, I would suck in deep the reek of workingman's musk, ship's tar, and sea water. By my faith, I must confess it smelled like it issued from some flower to me" (48).

Bonn's movement, both toward the sea and to masculinity, is a turn against his prospects on land as a woman. He sees only two paths on land, either prostitution or marriage, both of which he regards with equal distaste. He sees himself as able to do the work of any man, but artificially limited because of the gender imposed on him. Seeing a happy pairing between performing masculinity and seafaring, Bonn resolves, "If I could not find work as a woman, I would take some other form. . . . Thus outfitted, I would join some trade of the sea" (51). Bonn soon joins a pirate crew and begins to learn the ways of men at sea. He quickly performs the gender he has chosen, learning the most gruelling chores first – swabbing the decks, unfurling the mainsail, throwing waste into the sea. Bonn no longer fears having to rely on a man for income. At least in the pirates' minds, they live not off their victims but "off the sea" (116). In this way, his prospects on land, where he would have been dependent on men, have been replaced not by independence (the great ruse of masculinity) but instead by dependence on the sea itself.

Bonn's use of gender to escape misogyny is made possible at sea because the sea is an important site for queer resistance; at least that seems to be Farley's argument. In his retelling of the story of Jamaica's sodomy laws, his Calico Jack Rackham reveals the secret of his persecution by Governor Woodes Rogers: colonial terror against pirates in the Caribbean. Farley says that Jack and Rogers "shared those things that men sometimes share on sea-voyages, when one comes to know one's fellows in a way one never would on land" (292). Here, Farley visibly aligns the oceanic environment with sex between men. "To [Jack], all flesh was flesh, and this episode was just one of many; but to Rogers, it was a moment of deep ignominy, of weakness, of sin, and it was his drive to purge himself that drove the Governor on his campaign to destroy [Jack] and all who sail'd with him" (292). Thus, Farley places Jack at sea, comfortable with his sexual activity, ashamed only in his choice of companion. We see little regret in Jack, who has a subsequent relationship with Bonn where he encourages Bonn's continued male gender presentation.

Rogers, on the other hand, gives up his life at sea to prosecute pirates, in Farley's telling, because of a grudge against the sexual liberty pirates created for themselves at sea. Jack, just as Jamaican as Rogers, opposes the British colonial rule of law. Rogers' turn to this law is presented not as the obvious choice but as a personal incompatibility with queer life at sea. With this, Farley suggests that a Jamaican identity can be found just as easily in resisting the colonial residue of queerphobia. We might return to the parahuman in considering the usual pairing of cultural bodies, especially legislative ones, with nation building. However, Farley's portrayal of Rogers aligns him with the British buggery law, not the Jamaican ocean. Through a parahuman lens that balances cultural and natural agency, we can see Rogers's return to the city as Jamaica's governor as no more Jamaican than Rackham's return to the sea as pirate.

We must be careful here; we are entering dangerous waters. Bonn may have found greater sexual freedom at sea, but Farley's fictional account is positively brimming with issues of consent. Farley engages very little with the character of Poop, who was "used like a woman, on occasion, by his fellows" until Read joined the crew and started to protect him (80). This is perhaps one of the blind spots in pirate historians and enthusiasts alike. Temporal distance distracts us from the fact that the verbs most closely associated with the group are not as triumphalist as we like to think. Instead, pirates are most notoriously rapists and pillagers.

Farley's bildungsroman is the best-case scenario for Bonn, but for many the sea was the site of a more violent undoing of gender. For a more sobering account of ungendering at sea, we can turn to Hortense Spillers's (1987, 72) "Mama's Baby, Papa's Maybe":

> Those African persons in "Middle Passage" were literally suspended in the "oceanic", if we think of the latter in its Freudian orientation as an analogy for undifferentiated identity: removed from the indigenous land and culture, and not-yet "American" either, these captive persons, without names that their captors would recognize, were in movement across the Atlantic, but they were also nowhere at all. Inasmuch as, on any given day, we might imagine, the captive personality did not know where s/he was, we could say that they were the culturally "unmade", thrown in the midst of a figurative darkness that "exposed" their destinies to an unknown course. Often enough for the captains of these galleys, navigational science of the day was not sufficient to guarantee the intended destination. We might say that the slave ship, its crew, and its human-as-cargo stand for a wild and unclaimed richness of possibility that is not interrupted, not "counted"/"accounted", or differentiated, until its movement gains the land thousands of miles away from the point of departure. Under these conditions, one is neither female, nor male, as both subjects are taken into "account" as quantities.

Farley is perhaps viewing the ungendering that happens at sea in his particular way because of a desire for a more optimistic narrative, but the ungendering that happens in Spillers's account is important to acknowledge as well. We might find some amount of resistive potential in this ungendering as one of the violences that was enacted on slaves. Gender and sexuality as solid identities are foisted upon those the white hegemony deems subjects, and Allewaert (2013) reminds us that the white hegemony did not view slaves as subjects. If we understand the binary categories of man and woman, heterosexual and homosexual as the inventions of white European science, none of the categories end up fitting a black Jamaican identity, either in Farley's account or Spillers's.

Historical Fictions

Disrupting for a moment the association with the sea, Farley allows Bonn and Jack to retreat to the Jamaican hillside, an erotic paradise that fosters the pirates' queerness – Bonn continues to dress as a man, and Jack expresses pleasure as they "would talk together in the rough cadences of men, even as [they] shared sweet intimacies" (250). The queering that happened at sea was not withheld from Jamaica but recognized as they put down their queer roots. During this time on land, Jack impregnates Bonn, who miscarries the child, but Bonn raises Read's child as his own, choosing to believe Read's claim that Bonn impregnated him through the shared wall of their jail cells. As Tinsley (2010, 165) notes about this complicated unsettling of gender and reproduction, "not only is Farley's Caribbean a 'natural' haven for queerness, the region's populace, far from a bastion of homophobia, is (partly) the offspring of that queerness".

While Farley's book is classified as fiction, he's not fabricating a new history to further a supposed gay agenda; he's rewriting history to show how much of it is fiction in the first place. In an author's note at the end of the book, Farley pushes back against critics who worry about drifting too far from the accepted history: "My version of Anne Bonny's story differs from the conventional version – which is not to say that it is in variance with the truth" (324). He critiques the agreed-upon history, largely taken from Captain Johnson's book *A General History of the Robberies and Murders of the Most Notorious Pyrates*. Writers of histories in the eighteenth century often embellished and changed stories to better appeal to their audiences, and these embellishments often wrote over details that were assumed not to appeal to a book's audience. Farley says, "I did try to remain faithful to the historical record I believed was true, but I also recognized that other parts of the record were probably flawed. So if an event could have happened and felt true, I followed it" (325).

We should take the same sceptical attitude toward history, allowing more expansive readings of national formation. Farley's is one such reading, disrupting the more popular "out of many, one people" version of history that keeps the ocean as a line of transit, with Jamaica acting as a "melting pot" of cultures and ethnicities that were picked up and transported there (Delle, Hause and Armstrong 2011, x). In Farley's recounting of history, the sea is not an empty vessel that is traversed but the origin of unique experience and its own actor, contributing to Jamaica's growth as a nation.

However, we must recognize Farley's as yet one more writing of history – one that gives little attention to the less savoury aspects of desubjectification at sea. Farley's celebratory queer Jamaican-ness is warranted, called for even, in the face of queerphobic iterations of Jamaican nationalism. Yet we must be careful not to let utopian ideas gloss over other moments that also need to be taken into account. Citing moments like those in Spillers's work may provide a richer take on the themes suggested by utopian reimaginings like Farley's. Queerness need not be triumphalist to be invoked; as with Allewaert's (2013) parahumanity, we may do more work to unsettle queerphobic narratives when we account for persecution at the same time as we account for resistance situated in that persecution.

Notes

1. I use masculine pronouns throughout the paper because it is how Bonn refers to himself throughout most of the novel, but the framing narrative at the beginning of the novel uses female pronouns for Bonn at the end of his/her life.

2. In the seventeenth century, sodomy referred to all aberrant sexual practices, not exclusively anal sex between men.

3. I use "queer" and "queerphobic" in this paper to indicate the inseparability of gender and sexual variance, especially in this novel. Though there are issues regarding the terms' ties to the Global North, they seem more useful terms for this analysis than the equally Western "LGBT".

4. She uses as evidence a quotation from over three hundred pages into the book.

5. The black crewmate is unidentified in the text.

References

Allewaert, Monique. 2013. *Ariel's Ecology: Plantations, Personhood, and Colonialism in the American Tropics*. Minneapolis: University of Minnesota Press.

Delle, James A., Mark W. Hauser, and Douglas V. Armstrong. 2011. *Caribbean Archaeology and Ethnohistory: Out of Many, One People: The Historical Archaeology of Colonial Jamaica*. Tuscaloosa: University of Alabama Press.

Farley, Christopher John. 2005. *Kingston by Starlight: A Novel*. New York: Three Rivers Press.

Fink, Micah. 2013. *The Abominable Crime*. New York: Common Good Productions.

Gilroy, Paul. 2004. *Der Black Atlantic*. Berlin: Haus der Kulturen der Welt.

Puar, Jasbir. 2007. *Terrorist Assemblages: Homonationalism in Queer Times*. Durham, NC: Duke University Press.

Spillers, Hortense. 1987. "Mama's Baby, Papa's Maybe: An American Grammar Book". *Diacritics* 17 (2): 64–81.

Tinsley, Omise'eke Natasha. 2010. "Gender Pirates of the Caribbean: Queering Caribbeanness in the Novels of Zoe Valdes and Christopher John Farley". In *Hispanic Caribbean Literature of Migration: Narratives of Displacement*, edited by Vanessa Pérez Rosario, 153–68. New York: Palgrave Macmillan.

7.

Iconicity and Eroticism in the Photography of Archie Lindo

O'NEIL LAWRENCE

In 2008, while working at the National Gallery of Jamaica, I came across a small set of files focused on Jamaican photographers. Archie Lindo's file, which was among them, contained only two items: a photocopy of a *Jamaica Journal* article on Lindo by Martin Mordecai (1989) and a newspaper article on a posthumous exhibition ("Archie Lindo Photos on Show", *Gleaner*, 27 January 1998). Lindo, a descendant of the white Jamaican upper class, was born in 1908 and was primarily active as a photographer in the 1950s, 1960s and 1970s. My attention was originally attracted to the photograph *The Irish Moss Gatherers* (figure 7.1), an undated image from the mid-twentieth century that depicts three nude black men standing on a beach: first, because it resonated on several levels with my own photography, which at that point utilized nude male iconography, and second, because until that point I had been totally unaware of the existence of photographs of nude Jamaican male subjects from the mid-twentieth century or earlier. In an interview conducted with Archie Lindo's cousin Donald Lindo, he revealed that the *Irish Moss Gatherers* was one of his most reproduced and collected images (interview with the author, 5 August 2014; hereafter "Donald Lindo interview"). According to *Jamaica Journal*, the work had received award(s), although it was not specified which.

My second introduction to Lindo's work was to his private archive of photographs that I became aware of while discussing potential research topics with a close friend. He showed me an album containing photographs that spanned the gamut from mildly erotic to pornographic, many with artistic qualities similar to the *Irish Moss Gatherers*. The focus of this article is the works contained in that private archive, a significant portion of which was never exhibited publicly, and a discussion of them in relation to his most famous nude photograph *The Irish Moss Gatherers*, which although thematically and stylistically related to his private archive is more aestheticized and complex in meaning than most of the others.

Figure 7.1. Archie Lindo, *The Irish Moss Gatherers* (c. 1950). Reproduced from scanned negative with permission from Susan C. Willingham (née Lindo).

Based on my current knowledge of Archie Lindo's other photographs, I am able to approximate the date of the photograph to the 1950s and to identify the beach as White Horses in St Thomas, where Irish moss is still harvested and sold today.[1] It is by far the most outstanding of a series of photographs that were taken by Lindo on that same beach, several of which involve the same men.[2] All three men in *The Irish Moss Gatherers* appear to be relatively young and look fit and muscular. Their hair is styled in a way that also helps to date the photograph to the 1950s or early 1960s. The man on the left has a cigarette in his mouth and the man on the right has a cigarette in his right hand, which is held in front of his chest; the men on the left and right are both holding Irish moss in their hands, as if to compare the quality of their catch, although this may have been staged.

Figure 7.2. Archie Lindo, *Untitled* (c. 1950s). Reproduced from scanned negative with permission from Susan C. Willingham (née Lindo).

The men stand in a close grouping as if they are conversing with each other. The man to the left is seen in full profile, the man in the centre of the grouping is seen frontally and the man to the right is at an angle, near profile, which again suggests that they were posed. All three men are nude but their nudity is covered by large jute bags; the man in the centre holds the largest one, and the bags are supported across their shoulders by a rough cord. The placement of the bags appears deliberate, as there is another photograph, possibly involving one of the same men on the same day, in which he is walking away from the photographer with his bag held to the side, thus not covering his genitals (figure 7.2).

The jute bags, though providing seemingly modest coverage of what would otherwise have been full frontal nudity, could also be read as exaggerated scrotums, which adds to the sexual allusions in the work. The natural lighting is harsh and the position of the shadows, which are very short, suggests that it is midday. This lighting creates sharp shadows on the figures and obscures parts of their bodies as well. The skilful draping of the figures and use of the natural light to moderate the nudity of the figures are a reflection of Lindo's photographic skills and strong compositional sense. Lindo prided himself on using only available light (Mordecai 1989, 26). The self-possessed nature of the men in this photograph suggests that this image should be viewed as a distinct category of portraiture that differs significantly from depictions of people of other racial and ethnic backgrounds. The difference, Richard Powell (2008) contends, lies in the social capital that stems directly from the black subject's power to subvert dominant racist representations by evincing such traits as self-composure, self-adornment and self-imagining.

The men are standing on a sandy beach with numerous rounded white rocks. The beach indents behind them and the coastline recedes behind the men. There are numerous trees, mainly coconut palms, behind them, and a hilly landscape is evident in the far background, in which a rocky outcrop falls to the sea. From a formal perspective, the composition moves the eye from left to right in a sweeping movement. This too indicates that Lindo was familiar with the principles of photography and composition.

The men in this image are at once monumental and relatable, the midday sun creating sharp shadows that make their bodies almost cutouts in their environment, which adds to the iconic quality of the image. The rough rocky beach emphasizes the primitive battle for survival against the environment. It is an almost timeless image, as the only elements that provide hints of the period are the hairstyles and the cigarettes. The image can thus be subjected to multiple readings: it can be homoerotic or simply

Figure 7.3. Sandro Botticelli, *Primavera (The Allegory of Spring)*, detail (1477–82). Reproduced from Wikimedia with permission.

homosocial, it can be representative of a transgressive sexuality or simply be another nostalgic representation of "old-time Jamaica".

There are precedents in Western art history for the type of arrangement presented in *The Irish Moss Gatherers*. Although the comparisons I am about to make may at first seem to be provocative, the image would have such resonance for those with knowledge of Western artistic traditions, as Lindo presumably had. One iconographic type that readily comes to mind is the Three Graces from Greco-Roman mythology, which has been a common theme in European art from Greco-Roman antiquity to neoclassicism, although this theme is quintessentially associated with femininity and white, European culture (Carr 1846).[3] One example can be seen in Italian Renaissance painter Sandro Botticelli's *Primavera* (*The Allegory of Spring*) 1477–82 (figure 7.3). While more elegant, the grouping and posing of the Graces in the *Primavera* is strikingly similar to the grouping of the figures in *The Irish Moss Gatherers*, and the interaction of the semi-nude, dancing Graces also has homoerotic, in this case lesbian, allusions.

Another example, this time from neoclassicism, is the Italian sculptor Antonio Canova's *Three Graces* (1814–17), in which the eroticism is much more pronounced (figure 7.4). In Canova's work, the figures are fully nude and positioned more closely to each other, embracing, with their faces positioned as if about to kiss, which suggests greater intimacy between the figures. *The Irish Moss Gatherers*, in contrast, is assertively male and they are not touching; its eroticism is thus more implicit than in most conventional examples of the Three Graces.

While the image of the Three Graces is usually associated with whiteness, there is one major exception in European art: William Blake's famous print *Europe Supported by Africa and Asia* (1796), which appeared in John Gabriel Stedman's book *The Narrative of a Five Year Expedition against the Revolted Negroes of Surinam* (figure 7.5). In this image, the prototype of the Three Graces is transformed into a multiracial grouping of three women: an African, a European and an Asian. This image suggests that colonialism had the potential to be beneficial to all parties involved. Importantly, the European woman is central, dominant and the one being supported, which suggests one of two readings. The first is that despite Blake's and Stedman's abolitionist sympathies, they still took European racial and economic superiority for granted. The second reading, using a revisionist historical perspective, suggests that the central figure representing Europe would be unable to stand were it not for its colonial interests in Africa and Asia. The multiracial aspect of the print is an important departure from the established iconography of the Three Graces and may have influenced subsequent reinterpretations. It is noteworthy that Edna Manley (wife of Jamaica's first premier, Norman Manley [1959–62], and a major contributor to the Jamaican Cultural Nationalist movement of the 1930s and 1940s)[4] was significantly influenced by William Blake (Boxer 1990). It is also likely

Figure 7.4. Antonio Canova, *The Three Graces* (1814–17). Reproduced from Wiki-media with permission.

Figure 7.5. William Blake, *Europe Supported by Africa and Asia* (1796). Reproduced from Wikimedia with permission.

that Lindo was aware of this print, although there is no evidence that this directly influenced the posing of the figures in *The Irish Moss Gatherers*.

Modern and contemporary artists have interpreted the Three Graces archetype in more provocative ways, and the image has appeared in queer art, as can be seen in a print and painting, *The Three Graces* (1978), by Delmas Howe that reinterpreted and subverted the classical precedents by casting the Graces as modern cowboys. As we have seen before, the arrangement of the Three Graces in most incarnations has potential lesbian implications. Howe has created an image with three men which, while not explicitly sexual, has obvious homoerotic overtones. The men stand casually with arms around each other's shoulders in a display of homosocial comfort in a field that appears recently ploughed, apparently illuminated by the mid-morning sun. They are all clothed in decreasing amounts of farm-appropriate denim, from shirtless overalls on the figure to the left, to cut-off shorts on the figure to the right. Howe's work is a more complex commentary on masculine stereotypes and their idealization in American gay pop culture, as was embodied by the Village People band.

More recently, the Three Graces iconography has been referenced by the African American artist Kehinde Wiley, who is best known for his academically painted canvases in which he provocatively places young black men from the hip-hop generation in poses and contexts that cite the Western artistic canon and its iconographies. Wiley is openly gay; the contradictions inherent in constructions of black masculinity are a major theme of his work, which reveals that there is space for gay identities and sexuality in hip-hop culture, despite its assertions of heterosexual hypermasculinity.

I cannot determine whether the apparent reference to the Three Graces in Lindo's *The Irish Moss Gatherers* is as deliberate as in these examples, but the comparison with his emphatically masculine fishermen is certainly striking and brings to the fore the homoerotic implications of the photograph. In Jamaican visual arts, Lindo's *The Irish Moss Gatherers* should be seen in the context of the Nationalist school, particularly the manner in which the black male body was represented and foregrounded as a national and racial icon from the 1930s to the 1950s. Some of Edna Manley's most iconic works, like *Negro Aroused* (1935), its companion work, *Prophet* (1935), and *Diggers* (1936) (figures 7.6–7.8), were completed in the mid-1930s. They emerged during the Nationalist movements that were beginning to change Jamaican society: the middle-class nationalism of Edna and Norman Manley's Drumblair circle (the epicentre of the nationalist intelligentsia in Jamaica at that time) to which Lindo belonged, but also the popular black nationalism that was propagated locally and internationally

Figure 7.6. Edna Manley, *Negro Aroused* (1935). Collection: National Gallery of Jamaica. Reproduced from photograph with permission from the Edna Manley Foundation.

by Marcus Garvey (whose philosophy of black unity and African cultural nationalism represented a pointed alternative to the "out of many, one people" cultural nationalism of Norman Manley).

In these Manley works, the black male body is iconized through form – the exaggerated arms and thighs of the figure – and through gesture, as a symbol of power and upliftment. The black male is envisioned almost totally in terms of his physicality, though the art history literature speaks about it as a work symbolizing the social and political empowerment of the black populace. Looking more closely at Manley's *Prophet*, I note the way

Figure 7.7. Edna Manley, *Prophet* (1935). Collection: National Gallery of Jamaica (photographed by Dennis Gick, c. 1937). Reproduced from photograph with permission from the Edna Manley Foundation.

in which she delicately details the nipples, navel and buttocks of the figure, while his genitalia are abstracted (or perhaps censored). While this may have been an aesthetic choice, it also suggests an ambivalent sexual attraction to the black male body on the artist's part.

The formal and conceptual similarities between these works and Lindo's *The Irish Moss Gatherers* may explain the positive audience response to the photographs. The harsh midday light in *The Irish Moss Gatherers* gives the bodies of the men a distinctly sculptural and monumental quality that parallels Manley's *Negro Aroused, Prophet* and *Diggers* and, as in these sculptures, the sexuality of the men is emphasized by inference rather than visibility. Though like Manley, Lindo's choice may have been an aesthetic one, it is also likely that the modesty in this photograph is what enabled him to exhibit this work, since it conformed to common notions of propriety, while others taken in the same setting were too sexually explicit to be exhibited. It is probably also because of concerns with propriety that very little critical attention has thus far been paid to the erotic subtext that seems to be evident in the work of Manley and several others from the Nationalist movement.

Another important point to note is that Lindo's photograph depicts men at work; the heroic representation of black labour was another, and in this case, well-recognized hallmark of the Nationalist movement. The physicality of Manley's shirtless *Diggers* working in machine-like unison, for instance, multiplies and emphasizes the ideal of the physicality and economic productivity of the black male. One of the unresolved issues within Jamaican Nationalist art is its unwavering and, given Jamaica's history of slavery and present-day realities of labour exploitation, surprisingly uncritical celebration of physical labour as a nation-building activity. Albert Huie's *Crop Time* (1955), for instance, provides a sweeping panorama of the modern sugar industry as one of the pillars of the Jamaican economy but does not even hint at the historical baggage this subject carries (figure 7.9).

In Lindo's photograph the physical power and prowess of the men are similarly emphasized and presented as part of an idyllic scene, with no reference to their poverty or the physical danger that their profession involves. Other than the homoerotic overtones, there is nothing that deviates from the Nationalist iconography of this subject. This seeming lack of social and historical self-reflexivity on the part of artists like Manley, Huie and, for that matter, Lindo, is surprising if we consider that they occurred during mounting challenges to the prevailing social and racial order presented by Garveyism and Rastafari. It, however, reinforces what has always been the main critique of mainstream postcolonial cultural nationalism: that it failed to challenge the social order at a fundamental level and instead reinforced the social dominance of the emerging postcolonial elite, particularly the coloured middle class, to which Manley and Lindo both belonged (Donald Lindo interview).[5]

The theme of black labour is also evident in Alvin Marriott's *Banana Man* (c. 1955), another iconic work from the Nationalist School by an artist

Figure 7.8. Edna Manley, *Diggers* (1936). Collection: National Gallery of Jamaica. Reproduced from photograph with permission from the Edna Manley Foundation.

Figure 7.9. Albert Huie, *Crop Time* (1955). Collection: National Gallery of Jamaica. Reproduced from photograph with permission from Christine Huie-Roy.

with a social background similar to Manley's and Lindo's that emphasizes the physicality of the black man and helps to solidify the icon of the black man as a labourer (figure 7.10). The literature discussing this work makes no reference to the clear sexual innuendo inherent within the sculpture; the suggestive way in which he holds the bananas is particularly phallic.

Similar questions arise when we consider *Banana Man*, which dates from the same period as Lindo's *The Irish Moss Gatherers*: are the sexual connotations accidental or deliberate? As with *The Irish Moss Gatherers*, uncritical references to black physicality, labour and sexuality are combined, and it is again interesting that these references appear so prominently in art that purported to challenge colonial racial stereotypes, including those regarding supposed black sexual prowess.

Images of black male Jamaicans engaged in manual labour have enjoyed particular popularity since the nineteenth century. Both "the fisherman" and "banana man" are popular archetypes in that context,

Figure 7.10. Alvin Marriott, *Banana Man* (c. 1955). Collection: National Gallery of Jamaica. Reproduced from photograph with permission from Alicia Bogues.

probably because they both represent key areas of economic activity in the island. A photograph of fishermen in Kingston Harbour from about 1885 by Juan Valdez Sr, a photographer of Cuban origin, is a good example of the many iconic representations of Jamaican fishermen in Jamaican art and photography that have been used extensively in tourism (figure 7.11). Colonial-era images of black labourers were generally more anthropological in their focus than their Nationalist counterparts, as can be seen in the famous Duperly and Sons photograph of banana loaders at work (c. 1900), although they also reinforce and arguably romanticize black male labour (figure 7.12).

There is no erotic subtext in Duperly's *Banana Loaders*, although there are other nineteenth-century images of black males that are more erotically charged, such as *A Negro Boy* (c. 1891–92) by James Valentine and Sons, but these are not associated with labour and physical strength (figure 7.13).

Figure 7.11. J.B. Valdez Sr., *Natives Fishing* (c. 1885). Onyx Collection. Reproduced from scanned photograph with permission from National Gallery of Jamaica on behalf of the Onyx Collection.

Figure 7.12. A. Duperly, *Banana Loaders* (c. 1900, postcard). Onyx Collection. Reproduced from scanned photograph with permission from National Gallery of Jamaica on behalf of the Onyx Collection.

Figure 7.13. James Valentine and Sons, *A Negro Boy* (1891). The Aaron and Marjorie Matalon Collection: National Gallery of Jamaica. Reproduced from scanned photograph with permission from National Gallery of Jamaica.

This changes in the twentieth century: Archie Lindo's *The Irish Moss Gatherers*, while not representing fishermen per se (Irish moss is a sea plant), bears comparison to other contemporary images of Jamaican fishermen that have been so common as images of Jamaican life that they can be regarded as iconic. Toni Frissell, for example, produced several images of Jamaican fishermen, presumably while on a fashion shoot in the mid-1940s. In her photographs, the musculature, physical power and beauty of the fishermen pulling in their nets is even more pronounced than in Lindo's image. The iconic theme of the fisherman also appears in other media, such as Barrington Watson's epic *Fishing Village* (1996–98) (figure 7.14). This image, created by a heterosexual artist well-known for his female-centred erotica, is also ambiguous regarding the depiction of male sexuality, particularly with regard to the curiously "classicized" depiction of the boys who are helping to pull in the boat in the centre of the image.

The fisherman and banana man themes in Jamaican art have primitivist implications, the fisherman more so than the banana man, which

Figure 7.14. Barrington Watson, *Fishing Village* (1996–98). Collection: National Gallery of Jamaica. Reproduced from photograph with permission from Doreen Watson.

is less "timeless" because it is associated with a modern agro-industry. Primitivism was an artistic movement during the colonial and Romantic eras, when artists yearned for a simpler, idyllic lifestyle to counter modern life's mechanistic violence, which both "othered" *and* celebrated the lives of people deemed to be closer to nature.[6] Fishing requires little technology and is a popular activity among those who live close to the sea and on islands that brings the fisher closer to nature. It is, along with hunting, one of the most ancient and "primordial" human economic activities, so it lends itself well to primitivist stereotyping.

References to sexuality are more obvious in the banana man theme, given the phallic nature of the banana, but they are also present in the fisherman, in which there are stronger homoerotic connotations, since fishing is often done nude, or at least semi-nude, and because the profession is typically a homosocial environment dominated by men working in close physical proximity.[7] Rex Nettleford (1978, 4) critiqued the Nationalist art movement, positing that "cultural nationalism ha[d] indeed been an 'ideological façade' to cover up the social injustices of induced poverty among the black masses and the continuance of the entrenched privileges of the Eurocentric few". What makes Lindo's work different, however, is the addition of a queer subtext, which may be more deliberately subversive. This queer subtext becomes more obvious when we consider some of his other photographs of black male nudes.

Related Archie Lindo Nudes

At least one other photograph by Lindo may have been taken on the same day as *The Irish Moss Gatherers*, involving some of the same men, again all in the nude, who in this image appear to be resting under the shade of coconut trees at the edge of the beach (figure 7.15). I found this image in Lindo's archives, which I have entitled *The Irish Moss Gatherers II* for the sake of easy reference, I do not believe it was ever exhibited, although the image is comparable in aesthetic quality and iconicity. There are six men in *The Irish Moss Gatherers II*, one of whom is almost completely obscured by the others and appears to be lying down with his arm under his head. The attention of the other five men appears to be on this partially obscured figure, and four of the five men appear to be expressing some sort of amusement. At least one of the men in the original *The Irish Moss Gatherers* is also in this photograph: the crouching man with the jute bag in the centre of the grouping.

Figure 7.15. Archie Lindo, *Untitled* (*Irish Moss Gatherers II*) (1950s). Reproduced from scanned negative with permission from Susan C. Willingham (née Lindo).

The seated man on the left of the composition is seen with his body in profile; his legs are tucked beneath him on the sand but his face and attention are turned toward the photographer. He is the only one of the figures who is not fully in the shade, and he is sitting on his jute bag. He is also the only one to engage the photographer/viewer directly; his brow is furrowed, perhaps due to the sun, or perhaps quizzically, hostilely or apprehensively. Generally speaking, however, the men seem at ease with each other, each other's nudity and with the presence of the photographer. The relaxed nature of *The Irish Moss Gatherers II* suggests that the subjects were not hapless victims of Lindo's voyeuristic tendencies but conscious and comfortable participants in the transaction, suggesting informed consent on the part of his models.

In *The Irish Moss Gatherers II*, the man who is farthest right in the composition has his back to the camera/viewer and is sitting with his legs folded underneath him. He supports his weight on his right arm, which causes his back to form a graceful curve. This is echoed by the man standing on the left. Together they help to frame the composition – more evidence of Lindo's keen use of compositional devices. The man who was on the right in the original *The Irish Moss Gatherers* and is in the centre of this composition is laughing and holds what appears to be a photograph. The partially obscured figure also appears to be holding a photograph above his head with his left hand. The photographs seem to be the source of the mirth in the picture: they could be images of the men taken by Lindo on another occasion. There are other photographs in the private archive, some of them more explicitly sexual, which appear to have been taken on the same beach and involve some of the same men. This, too, suggests awareness and consent.

The composition of Lindo's *The Irish Moss Gatherers II* again reflects Lindo's awareness of Western iconographic traditions, whether he staged the image accordingly or uncovered it photographically in an existing situation. It can be compared to the French nineteenth-century realist painter Edouard Manet's *Le Déjeuner sur l'herbe* (1862–63) (figure 7.16). The gender

Figure 7.16. Edouard Manet, *Le Déjeuner sur l'herbe* (1862–63). Reproduced from Wikimedia with permission.

roles are again reversed, with female nude figures in this painting. *Le Déjeuner sur l'herbe* was deemed shocking in its day because of its depiction of nude women and clothed men without this juxtaposition being legitimized by a mythological theme, as was European art convention at the time. In Lindo's photograph, all the figures are nude in a homosocial context, but their nudity is legitimized by their occupation and therefore less deliberately provocative than in *Le Déjeuner sur l'herbe*. However, in both images it is the seated nude figure to the left who engages the viewer with a frank stare, a compositional similarity that may not have been a coincidence.

Lindo's awareness of Western iconography is also evident in other images from his private archive that are more explicitly homoerotic (figure 7.17). The posing of a seated male figure seen from the back, for instance, can

Figure 7.17. Archie Lindo, *Untitled* (n.d.). Reproduced from scanned photograph with permission from Susan C. Willingham (née Lindo).

be compared to the French neoclassical painter Jean Auguste Dominique Ingres's *La Grande baigneuse* (1808), although this is again a comparison in which gender roles are inverted (figure 7.18). The posing of the figure, who appears to be an art model with some experience, also echoes the muscular

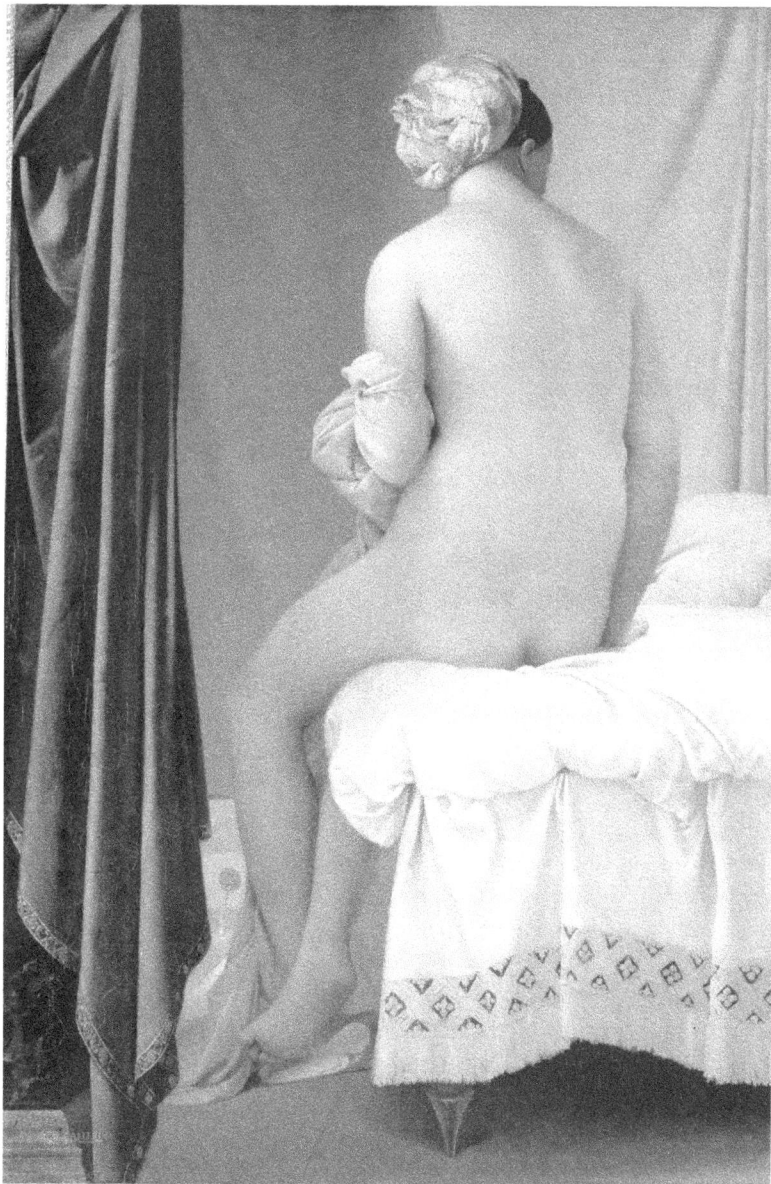

Figure 7.18. Auguste Dominique Ingres, *La Grande baigneuse* (1808). Reproduced from Wikimedia with permission.

but sensuous poses of Edna Manley's sculptures, which again underscores the argument that Lindo's imagery was in close dialogue with that of the Nationalist school (which was itself influenced by Western artistic traditions), even when he opted for more provocative sexual content.

The references to Western iconography in Lindo's depictions of black men suggest that there was a deliberately transgressive intent in his photography. In fact, the use of classical iconographies had long been a pretext and cover for the production of homoerotic work in Western art: "The thin ambiguous line between any man's admiration of such a (classical male) type and homoerotic attraction that is an object-oriented lust is the tightrope upon which Western societies have walked for generations" (Ellenzwig 1992, 14). Lindo added a more transgressive element to this strategy by inverting gender and race in iconographic types usually associated with femininity and whiteness. In his photographs, Lindo emphasized the muscular appearance of his black models without feminizing the masculinity of his subjects.

Lindo and Black Gay Erotica

The images by Lindo that I have discussed so far are eroticized but not sexually explicit. Some of the more explicit images in Lindo's private archive are equally aestheticized but others, especially the later ones in colour, lack obvious aesthetic and iconographic considerations and are more exclusively focused on the sexual content (figure 7.19). I have, however, seen none that depict actual sexual acts, which suggests that he may not have been interested in depicting sexual activity. This is an interesting paradox since Lindo would have been exposed to the liberating effects of the sexual revolution of the 1960s (though more explicit depictions of sexuality of course predated the 1960s).

Thus far, I have paid attention to the references to Western artistic iconographies. However, other iconographic references also warrant attention, especially in relation to Lindo's more private images. There are, for instance, particular types and categories that appear in mid-twentieth-century black gay erotica (erotica that depict black males for consumption by gay viewers, black or white). Images published by Jim Jager under the provocative and problematic title Third World Studio[8] (figure 7.20) and the photographic work of Craig Calvin Andersen, who produced collections of mail-order photographs and magazines focusing on black gay imagery from his photographic studio Sierra Domino (figure 7.21), are examples of this.

Figure 7.19. Archie Lindo, *Untitled* (n.d.). Reproduced from scanned negative with permission from Susan C. Willingham (née Lindo).

It is of note that both photographers were white. Especially in the case of Jager, there seems to be more than a hint of exploitation, as some of the models' French names and settings suggest that the photographs were taken in the actual "Third World" (such as Haiti). Andersen's photographs are both pornographic and highly aestheticized and are usually set in urban and semi-rural environments. Jager's work, on the other hand, is divided between a largely studio-based practice and photographs that appear to have been taken in a tropical environment and are generally less aestheticized than Andersen's work.

The black male in the majority of these images is represented in a masculine to hypermasculine way: muscular athletic bodies predominate, as do the stereotypically large and usually erect penises, and to a lesser

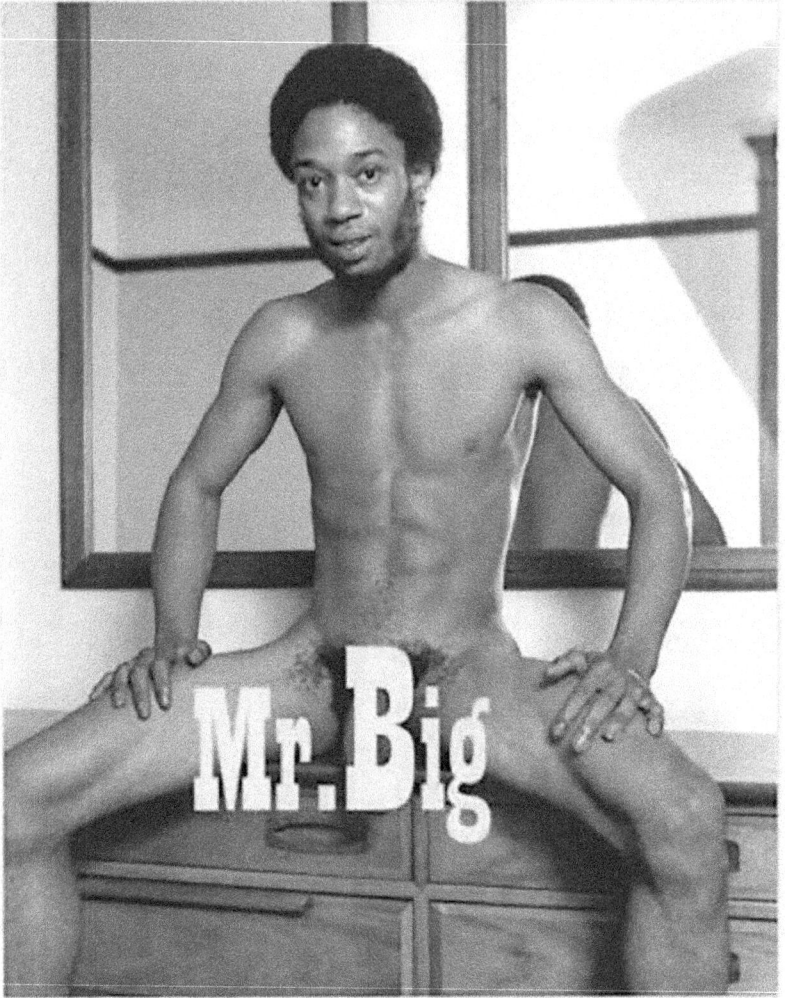

Figure 7.20. Cover of *Mr Big*, a collection of photos by Third World Studio (Jim Jager). Reproduced from Internet photograph with permission from Volker Janssen of Janssen Publishers.

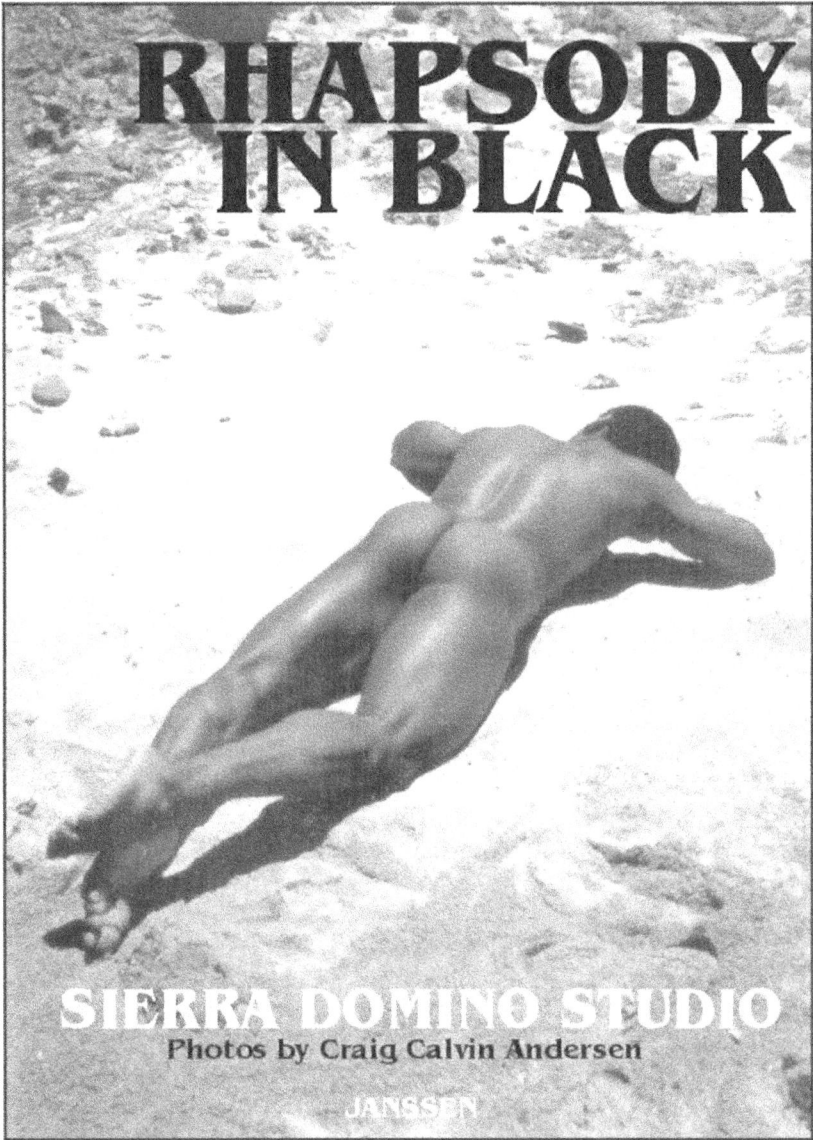

Figure 7.21. Cover of *Rhapsody in Black*, a collection of photos by Sierra Domino Studio (Craig Calvin Andersen). Reproduced from Internet photograph with permission from Volker Janssen of Janssen Publishers.

extent, the muscular large buttocks.[9] The poses in these photographs emphasize these characteristics. There are some typical poses, the most basic of which are full frontal or focused on the buttocks. There are variations on these shots usually involving lying down, sitting or standing, legs spread, bending over and any combination of these positions. Although the focus is usually on the genitalia in such images, the general muscularity and beauty of the body are also emphasized. Some of these images, especially those by Andersen, also reference classical Western art iconography, particularly in the posing of the body.[10]

The images in Lindo's private archive are generally consistent with these characteristics. There is a continuum beginning with photographs that have artistic aspirations like Andersen's (figure 7.22), to photographs that are closer to Jager's more matter-of-fact depiction of sexuality. These correlations suggest that Lindo was aware of the visual conventions of

Figure 7.22. Archie Lindo, *Untitled* (n.d.). Reproduced from scanned negative with permission from Susan C. Willingham (née Lindo).

mid-twentieth-century black gay pornography, although his photographs appear to have been produced for his private use, possibly for those in his intimate circle, but not for publication.

One feature of erotica generally – and gay erotica are no exception – is the use of verbal and visual puns that refer to penis size and sexual stamina, as on the *Mr Big* cover (figure 7.20), where the title is to be taken both literally and mischievously. The model's genitals are only partially covered by the large "B" in the *Mr Big* title. Such punning is also evident in a work from Lindo's private archive entitled *Light and Power* (figure 7.23), in which a standing, tall and muscular black male nude is seen from the back so that

Figure 7.23. Archie Lindo, *Light and Power* (n.d.). Reproduced from scanned negative with permission from Susan C. Willingham (née Lindo).

his genitalia are obscured, but juxtaposed with a very phallic lighthouse. These strategies allow for sexual content to be alluded to without actually having to represent it, using the power of association, and provided Lindo with a means of moderating and amplifying the meaning of the images. Within the context of the albums, this strategy proved to be powerfully transgressive in what was, despite the privileges Lindo enjoyed, still a prohibitive and secretive environment.

Owning and Collecting Black Gay Erotica

We can only guess at what prompted the creation of Lindo's images: the desire for personal consumption, the documentation of erotic and sexual encounters and, given the fact that he amassed a significant collection, also the sense of ownership of and control over the individual photographed. Naturally, the question of "ownership" is problematic in a postcolonial society with a history of black enslavement, and the question arises whether or not Lindo's photographs were exploitative. Similarly, as the furore about the nudity of Laura Facey's 2003 emancipation monument demonstrates, there are uncomfortable associations between nudity, sexual submission and slavery.[11] A case could be made that Lindo's photographs were exploitative, given his dominant social position, and that the men photographed were not fully aware of his intentions and the possible interpretations of these photographs. It is certainly of note that the identity of most of the men in Lindo's photographs is unknown, and it is obvious that most of these men were not of a high social status, which further suggests that they were disempowered in their relationship with Lindo and perhaps allowed him to photograph them because of the compensation that was offered.

However, from the images that I have reviewed, there appears to have been rapport between Lindo and many his subjects. The men do not appear to have been forced to pose for him. Images such as *The Irish Moss Gatherers II* further suggest that the men were well aware of the nature and purpose of the photographs taken. In fact, it could be argued that they were engaging in exhibitionist activities, as much as Lindo's may have been voyeuristic, that gave the models a measure of control. While I have focused on the images in landscape settings, a significant number of the photographs from his private archives were taken indoors, in what appears to have been Lindo's house or the beach cottage he often stayed at in St Thomas. This, too, suggests that the photographs were consensual and that there was some kind of relationship between himself and his subjects, even though that relationship may have been transactional.

The volume of negatives indicates that Lindo was an avid producer and collector of nude images of black men, to the point of obsession: it is necessary to consider what drives such collections. Susan Pearce, a scholar of the psychology of collecting, particularly images and erotica, states that "[t]hings collected are loved objects . . . collecting proves control over these objects" (quoted in Staiger 2005, n.p.). When such collecting involves images of people, further questions of objectification of course arise. Pearce posits that there are three major categories of collecting:

- systematic collecting: "an ostensibly intellectual rationale is followed, and the intention is to collect complete sets which will demonstrate understanding achieved",
- fetish collecting: "the objects are dominant". This is an "obsessive gathering [of] as many items as possible . . . to create the self",
- souvenir collecting: "the individual creates a romantic life-history by selecting and arranging personal memorial material to create what . . . might be called an object autobiography, where the objects are at the service of the autobiographer" (n.p.).

It would seem that the private archives of Lindo are generally consistent with the latter two categories. While Lindo was obviously producing and collecting images for personal erotic gratification and used his camera to act out and, presumably, memorialize his sexual desires and encounters, other motivations are also obvious. Lindo's photographs are engaging with the racial dynamics of his time and society and, as we have seen, with the Nationalist school's search for icons of Jamaican-ness.

As much as they reflect his sexual and racial fetishism, there is a romantic dimension to Lindo's images that idealize black masculinity, particularly in his earlier photographs. This is also evident in his literary work, particularly his poem *Bronze*:

You turned your head
And, statuesque, I saw you sit
As though you posed
For some great sculptor there;
God was your sculptor once,
The lovely bronze
He fashioned you from
Strong and rare. (Lindo 1944, 50)

The lyricism of this poem is also evident in the photographs of the Irish moss gatherers. The excerpt from the poem could almost be used as a caption for the images. The sexual tension evident in the poem appears to be diffused or legitimized by the constant references to God; diffused but not eliminated altogether, as one can easily imagine Lindo envisioning himself as the great artist and writer whose task was to capture and represent this "lovely bronze" beauty. The God references may also allude to his religious upbringing and the tensions this caused with his racially and sexually transgressive desires.

While Lindo's photographs are certainly problematic in terms of the social and racial hierarchies they represent and perpetuate, they also document the emergence of modern gay culture. Lindo was breaking sexual taboos in his societal context, given the prevailing sexual mores in the Jamaican society of the time.

As Allen Ellenzwig (1992, 3) has suggested, "To examine the male homoerotic in photography, then, is to seek a better understanding of the oppressions and accommodations men have faced in their social and sexual relations in the last century and a half – that is the very period in which these relations were undergoing their most dramatic legal, medical, psychiatric and social scrutiny." It is tempting to see Lindo's work in a similar light. There was a gay subculture in Jamaica that was more open than today, although there were also significant social restrictions that caused gay men to lead closeted lives.

I am left to wonder if Lindo was not more deliberate and groundbreaking in his representations than I had initially assumed. I should, however, also point out that Nationalist Jamaican art existed, contradictorily, in a legitimizing relationship with the Western artistic models it purported to oppose, and this, too, could be a factor in Lindo's photographs. There are clearly many unresolved tensions within Lindo's work: some are specific to him, but they also deepen our understanding of the tensions and contradictions in the work of the nationalist generation in Jamaica, which, while charting new ground and breaking taboos, was at the same time replicating colonial social hierarchies.

Notes

1. The term "Irish moss" denotes various types of edible seaweed. One of these, the actual Irish moss, or carrageen moss (*Chondrus crispus*), is a species of red algae that grows abundantly along the rocky parts of the Atlantic coast of Europe and North America, and was harvested for food purposes in Ireland during the

famine in the nineteenth century. The Irish moss harvested in Jamaica is part of the genus *Gracilaria*, a genus of red algae notable for its economic importance as a source of the thickening agent agar, as well as its use as a food for humans and various species of shellfish. In Jamaica it is used as the basis for an aphrodisiac drink (Mitchell 2011).

2. Donald Lindo said that at one time Archie Lindo rented a cottage from him in St Thomas. He may thus have been a regular visitor to the White Horses beach (Donald Lindo interview).

3. "The Graces (Euphrosyne, Aglaea and Thalia) are represented as young and beautiful virgins; they hold each other's hands and dance in a circle, indicating [a] perfect union and a perpetual renovation of pleasure. In their dancing attitude, we recognize the charms of personal dignity and elegant movement, without which even beauty is but a dead picture" (Carr 1846, 139).

4. "Archie Lindo was, in his personal and professional affiliations, and his artistic vision, closely associated with Jamaica's cultural nationalist movement. As David Boxer has argued in *Jamaican Art 1922–1982*, modern Jamaican art has its roots in the nationalist-anticolonial agitation of the 1930s and 1940s" (Lawrence 2014, 37).

5. Donald Lindo spoke extensively about the close relationship that Archie Lindo had with Edna Manley, particularly in her later years.

6. "Primitivism describes a Western event and does not imply any direct dialogue between the West and its 'Others'. In the context of modern art, it refers to the attraction to groups of people who were outside Western society, as seen through the distorting lens of Western constructions of 'the primitive' which were generated in the latter part of the nineteenth century" (Rhodes 1994, 8).

7. It may be tempting to associate the fisherman icon with the Jamaican slang term "fish" that refers to homosexuals. However, this seems to be a relatively recent development, and it is doubtful that there is a direct link to this longstanding homosociality. (I have found no clear explanation regarding the origin of this term.)

8. Jager's choice of this title for his erotic photography studio suggests a further separation beyond the racial to the social and political, which reinforces the dominant racial and social hierarchies in Western societies.

9. These elements are a hallmark of particular types of gay pornography as seen in the archetypical gay illustrations of Tom of Finland (Paglia 2009, 82).

10. For a more detailed analysis of types and developments of homoerotic photography, see Borhan (2007).

11. In 2003 the statue *Redemption Song* was unveiled at the newly opened Emancipation Park in New Kingston, Jamaica. The bronze statue, inspired by the quotation "Emancipate yourselves from mental slavery; None but ourselves can free our minds" (originally by Marcus Garvey and popularized in a song by Bob Marley), depicts nude male and female figures facing each other, hands behind their backs, looking skyward away from the troubles and concerns of daily life. The two figures stand in a pool of moving water, meant to evoke the symbolic cleansing of the psychological scars of enslavement. The statue sparked outrage from several vocal sectors of Jamaican society who wrote letters to newspapers and regularly called radio talk shows to voice their opinions. Concerns ranged from the suitability of an

artist of predominantly European heritage depicting the emancipation of Jamaica's largely black populace and to the supposed indecency and potential moral degradation that could be caused by the statues' nudity, particularly the male's exposed genitalia. Several commentators also felt the nudity and the close positioning of the statues too closely referenced slaves being stripped and sold naked on the auction block during the period of enslavement.

References

Borhan, Pierre. 2007. *Men for Men: Homoeroticism and Male Homosexuality in the History of Photography since 1840*. London: Jonathan Cape, Random House.
Boxer, David. 1990. *Edna Manley: Sculptor*. Kingston: National Gallery of Jamaica and Edna Manley Foundation.
Carr, Thomas Swinburne. 1846. *A Manual of Classical Mythology; or, a Companion to the Greek and Latin Poets, Designed Chiefly to Explain Words, Phrases and Epithets, from the Fables and Traditions to Which they Refer*. London: S. Marshall.
Ellenzwig, Allen. 1992. *The Homoerotic Photograph: Male Images from Durieu/ Delacroix to Mapplethorpe*. New York: Columbia University Press.
Lawrence, O'Neil. 2014. "The Exotic, the Erotic and the National: The Black Male Body in the Photographs of Archie Lindo". MPhil thesis, University of the West Indies, Mona, Jamaica.
Lindo, Archie. 1944. *Bronze: Short Stories, Articles, a Poem, and a Play*. Mandeville, Jamaica: College Press.
Mitchell, Sylvia. 2011. "The Jamaican Root Tonics: A Botanical Reference". *Focus on Alternative and Complementary Therapies* 16 (4): 271–80.
Mordecai, Martin. 1989. "Archie Lindo: Interviewed by Martin Mordecai". *Jamaica Journal* 21 (1): 20–37.
Nettleford, Rex. 1978. *Caribbean Cultural Identity: The Case of Jamaica, an Essay in Cultural Dynamics*. Kingston: Institute of Jamaica.
Paglia, Camille. 2009. "Sex Quest in Tom of Finland". In *Tom of Finland XXL*, edited by Dian Hanson, 81–82. Cologne: Taschen GmBH.
Powell, Richard. 2008. *Cutting a Figure: Fashioning Black Portraiture*. Chicago: University of Chicago Press.
Rhodes, Colin. 1994. *Primitivism and Modern Art*. London: Thames and Hudson.
Staiger, Janet. 2005. "Cabinets of Transgression: Collecting and Arranging Hollywood Images". *Particip@tions* 1 (3). https://www.participations.org/volume%201/issue%203/1_03_staiger_article.htm#_edn14.

8.

Brave "Battymen" and the (Im)Possibilities of a Straight Dancehall

CARLA MOORE

How do queerness and the dancehall (not so) secretly meet and shape each other? How do gay men in the dancehall exist across the various dancehall geographies and the colonial legislations that produce and police, all at once, masculinity, space and Afro-Caribbean sexualities? And how might we reimagine queer possibility if we deliberately centre the queer/MSM (men having sex with men)[1] dancehall participant as the holder, creator and conveyer of knowledge and thus as human? The following essay puts forth an intellectual ethnography of the dancehall as experienced by three participants: Cedric, age twenty-three, gay, participant in the dancehall for fifteen years; Jah Truth, age thirtyish, gay, gatekeeper and in the dancehall for eight years and Frederick, age eighteen, bisexual, participant and in the dancehall for three years.[2] Frederick and Cedric as dancehall participants, consume dancehall culture and reproduce it outside of the events but do not have the power to set the dancehall agenda (vis-à-vis introducing new dance moves, fashion, slang and other trends). Jah Truth's level of recognition, because of his job and high profile lifestyle, places him in the role of gatekeeper, which means he has the power to set the dancehall agenda, especially with regard to fashion. All three men are from low-income backgrounds, although Jah Truth now socializes and works in middle-class and upper-class circles and is financially well-off.

By centring MSM who claim space in the dancehall, this chapter unsettles the idea that dancehall and queerness cannot co-exist and pushes back at the idea of Jamaican MSM as imperilled, without agency, and always in need of foreign support for their liberation. In this way it interrupts what I refer to elsewhere as the homohegemony[3] of North American queer liberalism and expands notions of who is properly able to claim space in the queer diaspora. It also unsettles the overwhelming heteronormativity often ideologically and academically enforced on low-income Jamaican men, especially those in the dancehall space, as well as the overwhelming un-Jamaican-ness usually accorded to gay and bisexual and other MSM. Participants in this research reveal that rather than always being at odds with queerness, dancehall requires it: in the form of the gay man as musical fodder and also as black masculine gender nonconformity as sartorial excess, which is queer within a European masculine framework. Dancehall, as well as the ghettoes that inform it, becomes a site of potential liberation. The act of occupying the centre of the dancehall space, as well as family and community spaces by choosing not to "come out", creates strategic in/unvisibility[4] and, I suggest, constitute a type of modern-day queer marronage[5] that allows dancehall MSM to imbue the spaces with new meaning and possibilities. Within contemporary understandings of queer resistance premised, for example, on the disciplining and removal of offensive material by movements such as the Stop Murder Music campaign, the activities of dancehall MSM are groundbreaking: What would it mean if changes to the dancehall aesthetic, including the introduction of clothing formerly considered feminine, that have allowed MSM to move more freely through the space, were in fact initiated by MSM for this exact purpose? How does the complex subversiveness of queer dancehall offer an indigenous model of queer resistance?

Queerness Defining Dancehall Defining Queerness

Question: How do you define the dancehall space?

The space is almost like a profiling fashion show of the best of the best, it's like a little pageant. (Jah Truth)

Well the dancehall is straight. There is no point in time when I can see the dancehall as not straight. Even in the songs. I haven't seen the artiste to date who has sung about acceptance about homosexuality in the dancehall. I've seen where they have been acceptance [*sic*] of oral sex. Once upon a time oral sex was a no-no in the dancehall. Both artistes, female and male used to sing against it; bun [burn] it out. Now the males are supporting it. The female . . . not so much supporting it but it's like a tug-o-war. (Frederick)

When it comes to dancehall, it's all about being straight, a little of hype-ness, and behind that hype a lot of violence as well, showing who is badda [badder], who can defend themselves, who really can stand up and put up a fight against anyone. . . . At the same time, it involves a lot of enjoyment – high level of sexual enjoyment.[6] So basically the songs that are singing in the dancehall, if not sexually oriented, it involves violence but it can also be peaceful and productive. (Cedric)

The definitions of the dancehall show some variety. In one instance it is a site of "profiling" (displaying an enviable version of oneself) and in another instance it is a site for the working out of sexual resistances and taboos such as homosexuality, cunnilingus and fellatio. In a third instance it is a site for competition (which is a part of profiling), as well as enjoyment and violence. Sexual queerness – as nonconforming, nonreproductive behaviour – is made to disappear (through symbolic violence) as queer behaviours – performed as excessive masculine sartorial display – are called forth. Read differently, perhaps the one sexual performance or iteration must be silenced in order to compensate for the concessions made to other sexual possibilities. Thus dancehall, as a contested site of queerness, welcomes and symbolically refuses the MSM simultaneously.[7] The interviewees suggest that the dancehall is also, despite its violent and competitive features, a site for relaxation and enjoyment. In its reproduction of sexual disciplining as well as performative acts of display (profiling), the dancehall is produced as both colonial and anticolonial. It is a meeting ground for the interpretive legalities created by colonial and neocolonial laws as well as freedom-focused, Afro-Caribbean activities developed during plantation slavery.[8]

What is stranger than the assertion that the dancehall allows some queerness to emerge is the multiple ways dancehall is cited as needing queerness, in particular, queer men:

> Dem [gay men] help too wid di dressing, because mi see some yute [youths] whey [what] really know how fi put themselves together. Dem [gay men] love di tight pants, cause I never see a gay inna big clothes, so when dem come now, dem ever look good and dem fashion out. . . . Di [straight] man dem see how di [gay] man dem dress and dem run goh buy it and yu know sey inna di dancehall [it's about] who look good from who noh look good, and who appealing from who does not. (Frederick)

> Yes. Without gay men, half of them [artistes] can't write . . . they spend so much time writing about gays and bantering gays; if gays never exist, they wouldn't have anything to talk or sing about and half of them would not have careers. . . . [Plus] you have all these dressmakers, hairdressers and stylists and all that stuff who were inspired by a lot of gay things and gay people and even myself working in [the industry]. . . . It's not like you're gonna say let me give them [the public] a bit of gay and they don't know, it's more like ok, do society love a bit of gay sometimes? So let's perform for them and give them what they want – so it's really about what's in at the time and these [feminine-looking dance] moves are in and we can get a forward [popularity] from it, so let's do them and get a forward. (Jah Truth)

Queerness, rather than being marginal, is central to several aspects of the dancehall scene. Queerness as sexual practice and sartorial excess shapes the dancehall space, giving it the newness and "nowness" for which it is renowned. Queerness, or the denial of it, also offers stability to dancehall artistes, giving them constant creative fodder. The twin elements of economics and service to heterosexuality cannot be denied in these narratives. Specifically, queer men are accepted in the dancehall when they provide fashion worthy of imitation, service in the beauty and creative industries, and mockable figures for "heterosexual" dancers.[9] Thus, though queerness is permitted, it is allowed within strictly demarcated lines and is valued, it seems, as a characteristic of straight men.

These processes bring to mind the South African notion of "economic bisexuality" as documented by Xavier Livermon (2012): effectively male and female black South Africans were pardoned for homosexual behaviour if it was not premised on love but rather engaged in for economic gain. The economic bisexual retained heterosexual privilege and a normative gender role because the queer act was not queerness but rather queer sex by an otherwise straight person (306). The queer performances undertaken by assumed heterosexual dancehall participants allow them to transgress into the (economically fertile) realm of queerness without losing status because their heterosexual reputations remain intact. Economic bisexuality inadvertently or deliberately folds queer men's labour into compulsory heterosexuality as an adornment to attract (hetero)sexual mates or a performance through which straight actors can make more money. I argue, however, that the service queerness provides to heterosexuality does not diminish the subversive work it does by appearing in the first place. Such a reading, separated along gay/straight lines, threatens to reify unnatural binaries and cover over resistance work by queer dancehall participants through foregrounding (again) straight members. The presence of queer hairdressers, stylists and fashionistas in the dancehall space disrupts the received meaning of the space and radically expands the "who" of dancehall.[10] The salience of queer men to dancehall aesthetics unsettles discourses that claim gay Jamaicans do not exist, as time and time again supposedly straight dancers produce the queer man on their own bodies.

"Yu Haffi Be a Clown fi a Reason": Power and the Right to Queered Expression

The freedom to initiate queer expression is another issue discussed in some depth by all interview participants. The consensus is that status and power are necessary to legitimize the introduction of queer performance by straight men, especially with regard to fashion. Status is less important for the replication of the performance since all men in the dancehall space are accorded a de facto heterosexuality, and replicating queerness is read as an attempt to "stay in style" rather than a declaration of queer identity. Thinking through dancehall queerness moves the discussion of dancehall sexuality from compulsory heterosexuality to assumed heterosexuality (pending certain performances). The limitations of heterosexual expectation become sites of possibility for MSM who understand and capitalize on the norms within the space.

> Question: "If a man who has no money and no status came in an [avant-garde] outfit like the one that you came in, what would be his experience?"
>
> [P]eople would waa [want to] know who him be and if it too tight [they would assume] him a battyman . . . the only reason it could work for him is he's gonna come as a dancer. So him can't come as himself, he has to comes as somebody or as a foreigner or something; there has to be some underlying to it.[11] . . . You haffi sey him a foreigner, or oh yeah, he's into fashion, or yeah, he's a dancer; it has to be something. . . . You haffi be a clown for a reason. (Jah Truth)

Jah Truth, Cedric and Frederick all point to status, international travel and a desire to "not be left behind" as legitimizing dancehall's most recent queer turn. The metrosexual aesthetic, they opine, was introduced by Jamaicans who had travelled overseas, visiting foreigners and, in particular, dancehall artistes. The pre-approval provided by the artistes and other dancehall power players allowed the contradictory look to spread quickly through the space.[12] But as Jah Truth suggests, this particular "queer turn" is but one of many:

> Well, with fashion, I've seen the history because my mother used to love go dance; I grew up with a ghetto mumma [laughter] who love go dance . . . and the fashion has always been changed. Because I know [in] my father's old picture they have on tight pants. And [then] dem [dancehall artistes] sing say man pants fi have room. . . . Dancehall really surround fashion so much and anything is possible around dancehall because of the culture itself. Jamaica is not necessarily wanting to stick to what's wearing, they want changes. The average ghetto girl want to change her hairstyle, guys we don't have much hairstyle fi change and so forth, so as we get an opportunity to wear colour pants and get some changes, we jump on change. But fashion in dancehall has been ever-changing from I know myself and I know dancehall itself. It is going to take different shapes and different forms so I expected it [the new metrosexual wave].

Thus, as I have previously suggested, the dancehall as a black space has always been inherently queer. The men within it have always functioned in excess of traditional European masculinity and, moreover, have felt limited by it and have readily grasped opportunities to express themselves differently. But the meaning of queerness has changed significantly between Jah Truth's generation and that of his father. Jamaica, functioning as a part of the West, is affected by contemporary queer and related LGBTQ politics that positions queerness as a lifestyle and identity, rather than a practice. For example, the men in this sample locate themselves within the LGBTQ discourse by self-identifying as gay and bisexual. Despite situating themselves within LGBTQ discourse, though, their relationship with it is fraught. Frederick explicitly categorizes queerness as foreign:

> [Before] dem [Jamaicans] neva use to talk 'bout it dem neva use to have the homosexual thing. In the nineties when [Jamaican] people used to go foreign regular . . . yu neva need visa to goh England, yu just need an invitation – soh people go up dere and adapt to the style and bring it back and people start gravitate towards it and start to like it as like the porn videos. Is not everybody whey go up dere [to the North] dweet [turns gay]; the Internet have an influence pon the world too caw people go pon the Internet for different reasons, soh young people . . . when dem goh pon di computer, whey yu think dem looking at?

The implied relationships are telling. If queerness is perceived as coming into Jamaica along transnational lines, what are the received ideas about queerness that young men such as Frederick encounter? If we can agree that the brand of queerness most visible and most visibly reproduced by the media in the Global North locates such identities around "coming out", high fashion and body conscious identity, what is required of black MSM in order to be "properly" queer? And how would the need to perform that queerness have been contested by the baggy clothes and hypermasculine aesthetic of dancehall that preceded more recent queered trends? Moreover, queerness continues to be fed for some dancehall MSM by external images. Cedric, though recognizing queerness as not foreign to Jamaica, cites North American television shows such as *Degrassi* and *Glee* as informing his own understanding of queerness. *Glee* and *Degrassi* have the potential to open up and complicate queer identities, but they are still invested in queer as lifestyle/identity/preppy/pretty tropes. These Northern tropes, combined with direct and indirect associations within queerness as foreignness/ whiteness, continue to guide queer Jamaican men as they work through their own individual queer expression today.[13]

Recognizing the multiple and conflicting locations from which MSM speak also renders dancehall MSM intelligible and decentres Western imperialist understandings of both (queer) resistance and colonial respectability. I suggest that the internalization of some aspects of Northern queerness qua identity has complicated the relationship between dance-hall and queerness: it gives straight dancehall participants a list of char-acteristics that are "identifiably" queer (display of the body through tight clothes, close attention to grooming) while giving same gender–desiring Jamaicans an identical check list of legitimizing queer characteristics. Thus, while dancehall participants became aware of the often damaging power of queerness in the early 2000s – queer boycotts of dancehall artistes and events and international discourse that positioned Jamaica as a "back-ward" non-queer friendly nation – the local queer community also became familiar with the "look" and implicit demands of "legitimate" queerness. The end result, I suggest, was the creation of a class of MSM who could no longer easily access the dancehall space, not because of the homophobia, but because they looked (Northern) queer, and dancehall participants were already privy to this (Northern) look and could detect, mark and name it as queer. A group of men were now exploring a specific kind of gendered expression and identity that coincided with the rise of homo-antagonism engendered by Northern anti-Jamaican interventions and accusations of Jamaican homophobia; dancehall MSM were thus doubly barred from the space for their newly visible identities and their assumed queer practices.

Contrary to Northern belief, the dancehall space is not automatically repulsive to same gender–desiring people. Jamaican MSM who are raised in the ghettoes, who also participate in and inform dancehall cultures, remain a part of the dancehall community and desire access to the space. The dancehall is, in many ways, their "home". How then do they navigate the new tensions between their personal expression of self and dancehall's new landscape? I suggest the response is queer maronnage, which unfolds as a doubled effort to queer the dancehall space and the strategic deploy-ment of heterosexual signifiers in an attempt at misdirection. These queer practices are supported by "cultural labour" that will, perhaps, foster accep-tance within the broader communities. The first action, creating a queer space within a homo-antagonistic realm, emerges from rumours and stories. Living in the hybrid dancehall/queer space for years, I have been privy to the rumours of which artistes are same gender–desiring people and which artistes are not. While I will not name the artistes – even academic use of rumours must be sensitive – I strongly assert that the artistes most often cited by the interviewees and non-interviewees as responsible for importing the queer aesthetic are the artistes most often rumoured (within the queer community) to be MSM. In the process of importation, they continue the work of bringing Northern queerness into Jamaica but also a longer history of queered dancehall expression. These two factors push up against each other to create the specificities of the queer dancehall – the familiarity of sartorial queerness and the "foreignness" of sexual queerness – that give rise to queer marronage.

Rumours Dem Spreadin': In Defence of the Knowledge of the Oppressed

There is no measurable or apparent discursive "truth" about queerness in the dancehall. Dancehall artistes complicate queer culture, refusing to delineate its parameters and patterns. The homophobic nature of the space at the time this research is being conducted does not encourage visible queerness. To look too deeply would destroy the careers of some of these undercover queer importers – an outcome that neither the straight nor queer individuals in the dancehall are willing to facilitate. There are and have always been, however, rumours of same-gender desire and activities collapsing in on and momentarily characterizing specific dancehall artistes. With this in mind, if we imagine the "folk" as holders of knowledge, then we can imagine an entire world of knowledge that is closed off from those invested in respectability and appropriateness. The employment of rumour in an academic setting is an unlikely undertaking, but Toni Morrison (1984, 388) supports my thinking: "If my work is to confront a reality unlike that received reality of the West, it must centralize and animate information discredited by the West – discredited not because it is not true or useful or even of some racial value, but because it is information held by discredited people, information dismissed as 'lore' or 'gossip' or 'magic' or 'sentiment'."

This reading of dancehall marronage begins, unapologetically, in rumours. It is rumoured that the (secretly) MSM dancehall artistes are responsible for introducing the metrosexual aesthetic to the dancehall space. It is rumoured that one of dancehall's most prolific dancers, also responsible for propagating sartorial queerness, is secretly MSM as well. It is rumoured that many of the male dancers who are responsible for making particular "queer" looks universal to dancehall are secretly MSM themselves. What could this mean? It could mean that powerful (MSM) dancehall men, knowing the freedom the blind spots and marronage practices allow, queered the dancehall space. It could mean that (assumed heterosexual) dancehall artistes, equally subject to Northern queer discourse, also started experimenting with queerly gendered expression but were not chastised because of their privilege. It could also mean that the de facto heterosexuality assigned to dancehall artistes, coupled with their continuing homophobic performances, encouraged queerness in the space. It could mean that in the dancehall, queerness flourishes in plain sight, recoded as something else so as not to upset the dominant heterosexual narrative that invokes colonialism, nation and sexual respectability. At the very least, this means that a queerly influenced aesthetic, growing in mainstream popularity overseas, made its way into the dancehall on the bodies of dancehall men.

Undercover "Chi-Chi": Dancehall Queerness as Modern Day Marronage

I suggest that the behaviour of gay men/MSM in the dancehall constitutes a contemporary marronage: a deliberate hiding away "in plain sight" made possible through the superior knowledge of dancehall geographies. Specifically, the maroons (runaway slave warriors) of Jamaica "developed a superb system of espionage" (Campbell 1990, 7), which the Spanish attributed to their being "thoroughly acquainted with the region and so expert in the bush" (Wright quoted in Campbell 1990, 8). I suggest that MSM in the dancehall carry out maroon-like practices and resistances through their superior knowledge of dancehall geographies. MSM are intimately acquainted with the workings of homophobia through their exposure to homophobic performance as male socialization. The absence of a distinctive ghetto queer culture – of the kind that allows a person to be raised primarily in nonhomophobic settings – means both straight and MSM boys in the ghetto are raised within a context of neocolonial compulsory heterosexuality: they are privy to the (dangerous) signifiers of queerness as well as the (productive and appropriate) signifiers of heterosexuality. But, as Walcott (2007) states, "while black queers and black heterosexuals share a common historical past, how that past is understood and utilized in relationship to contemporary injustices can be quite different" (235). Thus, the call to compulsory heterosexuality is engaged as resistance activity rather than a demand for conformity, and plantation-era marronage practices are recast in the present day by black MSM in order to access liberation strategies.

The poverty-driven geographical restrictions of ghetto life, as well as the centrality of the communal street as a male social space, leave dancehall and ghetto MSM with very few places to hide.[14] They are necessarily in common space because in the ghetto almost all space in shared. As a result, dancehall MSM are close enough to the homophobic "performers" to parse projection from actual objection. Thus, knowing where they do and do not have spatial freedoms corresponds with where queerness can and cannot exist. In order to exist across the (questionable) divides between Jamaican (black), inner city and queer, Jamaican MSM who are active participants in the dancehall must practise unvisibility: being present and absent at the same time. In these spaces their activities are bold, brave and even contradictory, stemming from their locations at multiple sites of radical subjectivity: blackness, queerness, Global Southness and poverty, which are differentially articulated within the context of an assumed heterosexual masculinist geography. Within these geographies they activate their superior knowledge for queer marronage, living in what I refer to as the blind spot.

Yu Haffi Out an' Bad: Living in the Blind Spot[15]

The genesis of queerness in the dancehall may be "unclear" or fuelled by rumours, but all three participants agree upon the changes it brought for MSM in the space. Below they respond to the following question: "Have the changes to the look of the dancehall made it any easier for you to navigate the dancehall or to be in the dancehall space?"

> Yeah, it make a difference, caw me know say now me can go inna mi tight pants and mi go inna mi tight clothes and nobody naw look-look pon mi because everybody a dweet [do it]. . . . It mek it much more convenient fi me so mi can just nicely fit in. (Frederick)

> I would say definitely yes because a lot of the stuff that they're wearing right now, they can get away with it. Once upon a time you couldn't get away with it; you'd be called battyman, gay, boom bye-bye. I'm not saying that they are not saying it, but it's a different level now because everybody is accomplished, everybody waan top dem game . . . in those days, you could come out in a t-shirt, a little pull-up t-shirt with some stripe and you're high fashion but nowadays, high fashion dash whey; everybody a high fashion now soh yu haffi come out like a clown. (Jah Truth)

> Yeah, because you can easily fit in now, you don't have to tell yourself that you don't [or that] your clothes look too tight because it's already in. I'm a fashionable person, I like to express myself in various dimensions of fashion, I'll dye a part of my hair in brown and another part in purple or a little tip of red, not just for dance but for everyday look. People don't even look, and if I'd done it ten years ago, people would be saying "you dye you hair?!" (Cedric)

The changes to the space have made it more accessible to MSM who express themselves queerly, and participants all agree that there has been an increase in the number of MSM men in the space since the changes. They feel less at risk because everybody looks queer. Imagine, for a moment, that these changes were not commandeered by MSM but rather initiated by them; the liberatory power of those actions would be awe-inspiring. A class of men who actually changed a space and its geographic meanings by moving themselves from hypervisibility and unvisibility (because they were always called up in the space but never allowed in it) to invisibility and, with this, blending in with the other men in the space by encouraging those men to express themselves queerly. Even if the initiation of queer expression cannot be attributed to queer men, it is certain that they have inhabited it for their own resistance activity. By claiming more space in the dancehall, they propagate and modify the existing queerness, expanding the "acceptable" masculine gendered expressions in the space within the blind spot of assumed heterosexuality. In so doing, they have made the space accessible to even more queer men and alternative sexual practices.

Man a Gangsta: Symbolic Violence as Dancehall Masculinity

There have been some gains for queer men in the dancehall space, but despite being queered the dancehall is still not visibly queer-friendly. Queer men are, therefore, still required to deploy certain heterosexual markers. The performance of homophobia, though seemingly the most straightforward way to assert compulsory heterosexuality and straight masculinity, is not preferred. All three participants acknowledge that they do not partake in the "bunning out" of gay men through song or symbolic gunfire; they also remark that several straight participants ignore it as well. Rather than denouncing homosexuality explicitly, they perform heterosexuality through asserting masculinity, violence and "cool pose":

> When I get to dance . . . I just stand, listen and look; I might have a cup in my hand drinking. . . . Where I might be dramatic and as my friends would say, over-the-top, I don't behave that way in the dance. When I go to dance I love the mix-up, so I will watch because I know who and who don't really chat. I like the excitement and when it's time to dance, I dance. One thing I can assure you, I never hear one of those homophobic songs play and buss a blank, I just act still and I'm not the only person acting still, some straight also act still. (Cedric)

The terms "thug" and "gangster", as synonymous with heterosexuality, also appeared repeatedly in interviews:

> I know this guy in the ninth grade and the way him move and how him talk, mi can definitely know say him a one a da person deh [queer]. But how him move and how him behave, dem [other students] always a trouble him and waa [want to] beat him. But how me move now, most of my friends at school now can never know that because how me move, mi just move like a gangster. (Frederick)

> Even with all the dance moves and the tight clothes, you can't be posing like a girl you have to thugs it out. (Jah Truth)

Moving like a gangster and "thugsing" it out are psychological and physical undertakings premised on the restriction. For Jah Truth it means only dancing in certain ways, avoiding "feminine" gestures, and adopting a "masculine" demeanour. Interestingly, the male dancers at the centre of the space who have power by virtue of their role in the dancehall, actively adopt the gestures and postures he avoids. Yet when they stop dancing they too return to the "rude boy" pose.[16] Frederick also replicates these kinds of gestures but only when he is wining and gyrating with a female partner. Jah Truth, despite his gatekeeper status, is not a male dancer and unlike Frederick, no longer lives in the ghetto. He is also functionally "out" in some dancehall circles. As a result, despite his power, his relationship to the space is modified and there are new prohibitions placed on his body: he can no longer access certain forms of expression. Being gangster means adopting a "not to be messed with" profile that implies violence. The message is that there's nothing funny. Funny here implies the jovial (funny as in amusing) as well as the sexual (funny as in sexually queer). In Jamaica, gay men are referred to as "funny guys" and are identifiable by their (womanish) gaiety brought about by their ignorance of (black) reality: the rightness of heterosexuality and the dangers of the Northern "easy life" (which black men attempt to access through queerness) which makes men soft (and queer). Living in the ghetto often produces and requires a masculinity that is necessarily serious, concerned with survival and prepared to do whatever is necessary to ensure safety. Given these conditions there is little space for public joviality, as softness is taken as weakness. In order to fit in, the gay man must perfect projecting this brand of serious (read: potentially violent) masculinity.[17] For Jah Truth it means limiting his dancing body to only a certain set of identifiably "masculine" moves.

The geography of these performances is significant. Both Frederick and Cedric report that they are most comfortable on the borders of dancehall's inner circle. Both choose that space because it is the site of highest activity and "drama".[18] Frederick avoids the outer boundaries of the dancehall space because that is where the thugs, gangsters and gunmen hang out. They intimate, then, that for a person attempting to perform thug but who is not a thug, the centre of the dancehall is most productive. I suggest that the location is already a site of performance because of the ways the seal is used in spiritual ceremonies and the dancehall itself; it is always already an acknowledged site of projection, fantasy and alter/native universes where a person displays who they might be rather than who they are in their daily lives. The history and geographies of the seal, as a centralized and stage-like location of theatrics and repossession, make it more attractive for queer men/MSM. Specifically, it is the ideal site for deployment of heterosexual signifiers because, from that location, their performances of heterosexual masculinity, which signify who they "might be", are amplified within the dance and thenceforth into the community and beyond: the unquestionable "straightness" of the performer is cemented into the minds of all viewers. While the absolute centre of the seal may be too active and require a type of performance certain MSM are unwilling to undertake, the edges of the seal are just as visible and just as productive.

By undertaking these performances, dancehall MSM secure a position within the heterosexual dancehall while refusing compulsory heterosexuality. By moving (undetected) from the metaphorical fringes of the dancehall into its place of highest visibility, they trouble the division between margin and centre: "Pratibha Parmar argues that creating identities as black woman is not done 'in relation to', 'in opposition to', or 'as a corrective to' . . . but in and for ourselves. Such a narrative thwarts that binary hierarchy of centre and margin: the margin refuses its place as 'Other'" (Keith and Pile 2004, 187).

Dancehall MSM's refusal to be defined in opposition to their community or to be held up by their community as the outer limit of black sexuality spurs them to action. Retrieving themselves from the binds of compulsory otherness, they elide heterosexuality yet claim space that is normally preserved for privileged heterosexuals. They create space for queerness by using the power engendered by the blind spot that acts in opposition to queer visibility and, instead, deploys queered optics.

There Are (Still) No (Visible) Queers Here: The Underside of Marronage

The process of acquiring geographic privileges, as is usually the case with subaltern communities, has been at some cost. While the dancehall space has begun to look more queer, the ritualized performance of homophobia has retained its salience in many spaces, and the actions of dancehall queers to retain heterosexual privilege may not explicitly disturb the overarching moral expectations that emerge from colonial scripts of sexual respectability. It is telling, however, that the purpose and productivity of homophobic performance has changed over time. Jah Truth refers to the dancehall as "pretentiously homophobic", saying that homophobia is now a tradition in the dancehall space. He recognizes homophobic music as not always being a representation of how artistes feel but rather as texts that are "saying and doing things that everybody can agree on".[19] Cedric, in response to my question "Is dancehall music a true reflection of how Jamaicans feel?", explains:

> No. Sometimes not. I think it's for the hype and for the music to sell or it's just a character. The world is a stage and we are all performing. Sometimes actors take on roles that they don't like . . . in terms of the dancehall, you want your music to sell . . . the society accepts homophobic music; you just do as the Romans do. The artistes want to know that if fifty dances are held, you get booked for thirty or forty. If you go sing something that the people don't want to hear, nobody naw book you. You wouldn't even get radio play.

It is possible that the actions of dancehall MSM have changed the levels of real homophobia in the space. But despite its presence as performance (versus action), homophobia still persists. Participants report feeling safer inside the dancehall than outside, yet the lack of safety outside the dancehall is influenced by the music projected from within the dancehall.[20]

The queer labour to claim (hetero)sexual space in the dancehall is thus muddled. Marronage, as a slave-era undertaking, was equally complicated. Over time maroon communities signed treaties with the British government agreeing to return runaway slaves in return for their own freedom. In the Morant Bay Rebellion of 1865, it was the maroons who tipped the scales in favour of the British through their activities against other blacks. Their superior knowledge of the land was exploited by the British to defeat Paul Bogle and his black rebels (Hutton 1996, 30). Though maroon communities emerged as an important location of liberation for the enslaved, the maroons' actions to secure their own freedoms made them complicit with the oppressors. Thus, while they freed hundreds of black slaves, they acted against them as well. While very different, the complex parallels between the actions of the maroons and dancehall queers are worth noting: though MSM in the dancehall do not "bun fire", their selective projection and decisions leave the impression that there are no gay men in a space that is unquestionably heterosexual yet always being invisibly queered.

Despite the complications of dancehall queerness there is still the possibility for change. The work of shifting the dancehall does not only happen in the dancehall space itself; it also happens in the communities that inform dancehall music/psycho/land/scapes. By eschewing out-and-proud politics, MSM in the queer diaspora opt for a space at "home" in their communities. By remaining in the space unannounced, they access a community that is often denied to black queer people within the black community. They are also able to change the meaning of "home". The issue is messy: MSM are able to remain in the dancehall space because they deliberately deploy heterosexual signifiers. But two participants imply that though they would never come out in the dancehall space, individuals in their communities know they are not straight and remain committed friends.

> Question: Do you feel that people are under more pressure to act like they are homophobic in the dancehall or outside in the community?

> Well it's kind of a balance because [in the community] they deem you as being gay by basically your lifestyle: dem no [they don't] see you wid no woman or a look [pursuing] no woman; because you might look good and still naw look [pursue] no woman. And yet still you have a lot of straight friends who will still talk to you in the open. You live in a community and they know you, and know that you are a nice person, they like to talk to you so they don't pay that any mind. (Cedric)

For those employing a human rights framework, which demands confession, visibility and (near absolute) knowability, the value of this community-based acceptance may be lost. But Xavier Livermon (2012, 299) suggests that for many black queer people "cultural belonging" may be just as, if not more, important and productive than certain understandings of human rights. Indeed, because blackness and same-sex desire cum queerness have been historically and contemporarily created as mutually unintelligible, the "cultural labour" required of black queer people must be directed at relocating queerness inside blackness as a legitimate part of (diasporic) African cultures, especially in the imaginaries of their peers. Thus, "[w]hile the state can create rights through legislation, it is only within the spaces of black communities that real protection lies" (Livermon 2012, 304). The work of securing the acceptance and protection of peers is integral to the liberation of black queers. Additionally, since these same communities create dancehall music, peer-group acceptance of queerness by community members will necessarily have a positive impact on dancehall's dealings with sexual difference.

The relationships between dancehall and queerness are complex. Dancehall MSM inhabit the dancehall space for various liberatory activities, some of which can be read as complicit in perpetuating dancehall's homophobic performances. I maintain that the resistance work must be read as just that: resistance. In order to honour these difficult liberatory possibilities, we must decentre received notions of "proper" or "effective" resistance and recentre the experiences of those who inhabit and embody multiple sites of oppression, as well as those who do not necessarily conform to identity politics. Also important is the cultural labour undertaken by dancehall MSM to secure space as same gender–desiring subjects in their own communities. Their work bleeds over into the dancehall and is just as responsible for changes to the sound of dancehall as international intervention or other local-global political initiatives. Dancehall MSM claim space for themselves as themselves: as same gender–desiring people who, in part because of the geohistorical framings of black sexualities, do not engage in an explicit "coming out" or identity claim rituals. And with this, they change the meaning of dancehall space for all those within it.

Notes

1. While I recognize the limitations of the term "MSM", especially given its medicalized history, it is a useful term since it describes behaviour rather than depending on identity categories. It is also a term that is popular in the Jamaican landscape, and it is my intention to write in a way that is sensitive to our specific use of language and other contexts.

2. All names have been changed.

3. "Homohegemony" is a term I coined while writing my master's thesis from which this article is drawn. The term refers to the contemporary iteration of white, middle-class, male, Northern out-of-the-closet queerness that holds great cultural currency and is presently being deployed as the "right way" to be queer. Kyle Jackson (2014), who also researches queerness and Jamaica, came to the same term in his own work. Our theories differ, however, in that his concept is more closely tied to homonationalism while mine takes up homohegemony as a function of neocolonialism.

4. My use of the term "unvisible" echoes Katherine McKittrick's (2006) discussion of black women's geographies, specifically her discussion of Linda Brent, a slave woman who hid herself in a tiny garret for several years to escape her abusive slave master. From that tiny space she observed her children's lives as well as her master's search for her that she thwarted by having misdirecting letters sent from other states. In that space, "Brent is everywhere and nowhere, north and south, unvisibly present across the landscape, in the last place they thought of" (42). Just as Brent is both unseen and a felt presence, I argue for the unvisibility of Jamaican MSM. Even when they are not physically present in the dancehall, their presence is invoked, and it is their presence that stretches across and defines the dancehall space. They are not seen but are still there and materially shaping the space – unvisible.

5. Ronald Cummings (2010) and Ryan Joyce (2017) also employ the term "queer marronage" in their work.

6. Cedric also uses the dancehall as a site of escape from the many violent experiences of his life, including witnessing several murders. For him the dancehall is a liberatory space where he goes to forget himself. That he seeks liberation in a space reputed for rigid policing and restriction of MSM indicates that much is

left unsaid in how the dancehall space is presently treated in academia and human rights discourse.

7. What I find interesting about this discussion is the way the dancehall continues the previously mentioned work/politics of the street, signifying what is not acceptable, building reputation (through profiling) and initiating participants into the realm of black sexuality. Dancehall venues are often street corners and entire streets. In fact, the "street dance" is a popular type of dancehall event that regularly co-opts a particular street for that purpose. I suggest that the persistence of the street continues to shape the dancehall, in that the hypermasculinity of the dancehall is shaped by the masculinity required to survive in the openness of the community street.

8. The dancehall, therefore, claims space in a genealogy that includes, among other things, the juke joint and the black church. For more on this, see Beckles (2002) and Stanley Niaah (2004).

9. Admittedly this refers to a specific brand of queerness that is not stereotypically masculine. There are probably many other visibly gender-conforming queer men existing in and contributing to the dancehall in still unexplored ways.

10. The tense relationship between dancehall and queerness is blurred along class lines. Jah Truth, for example, as a powerful member of the dancehall industry is "allowed" to tie his queerness to his queer male body *and* receive validation differently. His role in the fashion industry, coupled with his power (through numerous television appearances), allows him some flexibility to admit that his queer expression is a result of his (sexual) queerness. It is to be noted, however, that his queerness functions to promote several dancehall artistes, which may allow him these "freedoms". But even so he admits he "butches it up" for sessions in the ghetto and is more relaxed "uptown".

11. The denotation of the queerly presenting person as a "somebody" implies they are of high social and economic status. The denotation as a foreigner is less simple. Foreigner in itself implies a kind of status, especially white foreigners. Their actual class and geographic privilege is negligible; they are imbued with power based on their white skin. Thus, their performances are taken seriously as indications of what is happening "out there" away from dancehall and as fodder for dancehall diversification. The foreigner is also excused from the rigid gendered and sexual boundaries of the dancehall based on the assumption that they may not know them or, in some cases, may not know "better".

12. On the role of the dancers: "they have a part to play in it. They want to be distinctive, they want to sell themselves, *their image as a celebrity*, so basically, they have to change their image and look different so not only the tight clothing . . . dem start tone dem face and skin . . . a lot of young girls see it and sey it look nice, cute and all a dat. Young girls run dung di dancers them, run dung di bwoy dem wid it so" (Cedric). The dancers are imbued with an always already existing heterosexuality: their activities and the activities of boys who imitate them are for the attention of women and girls. The assumed heterosexuality of dancehall's core participants, coupled with their power, allows them to express queerly without fear of repercussion.

13. It is important to recognize that the ways in which dancehall queers inhabit LGBTQ identity is markedly different from white, middle-class, Northern subjects. Some do not feel compelled to come out and do not think their deployment of certain heterosexual performances delegitimizes their bisexual and gay identities: "I would say [a person is] gay, because interest lies with the same sex, it doesn't matter if it's mentally gay or physically gay and it can be financially gay" (Jah Truth). In this way, Jamaican MSM expand commonsense understandings of LGBTQ positionalities while locating those identities within black communities.

14. Barry Chevannes (2003, 231) researched the role of the street in the socialization of Caribbean males, especially those from working class communities, and found "the perceived need, particularly in the poorer communities, to use the Street as a training ground in male survival skills. Moreover, it is a necessary part of male sexual initiation." The street is central to most men, straight and MSM, in working-class communities and, as such, both sets have the same intimate understanding of appropriate Jamaican masculine expression. It is also the site for the transfer of compulsory heterosexuality as a norm. This is exacerbated in poorer communities by a demand for hypermasculinity that is informed by (feminizing) poverty. The street is a site for the local interpretation and application of (persistently) colonial law.

15. For more on dancehall's "blind spot", see Moore (2014). I theorize dancehall's geo-psychic blind spot in my other work. Specifically it refers to the ways heterosexual expectation, homophobia and the musical and physical geographies of the dancehall combine to create the idea that anyone who dares enter the space must be straight since gay men enter at the risk of death. This creates a blind spot wherein everybody who enters is assumed straight and which allows MSM some space and access.

16. For more on the history of coolness and cool pose in black communities, see hooks (2004) and Majors and Billson (1993).

17. For Frederick, pseudo-violent profiling is coupled with ensuring the safety of his reputation by having a girlfriend at school. In his community, he uses his academic pursuits to explain not having a girlfriend, and since he is a good student, he is excused. The substitution of productivity for reproductivity in accessing value is a theme that persisted throughout the interviews. Frederick noted that the boys in the "fast stream" of his school were pardoned for not having girlfriends because they were "nerds".

18. For more on the geographies of the dancehall and how they are used by MSM, see Moore (2014).

19. All three participants agreed that if an artiste's career is failing or if a young artiste is trying to gain popularity, homophobic music has the most cultural currency – it sells. Despite the presence and salience of homophobic music partying/girls tunes are the most popular today. Usually several homophobic songs are played in a segment, gayness is symbolically burned out of the space and the party resumes. Thus, the image of dancehall's rabid homophobia projected internationally needs to be tempered and brought up to date.

20. The feeling of safety inside the dancehall is attributed to two things: the assumption that all men in the space are truthfully conveying their sexualities, which diminishes policing (Jah Truth) and a shared economic imperative to keep the party going (Cedric). Starting a fight of any kind will disrupt the party, which means the promoter, the selector and vendors will lose money. Based on a shared understanding of the need for money, as well as the possibility of a backlash from the participants directed toward the fighters, altercations are limited in the dancehall space. Cedric also implied that fighting was minimized because of the purpose of the space – for relaxation and enjoyment – which no one wanted to disrupt with unnecessary violence. With that being said, there are still incidents of gang and other violence in the dancehall space and homophobic violence remains a possibility.

References

Beckles, Hilary. 2002. "'War Dances': Slave Leisure and Anti-Slavery in the British-Colonised Caribbean". In *Working Slavery, Pricing Freedom: Perspectives from the Caribbean and the African Diaspora*, edited by Verene Shepherd, 223–46. Kingston: Ian Randle.

Campbell, Mavis C. 1990. *The Maroons of Jamaica 1655–1796: A History of Resistance Collaboration and Betrayal*. Trenton, NJ: Africa World Press.

Chevannes, Barry. 2003. "The Role of the Street in the Socialization of Caribbean Males". In *The Culture of Gender and Sexuality in the Caribbean*, edited by Linden Lewis, 215–33. Gainesville: University of Florida.

Cummings, Ronald. 2010. "(Trans) Nationalisms, Marronage, and Queer Caribbean Subjectivities". *Transforming Anthropology* 18 (2): 169–80.

hooks, bell. 2004. *We Real Cool: Black Men and Masculinity*. New York: Routledge.

Hutton, Clinton. 1996. "The Defeat of the Morant Bay Rebellion". *Jamaican Historical Review* 19:30–38.

Jackson, Kyle. 2014. "The Construction of Black Jamaican Masculinity in a Neocolonial Imaginary: Canadian 'Homohegemony' and the 'Homophobic Other'". *Caribbean Review of Gender Studies* 8:209–34.

Joyce, Ryan. 2017. "'Bitch Out of Hell': The Queer Urban Marronage of Assotto Saint". *Women and Performance: A Journal of Feminist Theory* 27 (2): 176–93.

Keith, Michael, and Steve Pile. 2004. *Place and the Politics of Identity*. London: Routledge.

Livermon, Xavier. 2012. "Queer(y)ing Freedom: Black Queer Visibilities in Postapartheid South Africa". *Gay and Lesbian Quarterly: A Journal of Lesbian and Gay Studies* 18 (2–3): 297–323. doi:10.1215/10642684-1472908.

Majors, Richard, and Janet Mancini Billson. 1993. *Cool Pose: The Dilemmas of Black Manhood in America*. New York: Simon and Schuster.

McKittrick, Katherine. 2006. *Demonic Grounds: Black Women and the Cartographies of Struggle*. Minneapolis: University of Minnesota Press.

Moore, Carla Kathleen Martina. 2014. "Wah Eye Nuh See Heart Nuh Leap: Queer Marronage in the Jamaican Dancehall". MA thesis, Queen's University, Kingston, Ontario.

Morrison, Toni. 1984. "Memory, Creation, and Writing". *Thought* 59 (4): 385–90. doi:10.5840/thought198459430.

Stanley Niaah, Sonjah. 2004. "Kingston's Dancehall: A Story of Space and Celebration". PhD dissertation, University of West Indies, Mona, Jamaica.

Walcott, Rinaldo. 2007. "Homopoetics: Queer Space and the Black Queer Diaspora". In *Black Geographies and the Politics of Place*, edited by Katherine McKittrick and Clyde Adrian, 233–46. Toronto: Woods.

Part 3.

Telling Stories, Finding Self

9.

In Search of the Dead
(Un)Marked Graves and the Sea of We

THOMAS GLAVE

We had left the car parked just off the main road, or rather, off the paved road wide enough to accommodate one car comfortably – some hundred or so yards back – amid thick bush, as most Jamaicans would term the sprawling green growth that offered no apology for its threat to sooner or later overwhelm everything within reach. We were walking, my cousins and I, toward the enormous deconsecrated church, known as St George's Church during its most active years in the nineteenth century and now referred to by people in the area, in the district of Mile Gully, in that part of Manchester parish in central Jamaica, as the duppy church: the "ghost" or "haunted" church.

It was a huge skeleton of a ruin, its clearly once-elegant (some would say imperious) front and structure worn down by time, neglect, isolation and Jamaica's unforgiving sun and rains. Now, in our time, various people in the area still believed that the Lord continued to cast His almighty gaze down upon that once proud but desolate shipwreck considered to have been holy in earlier unholy times, erected by human hands on supposedly sacred ground upon which, for miles in every direction, human beings had been tortured and brutalized for centuries in order to enable the nurturing of sugar cane, from the time of Spanish ships' arrival on this island in the fifteenth century until not so long ago. If the Good Lord did still cast His all-knowing gaze through that roof that had long ago surrendered its bones to the elements, it was always accompanied these days by glances from the indifferent moon – in fact, the same moon that had finally resigned itself to having to drag the sea behind it through all its travels across the world, yet had never uttered a word, not even a whisper during the last few centuries when uncountable numbers of dark bodies had either been hurled from ships' decks by crewmen into cold dark sea-waves – bodies still alive or in some state of dying – or when those bodies' rightful owners became convinced (or hoped) that immediately upon feeling the chilly salty water

Figure 9.1. St George's Anglican Church ("duppy church"), Mile Gully, Manchester, Jamaica. Photograph by the author, January 2015.

engulfing their thrashings and filling their lungs they would awaken back in the other green place from which they had recently been snatched, those dark cold waters becoming a silencing sea of death and transfiguration for those who had been pitched from the decks and the ones who had chosen to hurl themselves overboard.

In other writing, reflecting on history and its many horrific maritime journeys, desperate leaps overboard and indescribable attempts at trans-figuration and deliverance, I have referred to the sea most critical to my earliest memory, the Caribbean, as the Sea of We: a body of amnesiac water critical to those of us descended from the Africans transported over it across centuries into the horrors and agonies of "New World" slavery. In this regard the Caribbean, like the Atlantic, exists as a sea filled with our historical bodies: an abysm filled with who will ever know how many nameless, faceless corpses in how many forests of the dead down there: forests that I have imagined in other writing as forests of reaching arms, reaching upward, reaching toward light or toward the primordial darkness lodged between stars that some consider a darkness of redemption. Forests of outstretched arms and hands reaching toward a memory *not* filled with sweltering rat-filled ships stinking of death and disease and packed beyond imagining with the cargo that in our time must be named, spoken of, must never be forgotten. Forests of reaching arms very far down there reaching upward for memory *not* filled with the "undreamable dreams" and "unspeakable thoughts, unspoken" suffered by both the living and the "black and angry dead" in Toni Morrison's novel *Beloved*. Forests of reaching arms that exist surely in even greater numbers in the Caribbean's big-bellied and more ill-tempered cousin, the colder, darker Atlantic Ocean, another vast and equally unmerciful Sea of We.

It was with the Sea of We and its incalculable forests in mind that I accompanied my cousins on that distant afternoon a few years ago to the crumbling Mile Gully once-holy skeleton in whose churchyard lay buried – in a marked grave – the long-decayed body of my paternal great-great-grandfather, Stephen Sharp Glave, a white man from North Yorkshire, England. As a younger son in a family of several younger sons determined to make his own fortune, he departed England in the year 1831 (so my family has roughly ascertained) for the realm's then-slave colony of Jamaica, to assist his ailing and aging uncle Stephen Sharp in the management of a plantation in the colony's parish of Manchester.[1] With the help of my noisy cousins always so easily alarmed by the possibility of duppies (fear of duppies an unfortunate phobia to possess in a country like Jamaica, which is filled to its treetops with them), I eventually located his cracked century-weathered gravestone in the weed-choked yard. Upon its grey sun-punished stone could still be read the words,

> To the Memory of
> Stephen Sharp Glave
> Who Died on the
> 1st April 1873
> Aged 58 Years

Several months and in some cases years later, I would tell only a few closest friends how strangely moving and eerie it was to encounter one's surname, particularly in the name of an ancestor and in this instance a white English one, on a nineteenth-century gravestone embedded in the stony earth of what had been a slavery colony. Unsettling to contemplate the fact that this man's DNA unquestionably resided in my body, as it had resided in my father's and paternal grandfather's, and in the bodies of many other (though not all) Jamaican Glaves. Moving and eerie enough to cause the breath to quicken in the afternoon's shimmering heat and the descendant's tongue to fall silent. The fact was that this was a great-great-grandfather about whom I knew almost nothing except the reality of

Figure 9.2. Gravestone of Stephen Sharp Glave (1815–1873), churchyard of St George's Anglican Church. Photograph by the author, January 2015.

his skin colour and his origins in Lythe, North Riding, Yorkshire, where he had descended from a line of people whose social standing in the English class system of that time remains uncertain to us in the twenty-first century (although we know for certain that they were in no way aristocrats). Their genealogy from the year 1742 until the present day had included six Thomas Glaves – Thomas being the male "Christian" name most often repeated in the family. Thanks to pertinent historical and municipal Jamaican records not having been destroyed in the infamous 1925 fire that eviscerated the British colonial administration building in Jamaica's former capital, Spanish Town, I had learned some time ago that Stephen had made clear in his will, dated 25 February 1873, a mere five or so weeks before his death, that any of his several children who married what he had named in his will as a "Black" person – capital B – would be summarily disinherited, as he shortly thereafter proceeded to do with one daughter, Maria, who married one (apparently Black-with-a-capital-B) Lionel Henriques. By the years just before his death, if not before, Stephen had managed to acquire a large amount of land and some wealth; he bequeathed his transgressing Black-with-a-capital-B-marrying daughter Maria five acres of land, a mule and the right to pasture a cow on

Figure 9.3. Gravestone of Stephen Woofe Glave (birth and death dates obscured), churchyard of St George's Anglican Church. Photograph by author, January 2015.

every Glave property in the colony. This was far less than what her siblings William, Thomas, Frances, Charles, Edward and Eliza received, each of whom ostensibly opted for a path of lesser resistance and more ensured inheritance by deciding to marry exactly whom they chose, including Black-with-a-capital-B individuals, *after* their father's death. A fifth son, Stephen Woofe Glave, died in his early twenties in the year 1865 and is buried not far from his father in the churchyard.

The woman who bore and raised Stephen Sharp Glave's children we know in the family only as Catherine Wright: a brown or "mixed race" woman, my great-great-grandmother, who may or may not have been Stephen's legal wife. The specific contexts of the initial encounters between Catherine and Stephen remain unknown, but it seems clear that they occurred sometime after the full and official "emancipation" of Jamaica's slaves in 1838. I have asked in previous writings if Catherine might at some point have lived as a slave – been born a slave – before emancipation (Glave 2013). Whatever her legal status at the time of her initial encounters with Stephen, did she inhabit a role as Stephen's "woman", so to speak, or one of his women? (And what might it have meant to have been his "woman" or "one of his women" as a brown or mixed-race Jamaican woman, possible former slave and possible child of slaves – or not – connected to a white Englishman in the recently "emancipated" slave colony? What would have been the erotic, economic, social and pragmatic parameters of such a connection?)

What did she look like? What did he look like? We have no portraits, no photographs of either individual. Did they have conversations, as, beneath so many punitive suns, the lively post-slavery colony and its many living and dead moved about them? If one imagines a nineteenth-century white male from North Yorkshire, England – in this case one Stephen Sharp Glave, a paternal great-great-grandfather who may or may not at the time, or in our present time, have repudiated one for one's own skin colour, a skin colour for which his semen deposited inside Catherine's body was partly responsible – if one imagines such a man rubbing and grinding and even making the grunting noises some people are known to make during sex above or below or behind or in front of Catherine, the woman whom he selected finally to receive his semen and into whom he obviously ejaculated time and time again, given the number of their progeny, if all those resulting mid- to late-nineteenth-century Glave children were his own – if one imagines such a man and such a woman in bed together or in a field somewhere becalmed by the overseeing moon, or wherever they found themselves when they "did it" – if one imagines all that as one attempts to imagine the woman's engagement (or not) in the activity and his engagement (or not) in the activity, and her and his feelings about and during the activity, and her feelings about the man in question and his feelings in regard to her, and her feelings about herself, that woman, my great-great-grandmother; and as one attempts perhaps impossibly, finally, really, to imagine her feelings about her own body – thoughts such as *Is this my body, my very own body, my body that belongs to no one else but me? Is it possible for me, Catherine, to possess my own body in the year 18–? I know that my name is Catherine,* she may or may not have thought: *What else do I definitely, absolutely know, aside from the fact that one day I definitely will die? I will die, and so will Stephen, and so will my children* – Did Catherine ask herself such questions at varying times (or not) as that man, my great-great-grandfather whom she knew intimately in quite specific shadings of that word, prepared to spend himself within her? And how did she feel about the foetus, the several foetuses that, whether for better or worse or both, soon developed in her uterus after the purposeful swimming of that man's ejaculated semen into her body?

Is it possible that the preceding questions – questions unanswerable in any exact or definitive way, with which one should exercise great care against the projection of one's own early twenty-first century prejudices and judgements in engaging – yet still questions that linger and take up great space in the mind of one of Catherine's and Stephen's descendants (me) as much as they linger in the pondering mind of the writer I also am – is it possible that these questions are, in addition to their being historical, literary, political and deeply personal questions, also metaphysical ones? In considering this latter possibility, I utilize the prefix "meta" (μετά-) from the classical Late Greek's meaning of "in addition to" or "beyond": meta/in addition to the physical, the historical, the racial and racialized, the coloured, the gendered, the post-slavery colony, and the later developments of "postcolonial" and anticolonial literatures, political thought and "postcolonial" theorizing that responds, in part, to some of that literature and political thought, and more. Meta taking into account the abiding Sea of We and its ongoing relationship to these ancestors – to their bodies and the bodies of their children but also the bodies of the ancestors' forebears – and to my body and those of us of African descent in this century whose ancestors were forced to journey across that sea and its Atlantic cousin . . . remembering that the Sea of We also holds grave, even dire, implications for those not considered to be of African descent. (Remembering also first and foremost that the Sea of We is a graveyard of profoundly unmarked graves, utterly lacking the dignity and presence of gravestones, the very purpose of which is to mark and commemorate – delineate – a site for memory.) For a writer living and working in the early twenty-first century, a writer unceasingly obsessed with these two ancestors both of whom died over 140 years ago and both of whose genetic mathematics thread intricate equations through complex geographies mapped in the twenty-first century writer's body – a writer in our time racially marked as black (or, in Jamaica, "brown" and identified by some in Jamaica as a "battyman") and trying to "figure it all out" – figure that which, partly due to the silenced voices of the dead and the invisibility of their faces, cannot ever be entirely "figured out" – and for one trying to make sense of what can never be fully understood, does such imagining of sex and history and one's own ancestors engaged in what today, with twenty-first century Western eyes, one cannot help but regard as a racialized sexual coupling, help in any way – that is to say, amplify and/or deepen in any way – one's imagining of and reflections on the enormous amounts of white men's semen ejaculated into black and brown and red and yellow women's vaginas, and also no doubt at some point down those women's throats, throughout hundreds of years of European conquest, enslavement and colonization of African, Latin American, Asian and South Asian, Amerindian and other Caribbean peoples? Does my own imagining of my white, English, North Yorkshire-originated paternal great-great-grandfather's loins depositing his seed securely between the legs and within the warm body of my brown (or at least, in the eighteenth, nineteenth, twentieth and twenty-first centuries, definitely not white) great-great-grandmother help in any way to imagine and make "sense" of, for literary/narrative/recounting purposes, if nothing else, the incalculable amount of British white men's repeated ejaculations through hundreds of years over and into the bodies of black women, brown women, yellow women, and others? Does such imagining and ultimate reality lend any irony and maybe mordant wit, to the wry joke I have sometimes made when visiting the United Kingdom: "And so here I am once again in England – or Britain – visiting my people." In that joke, "my people" has meant – and keeping in mind what Stephen Sharp Glave's ejaculations and those of others must mean – not only black British people of Caribbean, and specifically Jamaican, descent.

I did find Stephen Sharp Glave's grave that afternoon, and reached down, with a decidedly brown hand, to touch it.

Touched it while wondering: can one be disinherited in the twenty-first century by one's white English great-great-grandfather for touching his grave with a hand that is most certainly not white with a capital W, but Brown with a capital B in Jamaica and Black with a capital B in the United States and the United Kingdom? And if, eventually, my brown hand seeks union with a Black-with-a-capital-B man's in marriage or a non-marital joining, will that connection lead to a disinheritance that can span centuries as well as skin colours? Can disapproving ghosts, if they be hauntingly inclined, disinherit the living, even those whose differently coloured skin they never touched, never mind that the repeated thrustings of their nineteenth-century loins made that skin colour a reality?

In fact I choose to believe not.

But then what of my great-great-grandmother Catherine's grave? I never found it that afternoon. Never located it anywhere in that weed-choked, deconsecrated churchyard far out in nearly the exact middle of Jamaica, so that I might pass my brown hand over it in order to touch it, feel it, as if attempting to feel and hold the flesh and warmth of that brown or at least definitely not white woman, some of whose blood yet courses within mine. I couldn't find it, though I knew – know – it must be somewhere: the (marked? unmarked?) resting place of a faceless though, fortunately, not nameless, woman. And so it is that we cannot always find the dead whom we are seeking, especially if we don't know their faces, as is the case for those who rest, sometimes fitfully, within the Sea of We's dark forests of reaching hands. It remains largely unlikely that we will find them

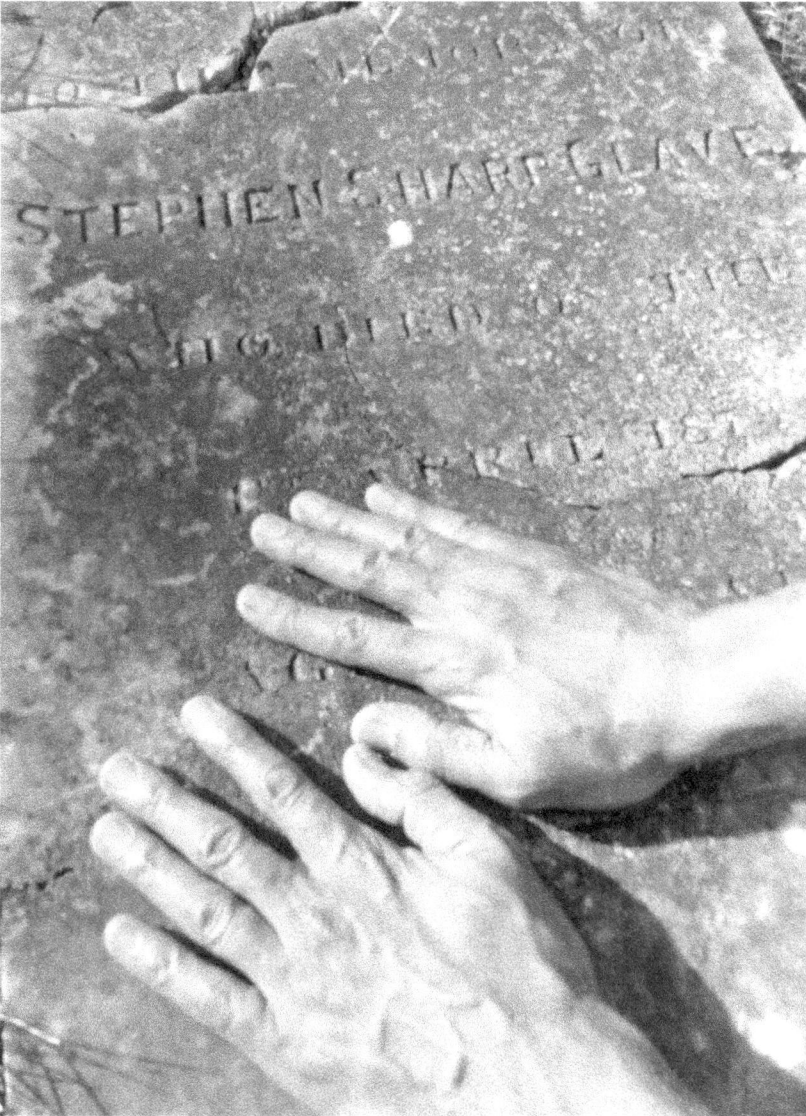

Figure 9.4. Thomas Glave's hands. Photograph by Michael Prescod, January 2015.

unless we are occasionally willing to live within the shadows, at the edge
of shadows, that regularly inhabit undreamable dreams, our own uneasily
dreaming bodies touched and – so some dreamers have insisted even after
death – held by incorporeal hands. They are always there, those dead. For
quite like the sea that stretches to the end of nowhere-ness and more out
there, they are for all time part of We.

The area around the duppy church in Mile Gully and the once-holy ruin in whose churchyard my great-great-grandparents and some other Glaves are buried, is believed to be haunted because of a catastrophic railway crash nearby in the town of Kendal in 1957: the worst train crash in Jamaica's history and in the entire Caribbean, that claimed the lives of almost two hundred people and left scores of others in seriously harmed condition.[2] It is averred by many in Jamaica, especially those who know the Mile Gully district, that the duppies of those many violently dead haunt the area and the skeletal church in particular. They haunt it with grief, but also rage over the sudden, cataclysmic end to their lives: a rage equalled only by Lucifer's when that beautiful, but prideful, angel was flung out of heaven by the Almighty Lord God directly toward the fires of hell. But the tale of a gorgeous angel's damnation and the rage of so many dead, and the more complete history of a now-deconsecrated dilapidated church built on a slight hill with a weed-choked churchyard overlooking a dirt road believed to have been made and maintained by slaves 275 years ago, are stories – like Stephen's, Catherine's, and even the vast spreading Sea of We's – for another day. Stories that, like drowned human beings, occasionally rise up out of dark cold water in search of a mouth, bodily flesh and a living tongue capable of speech: a tongue possessed of the gift, and sometimes the curse, of unflinching memory.

Notes

1. The Glave family is still working to determine the exact location of this plantation, the number of slaves and other workers it employed, its years of operation and what product(s) it produced.

2. The Kendal Crash has been one reason for the church's haunted reputation, but some Jamaicans familiar with the Mile Gully district claim that the church was feared to be a duppy den because of its long isolation, deconsecrated state (no longer holy, and thus more distanced from the Lord), neglected churchyard and gravestones, and general decrepitude.

Reference

Glave, Thomas. 2013. *Among the Bloodpeople: Politics and Flesh*. New York: Akashic.

10.

"What a Writer Is"

A Presentation Given at the Beyond
Homophobia Conference

ANDRE BAGOO

Let me begin with a poem I wrote three days after it happened:

Father's Day
Father's Day is coming and all I can think of is Orlando,
not the Virginia Woolf character who changed from a man
into a woman,
or Shakespeare's lover in the Forests of Arden
or Handel's opera sung by an alto castrato,
Orlando, the magic kingdom,
where the gunman mowed us down.

Father's Day is coming and all I can think of is Orlando,
all I can see is Orlando,
all I can breathe is Orlando,
the world is Orlando,
Orlando, Florida's natural,
no longer orange but red.
All those daughters and sons dead.
What are we doing for Daddy?
my sister Whatsapps frantically
What are we doing?
Orlando Orlando Orlando –

Though I "came out" years ago to friends, family and the public in a series
of newspaper columns, for a long time, I resisted the label "gay poet".
When it came to my creative projects, I told myself my work speaks for
itself. I am not a gay poet, I said, I am a poet, pure and simple.

But then the attack on the Pulse nightclub at Orlando happened. That week I found myself at the office of my day job, unable to work. I read about the circumstances of the shooting, about all of the victims. I read of one man, Eddie Justice. His last text message was, "I'm gonna die. Mommy I love you."

Whose life does not stand still when the spectre of such barbarity looms?

But while my world was rocked by this reminder of what is at stake in the battle for equality, all around me people were going about their business as if nothing happened. Worse, I saw first-hand how the Orlando tragedy was dealt with by elements of Trinidad and Tobago society. Whenever this attack was being discussed, gay lives were trivialized and ridiculed. How could people react this way? What was preventing them from seeing the humanity of Eddie as he lay in that bathroom stall desperately texting his mother?

I re-examined my life. The approach I had taken in my art began to look like nothing more than silence and, maybe, self-inflicted homophobia. It may seem strange, but for the first time in years, I turned to my poetry to seek relief. I had written poems in bad moods before. I had crafted sequences that dealt with love and relationships. But with "Father's Day" I tapped into both my intellectual mind and the blood flowing in my veins.

Susan Sontag (2007, 147) said, "It isn't what a writer says that matters, it's what a writer is."[1]

This conference has underlined the danger of a single story. But sometimes there *is* power in telling a single story: your story. Only when we all tell our stories do we see each other. A choir achieves beauty because different vocal ranges, different voices sing out.

Art, if it is really art, is at minimum concerned with the agenda of making life better. How do we make life better? We improve conditions now and for generations to come.

Yesterday afternoon in this room we all witnessed how the voices of intolerance are not afraid to speak out. All over the Caribbean the scales are already tipped against equality. In a situation where the scale weighs so heavily against us, our response must be directly proportionate and inverse.

In the weeks after Orlando, I quit my day job. I turned to gay writers like Thom Gunn, who reinvented himself again and again in his work. I turned to Kei Miller, Colin Robinson, Nicole Dennis-Benn. This is another answer: this sense of the choir. That sense is only made possible by visibility.

This is not to say every poem has to be the same; this is not to deny the power of mask and play or the poet's freedom to roam. This is simply to acknowledge the fact that civic life and artistic life are inseparable. I believe I should write the poems no one else in the world is in a position to write. I believe my peculiar experience as a gay man is what makes my work universal.

The claim is sometimes made that gay rights are a foreign import. But the very language I now use to talk to you today is a foreign import. Either we are human beings or we are not. Building a space to acknowledge our natural rights does not strip us of sovereignty – it radically empowers us. It allows us to act instead of being acted on. It lets us come closer to meeting our fullest potential as free, diverse nations.

I end with a new poem from my next book, *Pitch Lake*. This is a poem about Catullus, the ancient Roman poet who was supposedly in love with a woman named Lesbia. His poems disclose clear signs of his interest in men, to put it mildly. Yet, this aspect of his work has often been under-played. This piece brings together lines from some of his poems in order to reconstruct a different story about his life and the nature of his love for Lesbia. Kinda like how many gay women and men daily reconstruct our lives.

Catullus in Libya
At nights I removed my penis
but in the morning it grew whole again.
We sat at the shore, the sea's sulcus, & edged
into the light that burns the Sahara. Such women
that I love that I love such men: full of semen is my
purse, which pays the price and is paid in return.
I use them as if I had bought them for myself,
again and again their groins bursting
my anus
a flower at the furthest end of the desert
that plows through conquerors with petals.
Yet one day Libya I must flee, as I fled scorched
India, and deny the light that owns my soft marrow.
I will tell them of my love for her, this woman
of sand. My beheaded penis will not come
back like the sparrow on the cedar tree.
A bad rhyme I will be. Fuck me.

Note

1. From her acceptance speech, "The Conscience of Words", for the Jerusalem Prize delivered on 9 May 2001.

Reference

Sontag, Susan. 2007. *At the Same Time.* New York: Farrar, Straus and Giroux.

11.

"Hey Lara"

DOROTHEA SMARTT

Hey Lara, it's me.
Again. Broderick.
Again stannin' up outside.
Fool got flowers in he han',
some ole dutty wilting tings
he pick from 'long d'road.
Broderick! Go home na man!
No body doan waan you bout hay!
Move from m'place!!
If he doan heer – he gon feel!
My bruddas doan care bout Ernestine an' me
– she like a little brudah t'dem.
Can see she love me good-good,
care fuh muh, an' evryting – sweet me fuh tru.

Hey Lara! It's me!
Look 'e here! Broderick, down by d'water.
I washing d'Miss good clothes
and he come wid he foolishness –
'bout how he sorry he jus had to see me,
talk to me, got sumtin' to tell me. I lie
tell he I doan mine seeing he. Why I lie!?
– God's truth I feel sorry fuh de man.

Hey! Lara! Is me!
Broderick Knight! You hardears,
or ain't got nuh sense?! Ernie outside
talking t'he. Putting she self between me and he.
He eyes saufee-saufee pun me: *Lara is me!*
You know you love me woman! Hey Lara is me!

Hey Lara it's me, sorry but . . . But? But what?!
Now he take to following me bout!
He ain't got nuh wuk t'go look fuh?!
G'long man lef bout hay!
Whad-de-hell I want wid you?!
I tell he go 'way!
I did start to get jumpy-jumpy.
Ev'ry where I turn, I see Broderick
stannin' up, wid he long-face,
an he hat in 'e long-han.
Then he gone. Jus so.

Hey Lara! You ain't hear
Broderick gone Panama.
Gone t'mek heself a Colon Man fuh yuh!
Ernie an m'bruddahs laughing haard.
Ernie say they tek he down deh,
stan' up outside, mek he see through
the medical and ev'ry ting – sign off
in de Yankee bukraman book!
Fill 'e up wid s'much rum –
he was in Panama before he turn sober.

II.
The fellahs laughing: Doan obstruct we passage man!
Come all down from St Lucy, Moontown wid we las' cents
not a penny, jus we hard-wuk hands! We ready
to mek money, turn silver, and tek we place in de Worl'
Teetering on the deck, tossing up e'guts, confuse an' vex
as hell. Callin' fuh d'ship to tun back, callin' to he Lara.

On d'night-time breeze, comin' up from the Careenage.
She hear *Hey Lara it's me* . . .
I coming back fuh-yuh jus now y'hear?
And when I stridin' wid muh gold chain
panama hat, silk tie, black spats an' –
more money 'dan you see in yuh lifetime
is you gon come running wid, Hey! Is me! Lara!

Part 4.

Activism and Action

12.

Toward a Working-Class Queer Agenda and Leadership in Jamaica

ADWOA ONUORA AND AJAMU NANGWAYA

In this chapter, the working class is understood as the people whose existence is solely dependent on selling their labour in exchange for wages and who do not draw profit from the ownership of capital or productive resources. Even in situations where members of this societal majority are unemployed (actively or not actively seeking employment), their existence is largely shaped by the actual or potential relationship that they have with the means of production. They are decision-takers in the capitalist workplace vis-à-vis the owners of capital, and workplace relations condition the nature of the labouring classes' social status in the wider society. These wage slaves cannot access the type of social and economic policies and programmes that are able to improve the material conditions of their lives. It is for this reason that when we engage in the discourse on the working class, it is essential to go beyond the point of production. Rather, it is necessary to frame and include the experience of this class in its community setting. The reality of insufficient income to access decent and affordable housing results in residential segregation by class and income. As such, the members of the working class find themselves living together.

In the Jamaican context, many working-class LGBTQ people find it difficult being openly queer in these residential spaces. Their estrangement in society operates at multiple levels: from their working-class heterosexual counterparts as well as from their middle-class or petite bourgeois LGBTQ counterparts. This location puts the politically conscientized and class-conscious queers in a unique position to offer critical leadership and ideational insights and prescriptions on the interlocking nature of oppression across racial, gender, sexuality and class lines. Unfortunately, the traditional literature on class and class relations does not offer anything substantive on the condition of queers who are poor or from the ranks of the labouring classes.

History of the Queer Liberation Movement in Jamaica

The queer community in Jamaica is very much like other oppressed groups when confronted by oppressive conditions. A critical mass of its members tends to come together on the principal ground on which it is oppressed and participates in purposive collective action. In 1977 a number of queer-identified individuals started the Gay Freedom Movement (GFM) under the leadership of Chinese-Jamaican Larry Chang and a "small core of dedicated and committed individuals" (GFM 1981). Some of the goals of the organization were to "raise gay consciousness and awareness", "provide counselling and support to our oppressed brothers and sisters", "protest anti-gay oppression", "press for the repeal of the buggery law" and "remove homophobic prejudice and ignorance through public education" (GFM 1981). These LGBTQ activists had the goal of raising funds to operate a queer community centre and provide the basis for mutual aid and the delivery of social services (GFM 1981). The organization carried out activism in rural and urban areas. The GFM operated a prison support programme for incarcerated queers, produced the newsletter *Gaily News* and established an affirming gay youth movement support project. The *Gaily News* was distributed through subscriptions and the network of gay bars in Kingston. After several years of activism, GFM went out of existence in the mid-1980s. GFM is credited as the first organized queer liberation organization in the English-speaking Caribbean and is an important part of the struggle of Caribbean people for self-determination, queer emancipation in particular.

After a period of organizational silence, the Jamaican Forum of Lesbians, All-Sexuals and Gays (J-FLAG) was formed in December 1998. Larry Chang (2011) described a groundswell of interest in addressing queer oppression and said that he was impressed with the "calibre of people that were all involved" in this process. They were characterized as "young, bright, educated and intelligent Jamaicans" who "had language" to articulate the issues that gained traction. Their agenda was different from GFM in that "they took on a more constitutional approach" in advocating legislative change and a "human rights perspective".

The triggering event for J-FLAG was not an encouraging or welcoming one. In August 1997, sixteen prisoners who were identified as queers were killed by other prisoners after the commissioner of corrections, Major John Prescod, announced that condoms would be distributed to prisoners and guards to help combat the spread of HIV/AIDS. A prison rebellion erupted over the insinuation that some imprisoned men were having sex with other men, and the homophobic impulses of the men sparked a murderous rampage against their fellow inmates who were seen as gay. According to Lawson Williams (2000, 107), "there was a concerted effort by the 'men' (heterosexuals) in the prison to kill the 'boys'". The state skirted the homophobic imperatives behind the disturbances in the prison facilities. Thus, J-FLAG was born into an inflamed homophobic atmosphere. Public commentators such as Leachim Semaj, Mark Wignall and Barbara Gloudon made comments that amounted to telling queers that by being this public about their existence (abandoning the closet), they were making their private lives public and were unwittingly doing away with the time-honoured and effective survival strategy and societal understanding that queers should not be seen nor heard (Williams 2000, 108–9). Nonetheless, J-FLAG has valiantly carried out its mandate of advocacy to end the legal and cultural oppression of the LGBTQ community in Jamaica, notwithstanding its operation in a hostile and dangerous environment. It appears to be struggling to meet the needs and expectations of its diverse constituency as one of the better-known queer advocacy organizations in Jamaica. Chang (2011) stated that one of the major criticisms of J-FLAG was its failure to be heavily involved in the provision of social services, which was a major feature of GFM's underground activism. He said that J-FLAG's lack of access to financial resources was a problem but noted that the GFM carried out its mutual aid programmes in an even more exacting environment than today with respect to the material resources that were available.

Contemporary Environment and Priority Issues

In the repressively homophobic and militantly heteronormative social environment of Jamaica, one might easily pander to the judgement that all members of the LGBTQ community are in the same boat. The intervention of class, gender, (dis)ability, age, race and colour are factors of oppression that mediate the manner in which some LGBTQ members of the national community are able to shield themselves from the slings and arrows of outrageous (homophobic) fortunes. We are not in any way, shape or form begrudging anyone or a class of individuals being in a position to mini-mize the full impact of homophobic violence in Jamaica or elsewhere in the world. However, we intend to draw attention to the fact that if the agenda and leadership of a queer liberation movement are dominated by the petite bourgeois queer and they have not committed Amilcar Cabral's (1979, 136) "class suicide", the movement is likely to advance issues that are reflective of the bourgeois class. If these middle-class or petite bourgeois queers are mostly men, able-bodied and non-African or light-skinned, those who are effectively represented will be a small and largely privileged fraction of the LGBTQ community. In the report *Homophobia and Violence in Jamaica*, J-FLAG speaks to the existence of class privilege within Jamaica's queer community:

> The socio-economic class of LGBT Jamaicans is an important consideration for any discussion around anti-gay attitudes in Jamaica. LGBT people who fall outside the upper and middle class income brackets have neither the wealth nor the social capital to escape their circumstances. Life in Jamaica is therefore more difficult and dangerous for those made vulnerable by their socioeconomic status and whose vulnerability is further compounded by sexual orientations and/or gender identities which differ from the hegemonic norm. (J-FLAG 2013, 1)

It is our contention that the priorities of the largely working-class queer community in Jamaica would be better served if it assumed a dominant leadership presence in the queer liberation movement by including at the centre of the movement the fight to rid the world of class exploitation and capitalism. In their article "Homosexuality and HIV/AIDS Stigma in Jamaica", Ruth White and Robert Carr (2005, 354–55) highlight the reality of class differences within the queer community:

> Time and again, respondents reported that rich men who lived in the suburbs were protected from violence by their access to resources but that poor men "did their business in the street" and so were more "exposed" to police intervention, community exclusion and personal violence. . . . Poverty thus serves as a juncture between homophobia and HIV/AIDS stigma and discrimination such that poor men with HIV were assumed to have participated in homosexual acts and poor men who participated in homosexual acts were assumed to be HIV positive.

Class differences also affect who has access to the various types of capital that facilitate access to senior or major leadership roles in social justice organizations as well as social movements.

At present, Jamaica's queer liberation movement is led by the members of the petite bourgeoisie, both women and men. However, lesbians, bisexual and transgender women have raised objections to the domination of the LGBTQ agenda by queer men. This is unsurprising given the fact that queer men are also subjected to the same patriarchal socialization process that valorizes men and giving greater priority to the issues that are of importance to them. For example, the priority and resources given to the campaign to remove homophobic sections 76 (which punishes anal sex with up to ten years in prison with hard labour), 77 and 79 (which carry sentences of up to two years for men who demonstrate physical intimacy toward each other in private or public spaces) from the Offences against the Person Act is an example of bourgeois queer men focusing attention on an issue that is immaterial to the lived experience of working-class gay and bisexual men and lesbians as a group (Canadian HIV/AIDS Legal Network 2015). These sections of the act criminalize sexual acts engaged in by gay men and men who have sex with men. As such, sexual acts among bisexual and homosexual women are not illegal.

The proponents of the campaign to get rid of the "buggery law", or the relevant sections of the act, assert that this legal tactic has strategic value in the overall fight to end the legal, cultural and social oppression of LGBTQ Jamaicans. In Jamaica, homosexuality is not illegal under the law (Jørgensen 2016). It is gay men's intimate expressions of sexuality that are criminalized. However, sections 76, 77 and 79 of the Offences against the Person Act are normally conflated with the illegality of homosexuality, and individuals, organizations and institutions have embraced this incorrect and prejudicial outlook. J-FLAG (2013, 1) explained the legal context that contributed to anti-queer attitudes:

> Same-sex intimacy among males is illegal in Jamaica and is punishable by up to ten years in prison, with hard labour. However, the fine legal distinction that the law criminalizes the act of anal intercourse and not homosexuality is not a view generally held by the public. The popular position conflates the sexual act of anal intercourse (among men) with sexual orientation – in this case homosexuality. According to this cultural view, if anal sex is illegal then homosexual identities (whether male or female) are unlawful.

J-FLAG takes the pragmatic position that the removal of the anti-gay men sections of the act would assist in reducing the stigma that is attached to homosexuality and its deadly association with HIV/AIDS, which is contributing to the epidemic level of this disease in Jamaica for both heterosexuals and gay men (Amnesty International 2004). This argument in favour of getting rid of the sections of the law is not particularly convincing. In North America, the decriminalization of homosexuality did not prevent the early association between homosexuality and HIV/AIDS. It was mass public education and the communication of the fact that most of the people contracting this deadly virus were heterosexuals that led to changing attitudes, beliefs and practices with respect to the HIV/AIDS epidemic in this region of the Global North. It is hard for people to ignore the fact that their straight neighbours or straight people in the news are falling victims to this virus.

While the existence of the homophobic sections of the Offences against the Person Act might cause some health workers to feel apprehensive about providing services to gay men who presumably engage in illegal acts (Charles 2011, 13), or prevent some gay men from seeking the assistance of health care professionals, both groups are ignoring an objective reality in Jamaica. The police are not investing resources in the policing of sections 76, 77 and 79. Health care workers will not be charged for working with queer men, and queer-identified people are not going to be arrested or imprisoned for revealing their sexual orientation.

These sections of the law are not enforced; therefore, queer men are not being charged and imprisoned under this legislation (Human Rights Watch 2014). Bourgeois queer men are valorizing an issue that is of symbolic importance to them but has little or no relevance to the lived experience of working-class queers who struggle with accessing resources to meet their basic needs on a daily basis. Many Jamaican queers and allies are of the opinion that the repeal of sections 76, 77 and 79 would substantively improve the legal and social status of the LGBTQ community. They argue that the criminalizing of sexual intimacy among gay men provides a legal cover for the state to discriminate against this group of men and create and enable a social atmosphere that is hostile and discriminatory to queers in general (Human Rights Watch 2014, 10).

The decriminalization of sexual intimacy among gay men will not end the legal sanctioning of discrimination against queer-identified Jamaicans. The decriminalization of homosexuality in 1969 in Canada did not end discrimination in employment, housing, adoption rights, partner workplace benefits, access to the institution of marriage and other rights that heterosexuals take for granted. It was the government's and the courts' recognition of sexual orientation as a basis for discrimination that advanced LGBTQ rights in Canada. The pursuit of legal challenges to get sexual orientation and gender identity recognized as prohibited grounds on which queer Jamaicans may be oppressed would be the effective way to eliminate the state's legal support of homophobia.

Therefore, the goal should be to present an anti-queer discrimination test case before Jamaica's court of last resort, the Privy Council. This case would have a high likelihood of success. The jurists on the Privy Council are likely to strike down homophobic discriminatory practices and instruct the government to amend the relevant laws. It would be fitting for the antiquated holdover of British colonialism, the Privy Council, to strike a legal or constitutional blow against legislative-cum-structural homophobia, since Britain and its Christian missionary confederates were agents of the unholy alliance that imposed homophobia on Jamaican society.

Using the Privy Council might appear to be contradictory or in tension with progressive anticolonial, or anti-imperialist, political commitments. However, politicos must be cognizant of the objective fact around the world of the judicial arm of the state being the source of legislative advance for LGBTQ rights. Since it is the court of last resort, we are politically obligated to use all available means to advance the queer human rights agenda. Further, some critics of this approach might not have a problem with appealing to international organizations such as the Organization of American States and the United Nations to address the human rights question in Jamaica and elsewhere in the Caribbean. When the judicial arm of the state makes positive rulings on LGBTQ rights, it is not doing so out of love for the oppressed, but to advance the legitimation function of the capitalist state.

How Did We Get Here?

British colonialism created the enabling environment for prejudices against sexual and gender minorities in Jamaica with its introduction of legislation that criminalized male homosexuality. In 1864, Britain's colonial authority in Jamaica passed the Offences against the Persons Act that epitomized "British 19th century condemnation of homosexuality" (Charles 2011, 9). Societal attitudes toward queerness, or homosexuality, were shaped by Western imperialism's legal instruments and the white Christian institutions that were partners in the enslavement and colonization of Africans. These Christian churches in Jamaica contributed to the acceptance of anti-queer animus in the worldview of the Africans. The religious denominations provided the moral and religious cover that affirmed the hegemonic position that "sodomy and homosexuality were the antithesis of colonial respectability" (Charles 2011, 9). In the Amnesty International newsletter *OUTfront*, J-FLAG had this to say about the influence of religion on Jamaicans' perspectives on LGBTQ people:

> Christianity, often the Old Testament fundamentalist variety, is therefore deeply rooted in our culture, and denunciations of homosexuality are stock material in sermons up and down the country. In recent years the Rastafarian religion, which promotes a return to more natural living, has seen a growth in popularity. One denomination in particular, the Bobo Shanti, often takes a literal interpretation of the Bible. I don't wish to dismiss or demonize any religion or belief system as they are more complex than just a single issue such as homosexuality,

however, it is important to highlight the tremendous influence that these religions have on people's thinking and the way in which many people justify their
bigotry with religion. Singers such as Capleton, Sizzla and Buju Banton often
defend their homophobic lyrics which include incitements to violence against
LGBT[Q] people, by using their religious teachings as a justification. (Amnesty
International 2004)

In spite of colonialism's role in socializing Africans into embracing prejudices against the LGBTQ community, most Jamaicans claim the colonial
legacy of anti-queer oppression as a part of their authentic cultural beliefs
and practices. In the study *Outing the Center: Homophobia in Jamaica*, the
researcher Jamilah King (2006, 26) reveals that most of her interviewees
believed that "homosexuality was a western imposition introduced to
people of African descent during slavery". Those who hold to this view need
to engage in due diligence on this subject in order to avoid peddling ignorance in the public square. The West (Britain in particular) was hostile to the
practice of homosexuality. In fact, England's Buggery Law of 1553 made anal
sex illegal, carrying the death penalty (Charles 2011). When cultural workers
such as Bounty Killer make the claim that their position on homosexuality
or diverse gender identities is informed by their culture, they, as African
artistes, are appealing to the previously imposed morality and religion of
Europe and the West to justify their sexual prejudices and homophobia.
It is ironic that Britain has moved away from legal homophobia but the
formerly enslaved and colonized Africans whom it socialized to embrace
homophobia now view the indoctrination of the past as their own.

The human rights campaigner Peter Tatchell also highlights the contra-
diction of Jamaica's African majority embracing homophobia:

> Some defend violently anti-gay reggae music on the grounds that homophobia
> is "part of Jamaican culture". Racism was part of Afrikaner culture in apartheid
> South Africa, but that did not make it right. By this logic, we should also accept
> cultural traditions like pogroms, female circumcision, lynchings and honour kill-
> ings. In any case, homophobia is not authentic Jamaican culture at all. It was
> foisted on the people of Jamaica in the 19th century by British colonisers and their
> Christian missionary allies. There is no evidence the Africans brought to Jamaica
> as slaves were homophobic. On the contrary, homosexuality was common in
> many of the West African societies from which they were stolen. It became more
> or less accepted among many enslaved in their Caribbean exile, especially given
> the dislocation of traditional family life by the slave system. The prejudices and
> laws against homosexuality were imposed by the British. Yet most Jamaicans
> now claim homophobia is part of their own African-derived culture. They are in
> massive denial. ("It Isn't Racist to Target Beenie Man", *Guardian*, 31 August 2004)

It is clear then that Jamaica's dancehall cultural workers and the population in general are being selective about the colonial sexual morality that they choose to honour in practice.

Toward Public, Open and Principled Heterosexual Solidarity

Having discussed the role British colonialism played in shaping the anti-queer climate in Jamaica, we now turn our attention to examining the significance of socially dominant groups in the working-class queer liberation struggle. In particular, we focus attention on how queer-positive hetero-sexual progressives can openly, consistently and assertively advocate for LGBTQ emancipation and push back against the structural and institution-alized alienation fashioned by heteronormativity or a heterosexist society.

Jamaica has come a far way with regard to how Jamaican LGBTQ citizens are treated. However, this shift in attitude has been seen primarily among the middle class (Chambers and Chevannes 1991; Chevannes 1993). In an article in the *Economist* (2009) entitled "A Vicious Intolerance: Homophobia in Jamaica", the authors note a steady, positive change in police interventions in dealing with reports of homophobic violence. Even so, scholars rightly contend that this does not signal a sudden upsurge in open-mindedness in Jamaican society (Cowell 2011; Cowell and Saunders 2011). For the most part, the literature on the lived experiences of LGBTQ citizens in Jamaica shows that the dominant discourse remains one of violence, mistreatment and victimization at the hands of state and non-state actors. Also evidenced in the literature is a general unwillingness on the part of state actors and agents to accord queer-identified people the full menu of rights given to heterosexuals in Jamaican society (White and Carr 2005).

Ian Boxill, Joulene Martin and Roy Russell's 2011 *National Survey of Attitudes and Perceptions of Jamaicans towards Same-Sex Relationships* and the follow-up 2012 study concluded that there was little variance in perceptions about LGBTQ people between the two periods. The results of both surveys reveal a "persistent" and "strong" negative attitude toward sexual and gender minorities. The findings also suggest that a critical mass of citizens are opposed to changing the laws governing sexual conduct between consenting adults of the same sex (Boxill, Martin and Russell 2011; Boxill et al. 2012).

Charles (2011), in his analysis of representations of homosexuality in Jamaica, implicates the state in institutionalizing a normative sexual and gender hegemony. Echoing previous studies undertaken by international human rights groups, his position serves as a scathing indictment of law enforcement officers who he contends "are socialized like other Jamaicans to hate homosexuals" (12).

The work of Cowell and King offers insight into current attitudes of working-class Jamaicans toward sexual and gender diversity, and they discuss how dominant perceptions manifest in various social spaces, even among public policy actors (Cowell 2011; Cowell and Saunders 2011; King 2006). Their work details how the flames of anti-queer animus are fanned by public officials who make negative statements regarding LGBTQ citizens. According to a J-FLAG (2015) report, 64 per cent of politicians surveyed believed that homosexuality was immoral, 58 per cent thought gay behaviour should be illegal and 64 per cent agreed that LGBTQ people could be converted to heterosexuals. Almost two-thirds (65 per cent) would not support changes to decriminalize the current buggery laws, and 58 per cent would not support laws to ensure equal rights to LGBTQ people. Other scholars attribute the complacency exhibited by law enforcement officers in punishing those who visit violence on members of the LGBTQ community to their belief that homophobic attacks are a form of "biblical retribution" (Carr 2003).

Discrimination against queer citizens in Jamaica exposes itself in various forms that require intervention to ensure their protection and enable greater access to justice. A recent study entitled *Homophobia and Development: The Case of Jamaica* found that the vast majority of over three hundred LGBTQ people surveyed in 2015 believe discrimination is pervasive, and one in ten individuals identified a police officer as the perpetrator of the last incident of physical or sexual violence that they experienced (McFee and Galbraith 2016). Of those who experienced discrimination or violence, 51 per cent did not report their last incident of physical or sexual assault to the police. The largest proportion of individuals (41 per cent) did not report it because they did not think the police would do anything, and 30 per cent did not report it because they thought the matter was too minor. In addition, about one in four people feared a homophobic reaction from the police (McFee and Galbraith 2016).

Where harassment is concerned, the majority (61 per cent) did not report the incident to the police. Approximately one in five (19 per cent) felt too ashamed or embarrassed to report harassment. At the same time, 46 per cent of residents in Kingston reported that they felt that the police treated homosexuals worse than heterosexuals. The percentages in other parishes were as follows: St Andrew (16 per cent), St Thomas (19 per cent), St Mary (32 per cent), St James (32 per cent), Clarendon (28 per cent), St Catherine (22 per cent) and Trelawny (32 per cent) (McFee and Galbraith 2016).

The above data are telling to the extent that they implicate the Jamaican state in structural violence against LGBTQ citizens. They show that the police (as an arm of the Jamaican state) are incapable of securing the rights of queer and working-class citizens either because of low levels of trust or the belief that nothing will come of making a report. Data from Barnes et al.'s (2016) recent *National Victimization Survey* (2016) show that working-class citizens in general feel that the police in Jamaica are disrespectful and difficult to interact with. However, 23 per cent believe that homosexuals are treated worse by the police than are heterosexuals. This state of affairs is significant as it emphasizes the fact that discrimination against queer citizens cannot be divorced from the larger state-sanctioned structural gender-based violence meted out against working-class citizens. In today's Jamaica, citizens who deviate from the culturally expected gender roles ascribed at birth experience violence in the form of hostility, harassment, mob attacks, beatings, sexual assaults and murders (J-FLAG 2016). Moreover, individuals who are violent toward others because of their nonconformity to societal norms of sexual and gender expressions are not held accountable. The violence extends beyond the everyday interpersonal forms of violence, however. State actors and agents, in neglecting working-class queer citizens, are implicated in perpetuating structural violence that worsens the material conditions of working-class LGTBQ citizens whose daily existence is mediated by the violence of poverty, homelessness and inadequate access to health care and other social services.

It is for this reason we argue against an over-reliance on oppressive state mechanisms. As was stated in an earlier section of this chapter, the Jamaican state has a legacy of pandering to colonial respectability politics and an oppressive legal regime that safeguards bourgeois standards of morality, law and order. Thus, to do the necessary anti-oppression work that will give birth to queer liberation in Jamaica, we are of the view that, similar to historical struggles to secure women's rights and improved conditions and wages for workers, as well as racial justice for Africans and other racialized peoples, queer-positive heterosexual allies in Jamaica can play a crucial and substantive role in advocating and advancing the human rights status of queer Jamaicans.

In an article entitled "What White Allies Can Learn from Allies in the Gay Struggle", George Lakey (2017) highlights the important role privileged bodies play in social justice movements. He writes:

In the 1960s, white people showed we were allies by taking action – picketing racist realtors, boycotting to open jobs to black people, enlisting trade union friends to join the March on Washington, even sitting in and going to jail. That context of direct action was when the greatest progress against racism was made. Rustin argued that the choke-hold of racism cannot be broken as long as joblessness and poverty continue. Now we can see how correct he was; black scholars, entrepreneurs, celebrities and even a president can't really touch racism as long as fundamental institutions continue to generate it 24/7. Only powerful action campaigns can change institutions, and that's where the responsibility of the allies belongs. What better role for the privileged? Allies came forward in numbers, and still do. I can't tell you how many times I saw brave heterosexuals take on homophobia during struggles to win concrete gains for lesbians and gays.

Just as global struggles to end racism, sexism and class exploitation in the North necessitated the involvement of various allies, so too does the struggle for queer rights in Jamaica. People from socially dominant groups, heterosexuals in particular, must join forces with the LGBTQ community in organizing against multiple forms of oppression and state-sanctioned violence. The queer liberation movement in Jamaica needs queer-positive heterosexuals as the socially dominant counterparts of the LGBTQ community, to actively participate in targeted campaigns in order to bring about the much-needed changes that can bring about improvements in the human rights and material conditions of working-class queer citizens.

One way in which queer-positive Jamaicans or allies can help to reduce dominant anti-queer stigma and ensure that queer citizens have greater access to justice is by creating what Lakey (2017) calls "a spectrum of allies" within organizations in which they work. This can be achieved through consistent dialogue with strategic individuals in positions of power within these organizations. The 2016 debacle surrounding the manufacturer LASCO Distributors dismissal of an employee who made a homophobic tweet from the company's Twitter account following the historic win by 110-metre hurdler Omar McLeod ("LASCO Fires Employee Who Made Controversial Tweet about Omar McLeod", *Gleaner*, 17 August 2016), for instance, provided a prime opportunity for those in power within the private sector to demonstrate their commitment to instituting strategies that reduce anti-queer hostility. While apologies and public declarations are laudable steps toward stemming individual forms of violence meted out against queer citizens, the issuing of apologies and removal of individual employees does nothing to challenge systemic and institutionalized homophobia. An employee feeling emboldened enough to engage in a homophobic attack on an employer's Twitter account is an indication of the extent to which that organization is enabling anti-queer animus.

Companies like LASCO Distributors could do better than issuing a statement of apology and a promised sensitivity training session, as the individual employee's behaviour is but a reflection of the larger organizational environment and the external social environment. Therefore, people in positions of power within these organizations ought to commit to creating a queer-positive workplace backed by measurable goals and objectives. The preceding course of action would represent a serious act of reparatory justice and communicate to employees, and by extension those in the wider Jamaican society, that these businesses are committed to eradicating homophobic prejudice in their operations. It is much too easy for companies to compose statements of regret or apology or fire the transgressive employees. It is a completely different matter to carry out a systemic review of the organization's homophobic beliefs and practices to affect systemic changes that will make the employment space welcoming and empowering to LGBTQ workers.

Major companies or corporate citizens such as LASCO could provide a quota of employment placements for homeless queer youth and queer youth in general who would then see an improvement in their material conditions. This action would go a long way in terms of poverty reduction among working-class queer youth who experience high levels of homelessness (Human Rights Watch 2014) and unemployment. The preceding state of affairs is directly tied to their gender identity or sexual orientation and is prompted by their families expelling them from the household[1] or business enterprises' denial of employment opportunities to these youth. Since most of us spend a large proportion of our time in the workplace, interacting with colleagues who are queer in a queer-positive employment space could facilitate a higher level of understanding of, acceptance of and solidarity with members of the LGBTQ community. It should be noted that queer-positive workplaces would also have policies of affirmative action or employment equity hiring of other queer demographic groups across the job classification's system.

Companies and other workplaces could also include statements in workplace and relevant organizational documents on the companies' zero tolerance policy on homophobic language and behaviour. These organizations would also appoint equity officers to work with LGBTQ advocacy groups in hosting drop-in sessions and homophobic prejudice reduction workshops as a way to inspire dialogue and behavioural change around sexual orientation, gender and gender identity. This would be an exemplary show of queer allyship.

Public and private sector organizations could also issue statements calling on governments to undertake legislative measures that eliminate colonially imposed homophobic laws and practices that deny queer citizens their inalienable human rights. In the same vein, queer-positive employers, trade unions and other civil society organizations and institutions could issue public statements of solidarity with queer Jamaicans during the annual Pride Week in August. These companies could provide generous financial and in-kind donations to carry out queer solidarity public education initiatives and establish a fund to support organizations working to help homeless queer youth find shelter and stable forms of housing. Organizations could use social media to visibly display a statement on their commitment to ensuring equity in the workplace. They could also use the space to denounce discrimination on the basis of age, disability, gender, gender identity, race, class, religious belief or sexual orientation while at the same time reinforcing their commitment to tackling homophobic behaviour within the spaces under their jurisdiction. Companies could also use their social media platforms to openly encourage dialogue and greater understanding about the impact of homophobic violence.

Heterosexual allies could address and elevate the interests of LGBTQ from the labouring classes by engaging in a series of campaigns within private, public and non-profit organizations and major societal institutions. These campaigns would engage specific stakeholders with key messaging that connects the issues of poverty, chronic unemployment/ underemployment and precarious labour status, and inability to access the public health and education systems (issues that non-queer citizens also face) to the broader working-class struggle. The changes that queer-positive straight individuals or groups are seeking in these organizations and institutions must be structural, or systemic, in nature. We are not merely seeking attitudinal adjustment. The policies, processes and structures that engender homophobia must be swept into the dustbin with other outdated, prejudicial social relics.

Organizing Working-Class Queer People

There are a number of actions that can be carried out in order to affect the organizing of working-class queers in Jamaica and place them and their needs at the centre of the movement for queer emancipation.

Create and Strengthen Autonomous, Fighting Organizations

It is often said that there is strength in numbers. This well-known adage is apt when it comes to pulling together working-class queers as a collective force to address their priority issues and in crafting a programme of action to address them. This can be effectively done through the creation and strengthening of autonomous, fighting organizations that are the foundation of a militant and assertive queer liberation movement. Kwame Ture (formerly Stokely Carmichael) consistently proclaimed at public lectures that "organization is a weapon of the oppressed". It is through organizations that the oppressed (and even the forces of oppression) are able to build projects, programmes and institutions to pursue their interests (Nangwaya 2014). Jamaican working-class queers will remain socially alienated individuals clamouring for the full enjoyment of their package of human rights under middle-class queer leadership if they do not assert their right to self-determination in organizations under their own leadership. When oppressed groups develop effective and efficient organizations they are in a position to determine their priorities, establish the scope of their needs, marshal the material and human resources to meet self-determined goals, and disrupt, undermine or liquidate the existing state of the oppressive order that shapes their lives.

In spite of the well-meaning thoughts and actions of the largely middle-class–led queer human rights movement in Jamaica, its exclusion of a queer liberationist anti-capitalist critique of how capitalism impacts the lives of working-class queers and their heterosexual counterparts fundamentally affects the nature of its agenda for structural change that will ultimately transform the lives of the sufferers within the LGBTQ community. It is only a class conscious, feminist, anti-racist and intersectional working-class queer leadership that will produce a programme of action that will bring forth queer liberation.

Capacity-Building Training and Development Programmes

Many members of the working class do not have access to the broadest and highest quality of human capital. Race, class, sexuality and gender forms of exploitation serve as barriers to their acquisition of the knowledge and skills that would allow them to access the critical resources in society that facilitate maximum human development. According to the *Economist* (2017), and drawing on the pioneering ideas of the late American economist of human capital Gary Becker, "human capital refers to the abilities and qualities of people that make them productive. Knowledge is the most important of these, but other factors, from a sense of punctuality to the state of someone's health, also matter. Investment in human capital thus mainly refers to education but it also includes other things – the inculcation of values by parents, say, or a healthy diet." The prohibitive cost of formal education prevents most working-class queers in Jamaica from accessing high quality education, especially university education. Therefore, the critical knowledge, skills and competencies gained through advocating within organizations are denied. Jamaica's homeless queer youth, who are widely known as "gully queens", are an example of members of the working class who are not amply endowed with human capital like the petite bourgeois queer counterparts who run organizations such as J-FLAG ("The Gully Queens of Jamaica: How a Gay Community in one of the Most Homophobic Places on Earth has Literally Been Forced Underground into a Filthy Storm Drain", *Daily Mail*, 2 August 2014; Felsenthal 2016). In order to ensure that the working class has the relevant knowledge, skills and attitude to collectively lead their organizations and be a decisive force in the LGBTQ social movement, organizers ought to create training and development programmes. If we are committed to emancipation from below rooted in the experiences of the most socially alienated, it is incumbent on organizers to organize workshops that prepare the oppressed to take on strategic, ideational and operational leadership tasks throughout the organizations. Organizational tasks such as programme planning and development, public speaking, fundraising, mobilizing members of society, executing training and development activities, preparing reports and other organizational documents, serving as delegates or representatives in coalitions and alliances, and developing the ideological, philosophical and theoretical position of the organization are just a few concrete examples.

The reality, however, is that

> [o]ftentimes, our organizations do not set aside resources to train and/or develop their activists to do the required activities, which are necessary to achieve the goal and objectives of our struggle for emancipation. Organizers are left to learn through trial and error, someone informally taking them under their experienced wings as "mentees" or searching out learning opportunities outside of the organization. . . . If we want to create participatory-democratic organizations, we have to be deliberate about developing or expanding the skills of our activists. (Nangwaya 2013)

Systematic Engagement in Ideological and Political Development Work

While it is essential for working-class queers to have the knowledge, skills and attitude to carry out the pragmatic tasks of fighting for human rights and social and economic justice, the task of their ideological and political preparation ought not to be neglected. We live in societies in which the elite ideological domination of society is manifested throughout the key institutions of socialization as well as in the values, beliefs and behaviour of the oppressed. Some observers might categorize this phenomenon as "mental slavery", "false consciousness" or "hegemony". In spite of one's conceptual preference, the outcome is that even queers existing in a homophobic, patriarchal, capitalist, anti-African and racist society have embraced the ideologies of the political masters of society. Further, the working class is notorious for its limited class consciousness and, as such, is prone to identifying the interests and actions of the elite as aligning with theirs.

The above state of affairs can be transformed through the development of political education classes and the development of an anti-oppressive, intersectional curriculum that develops a counter-hegemonic outlook within the ranks of working-class queers. This ideological development programme would impress upon the participants that their interests, especially regarding political economy, are distinct from and in conflict with those of the elite. In spite of the homophobic thoughts and actions of working-class straight people, they are misguided potential comrades in struggle, not the enemies of working-class LGBTQ. They have more in common with each other than with middle-class straight people and queers. An ideological preparation programme would enable a mature and integrated class, sexuality, feminist and race analysis of oppression and liberation.

Queer-Positive Public Education Programmes

In spite of the high anti-queer animus in Jamaica, especially among working-class heterosexuals, the members of the queer community and heterosexual allies must carry out the work of developing a critical mass of queer-positive Jamaicans. It can be done through systematic public education about the lives of queer Jamaicans and the ways in which the oppression of LGBTQ individuals undermines the thrust for justice, equity and self-determination for the socially marginalized. Martin Luther King Jr (1963) captures the essence of the preceding assertion: "Injustice anywhere is a threat to justice everywhere. We are caught in an inescapable network of mutuality, tied in a single garment of destiny. Whatever affects one directly, affects all indirectly."

There is a strategic reason for mass public education. It is a way to win over our straight allies, especially opinion leaders and those whose actions can influence the actions of others to take a public stance in favour of queer liberation. We also want to encourage ordinary working-class Jamaicans to speak publicly about affirming experiences and relationships that they have with queer members of the national community. One of the authors has experienced such a situation in a course that dealt with the anti-oppression principle of Rastafari as articulated by Ras Ishon Williams (2008).[2] Students openly shared stories about their queer relatives and friends, not something that is often done in public. The value of hetero-sexuals publicly and assertively standing up for queer emancipation should not be underestimated.

Cooperative Economic Development

The oppressive class relations in society that impinge on the lives of working-class queers and their straight counterparts is the product of capitalism. This economic system has the inherent feature of dividing people into broad classes: the working class that sells its labour in order to survive and the economic elite that owns the means of production and controls the lion's share of the profit or wealth produced by the workers. Economic exploitation and subordination of the labouring classes is another principal trait of capitalism. The elimination of queerphobia and heteronormativity as a structural feature of Jamaica's institutions will not substantively change the economic condition of most queers from the working class. Therefore, it is essential for the working class and radical/revolutionary petite bourgeois queers to embrace and promote cooperative entrepreneurship and an integrated and comprehensive cooperative economic programme with three strategic goals: meeting the basic needs (food shelter, clothing, health care, financial services) of the queer community; developing a pragmatic basis for mutual aid and cooperation between working-class queer and heterosexuals; and putting into practice an economic model (cooperative economics, for example) that exists to meet the needs of members and not the pursuit of profit, as is the case with capitalist economics. Cooperative economics emerged during the Industrial Revolution as a way for workers and the poor to combat dehumanizing, greedy, alienating and exploitative capitalism. Their economic approach is committed to business or entrepreneurial activities that are focused on addressing members' needs, democratic member control of their economic organizations, advancing the welfare of the community and equitable sharing of the surplus or profit. The cooperative is the organizational form privileged by co-operators and it allows the working class or members to control capital in advancing their needs.

Worker cooperatives, similar to those used in Jamaica's sugarcane industry between 1975 and 1981,[3] could be deployed as the centrepiece of a development-from-below cooperative economic strategy that mirrors the approach of the Mondragon cooperatives in the Basque region of Spain.[4]

If this attempt at collective entrepreneurship through workers' control, ownership and management of a part of the Jamaican economy is placed on the development agenda by a section of the LGBTQ community, it would be creating queer-positive and affirming spaces that would provide the opportunity for day-to-day interaction and solidarity between queer and heterosexual Jamaicans. Heterosexual, working-class Jamaicans are economic pragmatists and will become members of workers' cooperatives that offer the hope of a better life, even with queers initiating or serving as a significant part of the leadership of this worker entrepreneurship experiment. We ought not to underestimate the value of social contact or interaction in reducing anti-queer prejudices in Jamaica.

A preliminary comparative research project by Keon West and Miles Hewstone (2012) on anti-gay men prejudices and intergroup contact found encouraging results among Jamaican post-secondary students. In their findings in the article "Culture and Contact in the Promotion and Reduction of Anti-Gay Prejudice", they tell us that "Although Jamaican participants reported more prejudice against gay men than did British participants, the results were encouraging in that Jamaicans' attitudes toward gay men appeared to be malleable. Contact was more strongly associated with positive attitudes in the Jamaican sample than in the British sample. Thus, although Jamaican sexual prejudice may be stronger than corresponding British sexual prejudice, it appears that change is possible" (58). Although the research findings came from post-secondary students and are unlikely to be representative of Jamaica's population, it should be noted that many, if not most, of the students in this sector are from working-class homes. Their families sell their labour in return for wages, and their working lives are impacted by the labour alienation experience,[5] notwithstanding the reality that many of them identify themselves as "middle class" based on consumption patterns and access to goods and services in the capitalist marketplace. If we look at these students' and their families' relationship to the means of production, we can see their working-class identity. They are also people with anti-LGBTQ prejudices, although their exposure to higher education might limit the likelihood of them using physical violence against members of the queer community.

In advancing cooperative economic development and worker self-management as an antidote to the neoliberal capitalist agenda, the working-class forces in the LGBTQ community would be offering strategic and organic intellectual leadership within the movement for social emancipation in Jamaica.

Concluding Thoughts

There is much that can be learned from developments in North America and Europe on the question of advancing the queer human rights agenda. It is clear that an intersectional, analytical framework, reflecting the one offered in the Combahee River Collective's "A Black Feminist Statement" (1982), which centres the different forms of oppression that impact the lives of African women, is essential in formulating a programme of emancipation for queer Jamaicans. We have highlighted the centrality of working-class leadership of the queer liberation movement in Jamaica in order to avoid replicating the respectability politics of the mainstream queer agenda in the Global North that seeks the removal of anti-queer personnel. Bourgeois, male, queer leadership will lead to a similar outcome in Jamaica. Therefore, a class-conscious, working-class, queer leadership working within an intersectional, analytical framework is the key to social transformation in Jamaica.

Notes

1. Charles (2011, 18–20) documents the case of a father whose son was suspected of being queer, inciting his classmates to beat him up.

2. Williams (2008, 20–21) states that the third principle of Rastafari calls for firm opposition to oppressive conditions. He asserts that "[a]nyone who has difficulty understanding the importance of fighting against oppression in all its forms, can never truly call himself or herself a Rasta".

3. The Jamaican experiment with worker self-management was carried out through over twenty worker cooperatives covering about five thousand worker members.

4. The Mondragon Corporation is a network of 102 cooperatives (mostly worker cooperatives) with a 2016 total revenue of over €12 billion, €427 million net investment and a total employment of 73,635 personnel. About 78 per cent of the personnel are worker members, and €22.6 million is devoted to social solidarity activities and projects. Read more at http://www.mondragon-corporation.com/en/about-us/economic-and-financial-indicators/highlights/.

5. Karl Marx's (1859) examination of labour alienation in his *Economic and Philosophical Manuscripts of 1844* still captures the experience of work life in the twenty-first century workplace. If we determine membership in the working class by the extent of labour alienation in people's lives, we might conclude that many university students come from working-class families. The document is available on Marxist.org at https://www.marxists.org/archive/marx/works/1844/manuscripts/labour.htm.

References

Amnesty International. 2004. "What Happened to 'One Love'? Prejudice and Homophobic Violence in Jamaica". *OUTFront*. Accessed 15 January 2020. www.amnestyusa.org/pdfs/Newsletter2004.pdf.

Barnes, Annmarie, Randy Seepersad, Jason Wilks and Scott Wortley. 2016. "The National Crime Victimization Survey (NCVS)". Report Prepared for the Ministry of National Security, Government of Jamaica. Accessed 15 January 2020. https://www.mns.gov.jm/content/national-crime-victimization-survey-ncvs-2016-final-report.

Boxill, Ian, Elroy Galbraith, Rashalee Mitchell, Roy Russell, S. Johnson and Lloyd Waller. 2012. "National Survey of Attitudes and Perceptions of Jamaicans towards Same-Sex Relationships: A Follow-up Study". Accessed 12 January 2020. https://ufdc.ufl.edu/AA00003178/00001.

Boxill, Ian, Joulene Martin, and Roy Russell. 2011. *National Survey of Attitudes and Perceptions of Jamaicans towards Same-Sex Relationships*. Kingston: University of the West Indies.

Cabral, Amilcar. 1979. *Unity and Struggle: Speeches and Writings*. Translated by Michael Wolfers. New York: Monthly Review Press.

Canadian HIV/AIDS Legal Network. 2015. "Constitutional Challenge to Jamaica's Anti-Sodomy Law: Questions and Answers". Accessed 19 February 2020. http://www.aidslaw.ca/site/wp-content/uploads/2015/12/Jamaica-constitutional-challenge_QA_Dec2015.pdf.

Carr, Robert. 2003. "On 'Judgements': Poverty, Sexuality-Based Violence and Human Rights in 21st Century Jamaica". *Caribbean Journal of Social Work* 2 (3): 71–87.

Chambers, Claudia, and Barry Chevannes. 1991. "Sexual Decision-Making among Women and Men in Jamaica: Report on Some Focus Group Discussions". Manuscript. University of the West Indies, Mona, Jamaica.

Chang, Larry. 2011. "Interview between Larry Chang and Thomas Glave". YouTube. Accessed 21 January 2020. https://www.youtube.com/watch?v=vqJb2ARl2hA.

Charles, Christopher. 2011. "Representations of Homosexuality in Jamaica". *Social and Economic Studies* 60 (1): 3–29.

Chevannes, Barry. 1993. "Sexual Behaviour of Jamaicans: A Literature Review". *Social and Economic Studies* 42 (1): 1–45.

The Combahee River Collective. 1982. "A Black Feminist Statement". In *But Some of Us Are Brave: All the Women Are White, All the Blacks Are Men: Black Women's Studies*, edited by Gloria Hull, Patricia Bell Scott and Barbara Smith, 13–23. Old Westbury, NY: Feminist Press.

Cowell, Noel. 2011. "Public Discourse, Popular Culture and Attitudes towards Homosexuals in Jamaica". *Social and Economic Studies* 60 (1): 31–60.

Cowell, Noel, and Tanzia Saunders. 2011. "Exploring Heteronormativity in the Public Discourse of Jamaican Legislators". *Sexuality and Culture* 15 (4): 315–31.

Economist. 2009. "Homophobia in Jamaica: A Vicious Intolerance". 17 September. Accessed 20 February 2020. https://www.economist.com/the-americas/2009/09/17/a-vicious-intolerance.

———. 2017. "Gary Becker's Concept of Human Capital". 3 August. Accessed 15 January 2020. https://www.economist.com/news/economics-brief/21725757-becker-made-people-central-focus-economics-second-our-series-big.

Felsenthal, Julia. 2016. "Meet the Gully Queens: The Transgender Women Defying Jamaica's Culture of Homophobia". *Vogue.* 10 November. http://www.vogue.com/article/ray-blk-chill-out-video-premiere-gully-queens.

GFM (Gay Freedom Movement). 1981. "Gays in Jamaica: A Position Paper". Accessed 15 January 2020. http://dloc.com/aa00001485.

Human Rights Watch. 2014. *Not Safe at Home: Violence and Discrimination against LGBT People in Jamaica.* New York: Human Rights Watch.

J-FLAG. 2013. "Homophobia and Violence in Jamaica". Accessed 17 February 2020. http://equalityjamaica.org/assets/homophobia_violence_in_jamaica_jflag_2013.pdf.

———. 2015. "Management Report on Awareness, Attitude, and Perception Survey about Issues Related to Same Sex Relationships". Kingston, Jamaica.

———. 2016. "Human Rights Violations against Lesbian, Gay, Bisexual, and Transgender (LGBT) People in Jamaica: A Shadow Report". Accessed 15 January 2020. http://tbinternet.ohchr.org/Treaties/CCPR/Shared%20Documents/JAM/INT_CCPR_ICO_JAM_22756_E.pdf.

Jørgensen, Sigrid. 2016. "Jamaica's Homophobia Forced 'Out of the Closet' by the Rainbow Flag". Council on Hemispheric Affairs. 16 June. Accessed 17 February 2020. http://www.coha.org/jamaicas-homophobia-forced-out-of-the-closet-by-the-rainbow-flag/.

King, Jamilah. 2006. "Outing the Center: Homophobia in Jamaica". Independent Study Project (ISP) Collection. Paper 380. Accessed 20 January 2020. http://digitalcollections.sit.edu/isp_collection/380.

King, Martin Luther Jr. 1963. "Letter from a Birmingham Jail, April 16, 1963". Accessed 10 January 2020. https://www.africa.upenn.edu/Articles_Gen/Letter_Birmingham.html.

Lakey, George. 2017. "What White Allies Can Learn from Allies in the Gay Struggle". *Waging Nonviolence.* Accessed 10 January 2020. https://wagingnonviolence.org/feature/white-allies-can-learn-allies-gay-rights-struggle/.

Marx, Karl. 1859. *Economic and Philosophical Manuscripts of 1844.* Translated by Martin Milligan. Moscow: Progress. Accessed 15 January 2020. https://www.marxists.org/archive/marx/works/1844/manuscripts/labour.htm.

McFee, Rochelle, and Elroy Galbraith. 2016. "The Developmental Cost of Homophobia: The Case of Jamaica". Accessed 10 January 2020. http://www.washingtonblade.com/content/files/2016/01/The-Developmental-Cost-of-Homophobia-The-Case-of-Jamaica_2016-1.pdf.

Nangwaya, Ajamu. 2013. "Message to a Younger Radical Activist: On Preparing for Organizational Leadership". *Pambazuka News.* 19 June. https://www.pambazuka.org/governance/message-younger-radical-activist.

Nangwaya, Ajamu. 2014. "Organization Is the Weapon of the Oppressed: Ferguson, Mobilization and Organizing the Resistance". *Dissident Voice.* Accessed 22 January 2020. http://dissidentvoice.org/2014/08/organization-is-the-weapon-of-the-oppressed/.

West, Keon, and Miles Hewstone. 2012. "Culture and Contact in the Promotion and Reduction of Anti-Gay Prejudice: Evidence from Jamaica and Britain". *Journal of Homosexuality* 59 (1): 44–66.

White, Ruth, and Robert Carr. 2005. "Homosexuality and HIV/AIDS Stigma in Jamaica". *Culture, Health and Sexuality* 7 (4): 347–59.

Williams, Lawson. 2000. "Homophobia and (Gay Rights) Activism in Jamaica". *Small Axe* 4 (7): 106–11.

Williams, Ras Ishon. 2008. "The Seven Principles of Rastafari". In *Rastafari,* edited by Rex Nettleford and Veronica Salter, 16–22. Kingston: Caribbean Quarterly Monograph.

13.

Pride, Vulgarity and Imagination

COLIN ROBINSON

> To paraphrase Trinidadian writer-activist Colin Robinson, the challenge is not
> simply to imagine the same-sex Caribbean but to imagine it imaginatively.
> —Omiseke N. Tinsley, *Thiefing Sugar: Eroticism between Women in Caribbean*
> *Literature*

I see my role today as sharing with you some of my most important groundings, looking back over two decades of organizing and thinking as a Caribbean gay activist, particularly the past eleven years since I joined the steering committee of CariFLAGS, and the seven since I helped found CAISO (Gosine 2015; Robinson 2012).

One preoccupation that has haunted all those years – and that I remember using to clap back to Thomas Glave's 1999 essay about imagination[1] – is the extent to which we in the queer Caribbean have become captives of others' narratives, which – I'm going to assert – has resulted in our catastrophic abandonment of imagining for ourselves. It is the thing I get into political fights over most often. I want to do so today as well, as it is the most critical challenge facing our Caribbean movement – it is as important as violence and social protection and mental health.

Far from anything academic, it is something my everyday activism repeatedly grapples with. I am eager for us as scholars and activists to see how we can use this unique space at Beyond Homophobias[2] to engage this together.

"I began to grasp the largeness of the work before us, the fact that we are not only creating essays or poems or stories, but the fact that we are creating culture. We are expressing ourselves as a people, and shaping the consciousness of ourselves as a people. We are creating ourselves" (Garrett 1986, 97–98). Those are the words of Daniel Garrett, reflecting on the African American gay men's writing group "Other Countries" he founded in 1986, and where I cut my activist teeth. The vision we created for one of our publications was to reach a boy hiding in the darkness of a basement reading James Baldwin by torchlight in a fictional place another writer, Reginald Jackson, called Boupaloupa, Mississippi (Robinson 2007). Granted, Caribbean young people now have American television and the Internet on their smartphones. But they also find themselves in the middle of a culture war for control over their bodies that did not exist when I was growing up.

When our teenagers turn for solace to the Internet that champions the hope that "it gets better" for American teenagers at risk of suicide (Meckler 2010), they find instead, in response to the murder of Dwayne Jones and young people like themselves, comments like this one on *GayStarNews*'s story on the murder (Morgan 2013): "Fuck dirty ass Jamaica."

Whether or not it is "the most homophobic place on earth", with a question mark, as in *Time* magazine (Padgett 2006) or "one of the most dangerous countries of the world for Trans and gender non-confirming individuals" in *National Geographic* (2017), what are we doing to counter a global movement's creation of such representations that are killing our young people's ability to imagine a future?[3]

What invests so many of us – straight and LGBTI – so deeply in the superlativeness and cultural particularity of our backwardness (Larcher and Robinson 2009), instead of the idea that we are not much different from any small place or any society that has been colonized?

I remember arriving in Kingston in 2000 and finding a breath-taking imaginativeness in the spaces LGBTI people were carving out for plea-sure and struggle that looked nothing like the standard representations of Jamaica (Robinson 2006). And over ten years in Trinidad and Tobago, I've witnessed how transformative it is when we show up to humanize ourselves, voice our visions for sharing the nation and connect to common values. We often do far too little of both across the movement. And more than ever we urgently need to domesticate the ideas we are fighting for, so we reshape not only our fellow citizens' sense of our depravity or others' sense of our states' barbarity, but *our own* sense of what our freedom looks like (Robinson 2007).

Why, when buggery laws in the region appear enforced for consensual conduct less often that the death penalty is for murder, do they operate as such a powerful fetish, commanding resources and attention far dispropor-tionate to their impact and displacing other policy targets that would impact more people (Robinson 2015)?[4] What are the responsibilities and roles of academics and activists in transforming or reproducing our dependence on these received ideas? As activists, do we turn to scholarship for political ideas and theories of change or just for data and clinical expertise for interventions? How as activists are *we* producing autochthonous knowledge?

At the end of the day, is the slow pace of change on sexual citizenship in the Caribbean because we have failed to be thoughtful enough about what we are doing and why? Are we still trying to use the master's tools to dismantle the master's house (Lorde 1983)?

I often experience others' impatience with questions about the analysis or strategy underlying our policy work, little interest in debating competing ideas, and a narcissism in litigation and policy decisions. As some of you know, the last time I was invited to participate in a plenary in a regional LGBTQI meeting and proposed to raise questions about self-determination, I was disinvited and my ticket cancelled. So I'm grateful to the conference organizers for providing a space for these provocations, despite some tensions in the run up to today.

How are we pooling knowledge and lessons? In solving shared problems like chronic urban homelessness (Henry 2014; Poyser 2015) or trans poverty, can we better turn to each other in generating and sharing understandings of local and regional problems, as will happen in some of the sessions here? How much of what we are doing is driven by funders' and partners' priorities and thinking rather than our own?

Finally, how are we safeguarding our own regional opportunities? The Caribbean, with generally weak nongovernmental organizations, now provides relevance and economic sustainability for a number of North American- and European-based LGBTI organizations that have leveraged significant state funding for new Caribbean initiatives at a time when victories at home are drying up donor resources. What is being "done for" us is now the currency by which LGBTI voters in those states hold their politicians accountable. Our own ideas play a quite limited role in this framework. And the one-here, one-there of our leaders embraced by these international projects have no real accountability to the region.

My simple call is for us to urgently rethink the politics of knowledge in LGBTI work across the region and to use our time together to explore how both the university and communities can contribute to more productive, grounded, strategic movements.

Acknowledgements

This chapter is an edited version of a presentation delivered at the opening plenary panel "Beyond Homophobia: Activism and Scholarship into the New Millennium", at Beyond Homophobia: Centring LGBT Experiences in the Caribbean, at the University of the West Indies, Mona, Jamaica, 26 January 2017.

Notes

1. In "Towards a Strategy of Imagination", a panel presentation at the University of Chicago symposium "Queer Islands?", 15–16 April 2005, I used Glave's essay to question whether "Caribbean LGBT activism, at home and in the diaspora, suffers from a severe lack of imagination, often stunting its authenticity", an imagination constricted by the twinning of a "disturbingly neo-colonial" and "reductionist" vision of Caribbean homophobia as "irrational, ignorant and inhumane" with neoliberal "faith in the universal human rights framework as a tool for liberation". In the presentation I assert that "[i]magination is as fundamental as power to liberation".

2. I insist on re-naming the event the way it was first communicated to me. This is consistent with an understanding of "the scope and complexity of how homophobias work differently across the region", as "activists and others living in the Caribbean have argued that there is a complex range of viewpoints and attitudes that must be accounted for in our defining of homophobias. . . . [T]here is certainly no uniform notion of 'Caribbean homophobia', but rather context is everything", with "specific nuances to space, place, identity, history, and politics. Hence, our use of the term 'homophobias' insists upon local understandings and contexts while expanding awareness of the differences and similarities across the region and its diaspora" (King and Nixon 2012).

3. Subsequent to the panel, I wrote about how even Jamaican writer Marlon James's (2015) coming-out at the pinnacle of his career encodes this (C. Robinson 2017).

4. In a more recent panel presentation, T. Robinson (2017) weaves together with her notion of "imagined lives" the vision of a "politics of imagination".

References

Garrett, Daniel. 1986. "Creating Ourselves: An Open Letter". In *In the Life: A Black Gay Anthology*, edited by J. Beam, 93–103. Boston: Alyson.

Glave, Thomas. 1999. "Toward a Nobility of the Imagination: Jamaica's Shame. An Open Letter to the People of Jamaica". *Jamaica Observer*, 9 January.

Gosine, Andil. 2015. "CAISO, CAISO: Negotiating Sex Rights and Nationalism in Trinidad and Tobago". *Sexualities* 18 (7): 859–84.

Henry, Balford. 2014. "MP Wants Help for New Kingston Homeless Gays". *Jamaica Observer*. 13 June. http://www.jamaicaobserver.com/news/MP-wants-help-for-New-Kingston-homeless-gays_16879080

James, Marlon. 2015. "Breaking Out: From Jamaica to Minnesota to Myself". *New York Times Magazine* MM60. 15 March. https://www.nytimes.com/2015/03/15/magazine/from-jamaica-to-minnesota-to-myself.html

King, Rosamond S., and Angelique V. Nixon. 2012. Introduction to *Theorizing Homophobias in the Caribbean: Complexities of Place, Desire and Belonging.* http://www.caribbeanhomophobias.org/node/6.

Larcher, A.A., and Colin Robinson. 2009. "Fighting 'Murder Music': Activist Reflections". *Caribbean Review of Gender Studies* 3:1–12. https://sta.uwi.edu/crgs/november2009/journals/akimadelarcher.pdf.

Lorde, Audre. 1983. "The Master's Tools Will Never Dismantle the Master's House". In *This Bridge Called My Back: Writings by Radical Women of Color,* edited by Cherrie Moraga and Gloria Anzaldúa, 94–101. New York: Kitchen Table Press.

Meckler, Laura. 2010. "Obama Joins 'It Gets Better' Campaign: Dan Savage Says: Make it Better". Washington Wire blog. *Wall Street Journal:* 22 October. https://blogs.wsj.com/washwire/2010/10/22/obama-joins-it-gets-better-campaign-dan-savage-says-make-it-better/.

Morgan, Joe. 2013. "Jamaican Cross-Dressing Teen 'Chopped and Stabbed' to Death by Mob". *Gay Star News.* 23 July. https://www.gaystarnews.com/article/jamaican-cross-dressing-teen-%E2%80%98chopped-and-stabbed%E2%80%99-death-mob230713/#gs.ku4RXZg.

National Geographic. 2017. "How Science Helps Us Understand Gender Identity". January. http://www.nationalgeographic.com/magazine/2017/01/how-science-helps-us-understand-gender-identity/.

Padgett, Tim. 2006. "The Most Homophobic Place on Earth?" *Time:* 12 April. http://content.time.com/time/world/article/0,8599,1182991,00.html.

Poyser, Andre. 2015. "Julian Robinson Seeks Solutions for Homeless Gay Youth in New Kingston". *Gleaner,* 19 May. http://jamaica-gleaner.com/article/lead-stories/20150519/julian-robinson-seeks-solutions-homeless-gay-youth-new-kingston.

Robinson, Colin. 2006. "Holding on to Another Jamaica". *Clamor Magazine* 37:81–83. https://archive.org/stream/clamormagazine37mult/clamormagazine37mult_djvu.txt.

———. 2007. "Sojourner: An Abandoned Manifest". In *Voices Rising: Celebrating Twenty Years of Black Lesbian, Gay, Bisexual and Transgender Writing,* edited by G.W. James, 6–11. Washington, DC: Redbone Press.

———. 2012. "The Work of Three-Year Old Caiso – Reflections at the MidPoint: Activist Report (Trinidad and Tobago)". In *Theorizing Homophobias in the Caribbean: Complexities of Place, Desire and Belonging,* edited by Rosamond King, Angelique Nixon, Colin Robinson, Natalie Bennett and Vidyaratha Kissoon. http://www.caribbeanhomophobias.org/node/6.

———. 2015. "The Fetish of Law". *Sunday Guardian* (Trinidad and Tobago). 21 April, A22. http://www.guardian.co.tt/columnist/2015-04-11/fetish-law.

———. 2017. "Imagining Leaving". *Guardian* (Trinidad and Tobago). 21 August, A20. http://www.guardian.co.tt/columnist/2017-08-20/imagining-leaving.

Robinson, Tracy. 2017. "Towards Sexual Equality: Dismantling Discrimination in Law and Practice". Presentation at panel discussion "Towards Sexual Equality: Dismantling Discrimination in Law and Practice", Faculty of Law, University of the West Indies, St Augustine, Trinidad and Tobago. 28 September.

Tinsley, Omiseke N. 2010. *Thiefing Sugar: Eroticism between Women in Caribbean Literature*. Durham, NC: Duke University Press.

14.

So

Queer Life Beyond and Against Homophobia

RINALDO WALCOTT

[E]ven as they tried to kill me with insults I moved outside their identity.
—Hilton Als, *The Women*

Gay identity is always forced to remember its origins in insult as soon as it makes
an effort to forget them.
—Didier Eribon, *Insult and the Making of the Gay Self*

Let me begin with the obvious. *Time* magazine's 2006 article "The Most Homophobic Place on Earth" (Padgett 2006) haunts this conference and quite frankly, haunts all of us who identify as Caribbean queers. The profound impact of the article is that it achieved what had previously been whispered, but not fully and openly uttered, that the people of the Caribbean region and principally Jamaicans, are homophobic beyond imagination and logic. This claim of Caribbean, black and African people's outsized homophobia has become one of the central conceits of Western rights-bearing discourses and the institutions that export them. The "most homophobic" claim is now globally cemented, despite not being based on much evidence to support its inference. Indeed, on close inspection one begins to realize that the claim of outsized homophobia takes its imprimatur from a much deeper and older historical logic of African and black peoples as savage and atavistic.

Now, please do not hear me as offering an apology for the actual violence of homophobia in the region and particularly in Jamaica, which has been specifically singled out as uniquely homophobic. Instead, what I am pointing to are the ways in which an already epistemic claim about African and African-descended people seeks its validation and verification in collecting certain kinds of evidence that makes other kinds of evidence that counters the claim not appear at all, or only appear as an anomaly. When we couple *Time*'s article with Human Rights Watch's two reports of 2004 and 2014, *Hated to Death* and *Not Safe at Home: Violence and Discrimination against LGBT People in Jamaica*, we are left with the impression that queer life is impossible in the Caribbean region. And yet we know that queer life exists in the region. So how do we make sense of this glaring incongruity? How do we notice and track queer life? What are the stakes for queer life in the region beyond and against homophobia? How do we know the Caribbean queer, and is knowing the Caribbean queer a necessary act? To attempt a response to those questions, I first want to return to my own memories of queer life in Barbados and work from there to attempt an arrival at Caribbean and black queer life that is both in the region and in the region's extensions. I hope what I mean by extensions will become clearer as I proceed, but let me say that the Caribbean region exists beyond its physical geography and thus its extensions must be accounted for beyond the region.

Queer Memories/Queer Barbados

Barbados is a queer society. When I search my childhood and young adult memory for queer people in Barbados I always recall and remember gay and lesbian people in all of the communities that I resided in before arriving in Canada. These queer people were neither ostracized nor, from what I could discern or remember from that time, lived in fear of their lives. What I do remember is that those queer people were particular types of queers, as I have now come to realize and understand. In all matters of queer sexuality they fit a then-prevailing stereotype of performing what was read or understood as inhabiting the gender that they were supposed not to *be* in some recognizable fashion. That is, the women behaved like "men" and the men behaved like "women". Gender and sexuality were inextricable in the mark and trace of how sexuality was understood as I now remember it. In this regard, their queer sexualities were known and their "abnormality" fit a frame of reference that ultimately did not disturb gender roles and performances in ways that called attention to the heteronormative punitive structure of the society. Indeed, their performance of gender and sexuality reaffirmed hegemonic gender roles. These queer people did not have to hide and thus they lived their lives out of the closet, as we now call it, in their communities. This particular frame of queer sexuality in the Barbados I came of age in was, however, mediated by other frames of queer sexuality that I later came to understand as undesirable.

In particular, in the Barbados I remember, the language of someone "liking little boys" was very much linked to an imagined specific kind of queer male sexuality. The phrase "liking little girls" was a claim that I never heard concerning queer women. The particular language of men "liking little boys" was launched at men who appeared to be men but were deemed otherwise, that is, they did not fit the male gender role in all the ways in which it was assumed one must fit. They stood outside normative sexuality because they had sex with other men, and members of the community knew that to be the case. While the language of "liking little boys" obviously spoke directly to the practice of paedophilia and therefore must be uncoupled from queer sexualities, it is important to recognize that it was not then tied to queer sexualities, and in many ways remains so, in Barbadian discourses and beyond, as a way to discredit nonheterosexual practices. It is what we might call a homophobic claim and one that is often invoked to mask acts of violence and hatred directed at same sex–loving men in particular.

Again, same-sex sex work was also ambivalently frowned upon, ambivalent because the question of the material sustenance was one that was valued in the transactional economy of money for sex. This particular kind of labour was often tied to the stereotypical "beach boy", but clearly, exceeding the beach sex economy was understood to trouble the much too settled patriarchal heteronormative gender roles of the society. Thus men who did not exhibit a nonnormative "masculinity" but were understood to be homosexual were seen as particularly vile and dangerous. The difference in status concerning the performative roles of gender in relationship to practices of sexuality indicates the normative frames of a specific and definable masculinity in Barbados and, one might argue, the larger Caribbean Basin. It is a masculinity that is defined in relation to fathering children, participating in multiple heterosexual relationships and adhering to whatever the prevailing codes of masculine conduct are for the specific time. Hegemonic masculine conduct never does involve same-sex love, even though it might involve the occasional same-sex "fling" with a gender-nonconforming person.

In this chapter, I mainly refer to "men", even though I should make clear that in my memories of queer people in Barbados in the later 1970s and 1980s, what we today call trans people, gender-nonconforming and nonbinary people abounded in Barbados. Indeed, as a child I recall my sisters speaking openly and excitedly about the Queen of the B shows that were regional competitive drag shows held at the Plaza cinema (I think). While always spoken about in a register of laughter, maybe even ridicule and definitely insult, I do not recall any notion that violence had to be enacted on the people participating in such events. A different sense of queerness, for lack of a better term, was operable. Indeed, as I hope to show, the language in use and on offer often fails to bring our full experience and our full selves into existence when sexuality and gender are at stake.

In at least two communities that I lived in in Barbados, gender-nonconforming people lived lives as tailors, dressmakers and independent food operators. These people hid neither their gendered performativity nor their sexuality, and adults in the community recognized them as members of the community with the same kinds of respect and dignity afforded them as other adults. Of course, that compact broke down in matters of community dispute, where insults would be hurled at these people. I shall return to this point shortly because I think insult is crucial to queer life.

What I am offering here is a truth claim that finds resonance in some of the scholarly research that has been done on Caribbean sexualities and in particular queer sexualities (see Murray [2006] and Sharpe and Pinot [2006]). For example, some scholarship points to the ways in which masculinity in the Caribbean is premised on a practice of heterosexuality that is often polygamous and often involves the rearing of numerous children (Kempadoo 2004). That my memories accord with those findings does not at all mean that my memory is correct: it might simply mean that I have come to remember such as being the case from the encounters with scholarship, memory-work and the queer circumstances of diaspora displacement producing the lie of nostalgia. But I don't think so.

The memories that I hold of late 1970s and early 1980s Barbados are mediated by another set of memories, those of the late 1980s and early 1990s. I remember being harassed particularly as a "buller" and "faggot" in that period in Barbados. The memories of such insults disrupt the more ambivalent story of queer inclusiveness that I remember as a child and sit in opposition to what is often understood as a Barbadian response to homosexuality as somehow uniquely different and milder than other parts of the region. A certain kind of Barbadian queer exceptionalism exists that is both a reality and that simultaneously obscures homophobia there. Between the vulgar homophobia of verbal harassment and the milder ridicule of insults, insults that required queerness to always appear "queer" or as an "act out of the ordinary" as a specific gendered performance, a number of possibilities lie, I would argue, for something else to emerge out of the region that are unique to it. For such to occur we must grapple with the complicated history of gender and sexuality in the region.

In Hilton Als's (1996) memoir *The Women,* he writes, "[b]eing an auntie man enamored of Negressity is all I have ever known to be" (9). He continues, "I have expressed my Negressity by living, fully, the prescribed life of an auntie man – what Barbadians call a faggot" (9). Als writes into being his queerness as an expression of his Barbadian family's circumstances in 1970s New York. Concerning his mother he writes:

> She had one friend who was an auntie man. Unlike other women who knew him as well, my mother didn't find her friend's sexual predilection confusing or anger-provoking. Besides, auntie men were not mysterious beings to her; in Barbados, most ostensibly straight men had sex with them, which was good, since that left women alone for a while. During the course of her friendship with Grantly the auntie man, she focused on him. Had she had access to other people besides her children, lover, employer, doctors, she might have been a fag hag, fond of auntie men, music, movies. (29)

Als's observation and memory of his mother resonates with me. I too have known Barbadian women whose focus on their auntie man would have constituted them as what we call "fag hags". The auntie man occupies a specific place and function as long as his masculinity is recognizable as a specific type of "queer". Als recalls the insult of "faggot" in his family as a disciplinary practice to keep him in line as a product of other contradictory and ambivalent forces in Barbadian and Caribbean social relations. I have always found Als's passage useful for mapping a particular cultural moment of Barbadian and Caribbean queer recognition that is unique to us with all its various troubles.

Indeed, while Als invokes "auntie man" without its demeaning qualities and "faggot" as a disciplinary term, I remember another term: the term is "so". To be *so* was to invoke in a nondemeaning fashion that one's sexuality and gender were nonhegemonic. Thus one would hear adults refer to someone as *being so,* said in a fashion not to demean them. It is the ontology of *so* that I, in part, want to pursue because I believe it cast a different light on Caribbean sexualities, especially queer and gender-nonconforming sexualities, in a way that does not pathologize but recognizes our own histories of living in the midst of communities of care and love that complicate contemporary narrative claims of outsized homophobia in the region and its extensions.

This chapter grapples with a Caribbean queer sense of being encapsulated in the Barbadian reference of *being so.* The utterance of *being so* is of the recognition of nonheterosexuality and is not necessarily deployed in the service of homophobia. In this chapter I argue that the Caribbean has within it modes of everyday ways of being that complicate practices of homophobia beyond and against the language of rights. I turn to *so* to begin to articulate what might be at stake for reckoning with Caribbean queer life beyond and against claims of homophobia.

Homopoetics

Being so does the work of what I call homopoetics. By homopoetics I have been attempting to develop and articulate a way of noticing Caribbean, black and African nonheterosexual practices and nonhegemonic gender performativity that is located in our unique relation to the partial imposition of European universalist humanism. I am interested in this kind of pursuit because I am convinced that European humanism cannot bring our full selves into being. Therefore, I have often turned in my work to the queer ideas of Édouard Glissant and Sylvia Wynter to articulate what I call, following them, homopoetics. Homopoetics allows me to read across various spaces and texts and to make truth claims that complicate narratives of memory but that also produce the intellectual and conceptual terrain to notice our ways of being unencumbered within other frames of subordination.

Most importantly, homopoetics allows me to find in Caribbean people's practices and ways of living the resources to both affirm our lives and the terms under which challenges can be made to Caribbean states and beyond to articulate a different kind of future and a different order of human life. Glissant and Wynter allow me to read the Caribbean beyond its geographical boundaries: not to empty it out, nor romanticize it, but to render its circulation and orientation worldly and global. More specifically, homopoetics allows me to engage discourses of homophobia both real and imagined in the context of what Miriam Smith (1999, 22) has called "rights talk" as a complicating disciplinary project of ongoing colonial and imperial conditions for the Caribbean.

In *Caribbean Discourse*, Édouard Glissant (1989, 120) writes, "I define as a free or natural poetics any collective yearning for expression that is not opposed to itself either at the level of what it wishes to express or at the level of the language that it puts into practice." Glissant's articulation of poetics is what I use to develop the idea of homopoetics. Also drawing from his *Poetics of Relation,* I extend his insights to think about "the homopoetics of relation", which for me is particularly urgent as HIV/AIDS continues to be a significant defining feature of the region, simultaneously alongside the aforementioned claim of the region's exaggerated homophobia. At the same time, this homopoetics is concerned with the relation and nonrelation between the epidemic of HIV/AIDS among African Americans, its devastating impact on the African continent and its increasing impact among black and African Canadians. Glissant (1989) claims two kinds of poetics: natural and forced. He proceeds to more fully define natural poetics:

> Even if the destiny of a community should be a miserable one, or its existence threatened, these poetics are the direct result of activity within the social body. The most daring or the most artificial experiences, the most radical questioning of self-expression, extend, reform, clash with a given poetics. This is because there is no incompatibility here between desire and expression. The most violent challenge to an established order can emerge from a natural poetics, when there is continuity between the challenged order and the disorder it negates. (120)

Glissant offers in his articulation of a natural, or free, poetics a method for "reading" and debate that might be useful for thinking Caribbean-ness, queerness and claims of homophobia within and across diasporic communities in the Americas. His natural poetics is an orienting device of sorts. It is a method of movement, it is a method of relation and it is a method of thought. The movement is not merely one of bodies but ideas as well. The relation is not merely one of identity; it is a relation of politics too. The thought is not merely one of ideas and speech acts, it is a queer insistence, or as Glissant (1997) puts it in another sense in the *Poetics of Relation*, it is a "that that" (159). The archipelago of the Caribbean is not merely a geographic space, but the Caribbean as an entity extends beyond its geography as a global reality – it is an extension in time and space, as well as into other spaces and places. For those of us who have any relation to the region (and that is all of us in the post/colonial modern world), what Sylvia Wynter (1992, 272) has called "the jobless archipelago", commitments can be complex and contradictory. Significantly for those of us who are nonheterosexual, those commitments and identifications pose difficult dilemmas concerning political expression and demands, cultural desires and identifications and relationships between place, nation and space – especially in the extensions.

The *Poetics of Relation*, Glissant (1997) claims, is an extension of *Caribbean Discourse*: "a reconstituted echo or a spiral retelling" (16) of the latter text. I read both texts as the impossible unspeakable spoken of the creole Americas. The impossibility of speaking the creole Americas is more about US regional imperial hegemony than it is about either a conceptual claim or an empirical material reality. Glissant and Wynter in my view come closest to uttering the Truth of the Americas and its creole-ness. Similarly, one might make the leap from Glissant's creole-ness to arguments about queerness as a relation–nonrelation to Africa, the colonial legacy and the postcolonial condition of imposition and disappointment and its sexualized orienting behaviours.

Why turn to the queer ideas of Glissant? He writes: "Creolization, one of the ways of forming a complex mix – and not merely a linguistic result – is only exemplified by its processes and certainly not by the contents on which these operate. . . . We are not prompted solely by the defining of our identities but by their relation to everything possible as well – the mutual mutations generated by this interplay of relations" (1997, 90). In Glissant's ideas I find links that help me and should help us all think both the melancholic morass of Caribbean homophobia and simultaneously the Caribbean's assumed heteropatriarchal assumptiveness, right along "rights talk" and a desire for rights. The debates taking place in the region and its extensions concerning homophobia are only so banal in that feminist insights, many of them homopoetic, still occupy an edge in politics and thought – in political thought and organizing. My ongoing surprise that feminism occupies the edge in the queer rights-talk debate in the region and its extensions tells me something about the work still to be done. In the extensions much is possible, including the production of what Glissant (1997, 144) terms "the chaotic network of Relation and not in the hidden violence of filiation".

In David Murray's (2012) *Flaming Souls: Homosexuality, Homophobia and Social Change in Barbados* he offers an anthropological account of Barbados, and in some ways the region, that appears to accord with the exceptional narrative of the place. I find in Murray's work moments of recognition and moments of disidentification that betray the limits of anthropology as a disciplinary orientation that cannot access the kind of turn I am attempting with *being so*. Murray's account is a curious one for a number of reasons. Drawing from his previous queer theoretical work on Martinique, especially the Foucaultian turn, and transnational feminist and queer scholars Jacqui Alexander and Kamala Kempadoo, Murray is aware of the ways in which his white male northern-ness curves his analysis and he, in the fashion we are now used to, acknowledges such. However, it is not Murray's whiteness that I take issue with: it is rather the way in which he invokes the North and simultaneously delimits the South. Let me explain.

Murray's account and questioning of homophobia in the region, and in Barbados in particular, appears as one we should embrace. It reads as nuanced, sensitive and weary of a Northern insistence that the Caribbean is a backward place on the question of nonheterosexuality. Murray questions such claims in a way that one might not take too much issue with. What does trouble is that the North that Murray writes from seems devoid of the Caribbean. Anthropology's still insistence on studying an Other means that Murray is not able to notice how the Caribbean extends into the North and how that extension shapes his analysis of the South. Indeed, had he been able to do so he would more substantively question the language of visibility and invisibility that he used and, furthermore, his delineation of "queens" versus gay and lesbians would largely not have held up as an analytic.

I want to suggest that Murray is not able to access the ontological conditions of queer subjecthood that *being so* is an articulation of. So while Murray questions the imposition of Euro-American logics of queerness on the region and thus the narrative of homophobia, his account does not shift the terrain at all. Murray's inability to shift the terrain from homophobia to *being so* in some ways marks the anthropologist's exclusion from a deeper orientation of and in Caribbean community and an inability to notice how queer Caribbean subjectivity articulates and performs itself in the Caribbean outside the region in places like the North. Indeed, had he noticed the Caribbean in his North, a much thicker account would have occurred. The account Murray (2012, 204) offers us is over-determined by his insistence, Foucaultian in nature, that "homosexuality was increasingly debated in public contexts at this historical juncture because Barbados faced major social and economic challenges in its marginal position relative to other international political and economic alliances such as the North American Free Trade Agreement (NAFTA) and the European Union (EU)". One wants to simply respond, "What's new here?" So what I am suggesting is we need a new theorization of the problem.

Let me give another example from the place of activism. The narrative of homophobia, despite Murray's best stated intentions, did not shift in his account. If we turn to Maurice Tomlinson's activism, a similar moment occurs. Tomlinson, a former Jamaican lawyer married to his white Canadian partner and now living in Canada, has emerged as an international activist and campaigner against homophobia in the Caribbean. One would be hard pressed to dismiss Tomlinson's claims around homophobic state laws and about violence and the general context of homophobia in the region. And yet his activism, based in a specific discourse of both rights and identity, can neither notice queerness as existing outside that paradigm nor acknowledge how Caribbean queerness works beyond the regional boundaries to resignify a more complex articulation of gender and sexuality.

As at least one face of a rights-based and rights-talk movement in and outside the Caribbean region, Tomlinson finds himself reproducing, in the most atavistic ways, the region and its people as outsized homophobes. Most recently in Toronto, his proclaiming that he feels safer with the police than in the black community cemented his atavistic approach to queer rights discourse. In making such a claim, Tomlinson did not only attempt to ignore the tremendous police violence that black, African and Caribbean people experience in North America, but he also displaced police violence in the region in a way that he clearly would otherwise not intend, I suspect. What this example highlights for me are the ways in which certain forms of activism are indebted to the now deep and unspoken logics of Caribbean, black and African savage atavism. That Tomlinson could imagine that Caribbean and Caribbean-descended queers in Toronto did not have a legitimate critique of policing and that they would understand their communities as the central locus of their oppression demonstrates a specific interpretation of Caribbean people that fits the "most homophobic place on earth" logic. It is obviously a logic that must be challenged, called into question and ultimately refused because the rights-bearing subject it imagines can only but reinforce ongoing white supremacist imperial relations of all kinds. The logic remains committed to our collective unfreedom.

I am, however, not simply providing a refusal that allows us to reside in normative Caribbean gender relations. I am offering the ontological position and utterance of being so as a buttress against anti-black and anti-African logics that place us outside of modernity and in need of rescue. So is a different kind of orientation for how we might approach both rights and homophobic violation. So requires us to think freedom, especially sexual liberation and gender performance beyond what we already have, to reinvent them anew, to crib from Wynter.

Tomlinson, now in the Caribbean diaspora, is an example of a certain kind of NGO economy of mobility that reproduces a white gaze and logic that renders the Caribbean backward. Indeed, his intervention into the Toronto public sphere has been characterized by an ongoing production of Jamaica and the Caribbean as singularly homophobic and at the same time revealing and misreading Caribbean queer politics and activism in the city.

Scholars like Cassandra Lord (2015) doing work on Pelau, a gay carnival-style band in Toronto's Gay Pride, in *Performing Queer Diasporas: MasQUEERade in the Toronto Pride Parade*; OmiSoore Dryden (2010) working on black, African and Caribbean queer blood, HIV and the blood bank's ban on people from HIV "endemic regions" (their language not mine) in, for example, "Canadians Denied: A Queer Diasporic Analysis of the Canadian Blood Donor"; and Beverley Bain's (2017) work on the history of Caribbean, black and African queer organizing in Toronto, "Fire, Passion and Politics: The Creation of Blockorama as Black Queer Diasporic Space in the Toronto Pride Festivities" put into stark relief Tomlinson's simplistic reading of the public sphere he now occupies. Importantly, Tomlinson fails to recognize how Africa rejoins her diaspora in spaces like Toronto. This overlooked comingling and rejoining allows for a different kind of fashioning and performance of gender and sexuality that rights talk in the mode of Tomlinson and his investors cannot even begin to make sense of. The orientation of Tomlinson's activism thus requires redirecting in a substantive way if it is to be capable of engaging *being so* as a potential mode of our future freedom.

Sarah Ahmed (2006), in *Queer Phenomenology: Orientations, Objects, Others*, writes, "[n]ow in living a queer life, the act of going home, or going back to the place I was brought up, has a certain disorienting effect" (11). Her insights on phenomenological experiences in terms of queer orientations help me problematize how memory informs my practices of queerness in diaspora. Significantly, this work is about how a queer diasporic Barbadian might speak to the project of rights talk and homophobia as a displaced subject whose sexuality, while formed in North America, is actually much more constitutive of the queer region of Barbados and the larger Caribbean than at first glance appears. I have resigned from "gay" as an identity category and a politics in favour of an orientation that is premised on a desire concerned with sexual and gender freedom.

In liberal, democratic societies, citizenship is the terrain over which governing is most aptly contested. Thus, any real and sustained changes to citizenship impact all, regardless of gender, sexuality, class and so on. Queer rights to citizenship must and should be a fundamental priority, but how those rights are attained is crucial for their sedimentation and cementedness to the nation-state. How these rights are attained becomes crucial for what kind of human we might and can become beyond the present expansion of what Wynter and McKittrick (2015, 23) call the "ethnoclass" of western bourgeois society. Indeed, if rights is the orientation, those rights must rethink the state in more fundamental ways; maybe undo the state as it presently works as arbiter of our beings.

In *Insult and the Making of the Gay Self*, Eribon (2004) suggests that insults work to constitute queer community. His insight is premised on a reading of the insult that is both internal and external to queer communities. Eribon points out that one subset of insults is caricature in its many forms. This particular kind of insult coupled with ridicule and an expected and assumed repartee was fundamental to the kind of homophobia that I remember as a child in Barbados. But importantly, queer subjecthood was expected to trade in the practice of insult both as repartee and as an expected element of marking itself as different. Homophobia was not premised on physical violence as much as it was the violence of verbal sparring. Insult and its practice were an ambivalent space of "freedom" and identity-making. But as Eribon (2004, 79) concedes, "gay identity is always forced to remember its origins in insult", which means that queers are never able to leave the insult behind. Rights talk's desire is to leave the insult, the wound and the injury behind, but the insult might be the orienting device that queers require to make identification into and make community. The work of the insult separates and disciplines, but it is also community-constituting, which makes it powerfully useful. Thus, the work of the insult can also be orienting, to recall Ahmed.

Many years previous, Makeda Silvera (1992) in "Man Royals and Sodomites" made it difficult to reclaim such names in any too easy fashion. The dreaded words "buller", "batty man", "chi chi man", "sodomite", "man royal" – and it goes on – are orienting insults, I would argue. Vile names that give meaning to acts of desire and pleasure censured through state and extra-state means. These names designate "behavior-directing signs" (Wynter 1990, 449) that mark same-sex love and desire as aberrant. In the age of HIV/AIDS, the subjecthood of the homosexual carries new meanings. Audre Lorde (1982), in *Zami: A New Spelling of My Name*, sought to reclaim and re-articulate in "biomythographic" terms "zami" as a metaphor for women's community that was both emotionally supportive and, when necessary, sexually satisfying. This move is not unlike Gloria Wekker's (2006) anthropological studies in Suriname concerning "mati-work". Less successfully, Wesley Crichlow (2004) in *Buller Man and Batty Bwoy: Hidden Men in Toronto and Halifax* attempts the social scientific reclamation of buller man and batty boy within a Caribbean extension – Canada. In his view, which is a view launched in opposition to clearly demarcated "white" ways of naming, black same sex–loving men must find names internal to their "cultures" which would be more appropriate than "gay", "queer", "faggot" and so on. I, therefore, do not fundamentally disagree with Crichlow, but I place a different emphasis on what can be reclaimed and the work the reclaiming is meant to do. Thomas Glave (2008) recounts in the introduction to *Our Caribbean* how at least two potential contributors pulled out of the compilation because the words "gay" and "lesbian" did not capture their sense of being. In my view much is in the name and how the name works to produce modes of being that work beyond subjection and its violent institution. To repeat, *being so*, I am suggesting, does the work of the ontological restitution of the sort that I am after.

Again, without suggesting an apology for homophobia in the Caribbean and its extensions – there exist places in the European West where queer theory and queer bodies meet hostility, even if there is a sense of gay and lesbian rights talk put into play in the governmental or state sphere – I return to the insights of Eribon's *Insult and the Making of the Gay Self*. Eribon (2004, xv) writes:

> In 1995, the year of the first enormous French Gay Pride, editorials in the press, from the right and the left, gave free rein to sentiments that can only be qualified as phobic. Gay Pride, they said, was a danger to democracy; the homosexual "separatism" that such events revealed threatened to "destroy the architecture of the nation". . . . Newspapers went on to . . . insult the field of lesbian and gay studies, which apparently represented a danger to knowledge, to culture, to thought and to the university.

Eribon's chronicling of such recent French responses to mass public expressions of homosexuals in the public sphere is, I repeat, not an excuse for the Caribbean. It is rather a challenge for all of us to think differently about the question of identity and rights talk. However, the enduring coloniality of queer life deliberately positions queers of the Global South as needing a helping hand from the North Atlantic that is most times not about genuine struggle to build community but about, as Gayatri Spivak (2004, 542) puts it in "Righting Wrongs", "that they must be propped up".

For me, insult is an opening to a conversation of sorts in Barbados, the Caribbean and their extensions. The insult rests in the refusal to sometimes name, as some Bajans do by refusing to utter or say the word "homosexual", to produce queer people as possessing a subjecthood, but I am suggesting that in their refusal or insult they too are giving queers a life. Some men and women are thus said to be *so* nonetheless, and as such, a recognition of a different kind of subjecthood, one that is not degraded nor invisibilized, as Murray thinks is the case. It is, however, a subjecthood not beholden to state management, accounting and regulation, but a subjecthood deeply embedded in the people's ethical ways of being with each other in community. *So* marks a collective ethical ontological condition that requires a different register of love and care, a register that is uniquely ours. In the homopoetics of such speech acts is an opening up, a poetics of language and talk and the origins of a new, yet old, personhood rooted in the queer modernity of the region itself.

Citizen practices and their state bestowal call for knowable identities, that is, how the managerialism of citizenship works. However, sexual practices, multiple and varied, as we all know, do not require a manageable identity for their practice. Contemporary human rights are based on a claim to identity – a knowable identity. The ethics of the situation calls for rights without identity claims. As Spivak (2004, 564) writes, "Indeed, the name of 'man' in 'human' rights (or the name of 'woman' in 'women's rights are human rights') will continue to trouble me." Let me then conclude with a reminder from a previous essay, "Queer Returns": "Sexual practices without attendant identities and a move that advances such a claim can pose new and important questions for the remaking of the late modern state. The Anglo-Caribbean queer movement has the potential to make such a contribution to our sexual politics in the 21st century" (Walcott 2009, 15).

References

Ahmed, Sara. 2006. *Queer Phenomenology: Orientations, Objects, Others*. Durham, NC: Duke University Press.

Als, Hilton. 1996. *The Women*. New York: Farrar, Straus and Giroux.

Bain, Beverley. 2017. "Fire, Passion and Politics: The Creation of Blockorama as Black Queer Diasporic Space in the Toronto Pride Festivities". In *We Still Demand: Defining Resistance in Sex and Gender Struggles*, edited by Patrizia Gentile, Gary Kinsman and L. Pauline Rankin, 81–97. Vancouver: University of British Columbia Press.

Crichlow, Wesley. 2004. *Buller Man and Batty Bwoy: Hidden Men in Toronto and Halifax Black Communities*. Toronto: University of Toronto Press.

Dryden, OmiSoore. 2010. "Canadians Denied: A Queer Diasporic Analysis of the Canadian Blood Donor". *Atlantis* 34 (2): 77–84.

Eribon, Didier. 2004. *Insult and the Making of the Gay Self*. Translated by Michael Lucey. Durham, NC: Duke University Press.

Glave, Thomas. 2008. *Our Caribbean: A Gathering of Lesbian and Gay Writing from the Antilles*. Durham, NC: Duke University Press.

Glissant, Édouard. 1989. *Caribbean Discourse: Selected Essays*. Translated by Michael Dash. Charlottesville: University of Virginia Press.

———. 1997. *Poetics of Relation*. Translated by Betsy Wing. Ann Arbor: University of Michigan Press.

Human Rights Watch. 2004. *Hated to Death: Homophobia, Violence and Jamaica's HIV/AIDS Epidemic*. New York: Human Rights Watch.

Human Rights Watch. 2014. *Not Safe at Home: Violence and Discrimination against LGBT People in Jamaica*. New York: Human Rights Watch.

Kempadoo, Kamala. 2004. *Sexing the Caribbean: Gender, Race and Sexual Labour*. New York: Routledge.

Lord, Cassandra. 2015. "Performing Queer Diasporas: MasQUEERade in the Toronto Pride Parade". PhD diss., University of Toronto.

Lorde, Audre. 1982. *Zami: A New Spelling of My Name*. Freedom, CA: Crossing Press.

Murray, David. 2006. "Who's Right? Human Rights, Sexual Rights and Social Change in Barbados". *Culture, Health and Sexuality* 8 (3): 267–81.

———. 2012. *Flaming Souls: Homosexuality, Homophobia and Social Change in Barbados*. Toronto: University of Toronto Press.

Padgett, Tim. 2006. "The Most Homophobic Place on Earth?" *Time*. http://content.time.com/time/world/article/0,8599,1182991,00.html.

Sharpe, Jenny, and Samantha Pinto. 2006. "The Sweetest Taboo: Studies of Caribbean Sexualities, a Review Essay". *Signs: Journal of Women in Culture and Society* 32 (1): 247–74.

Silvera, Makeda. 1992. "Man Royals and Sodomites: Some Thoughts on the Invisibility of Afro-Caribbean Lesbians". *Feminist Studies* 18 (3): 521–32.

Spivak, Gayatri. 2004. "Righting Wrongs". *South Atlantic Quarterly* 103 (2–3): 523–81.

Smith, Miriam. 1999. *Lesbian and Gay Rights in Canada: Social Movements and Equality-Seeking*. Toronto: University of Toronto Press.

Walcott, Rinaldo. 2009. "Queer Returns: Human Rights, the Anglo-Caribbean and Diaspora Politics". *Caribbean Review of Gender Studies* 3:1–19.

Wekker, Gloria. 2006. *The Politics of Passion: Women's Sexual Culture in the Afro-Surinamese Diaspora*. New York: Columbia University Press.

Wynter, Sylvia. 1990. "On Disenchanting Discourse: 'Minority' Literary Criticism and Beyond". In *The Nature and Context of Minority Discourse*, edited by Abdul JanMohamed and David Lloyd, 207–44. Oxford: Oxford University Press.

———. 1992. "Rethinking 'Aesthetics': Notes towards a Deciphering Practice". In *Ex-iles: Essays on Caribbean Cinema*, edited by Mbye Cham. Trenton, NJ: Africa World Press.

Wynter, Sylvia, and Katherine McKittrick. 2015. "Unparalleled Catastrophe for Our Species? Or, to Give Humanness a Different Future: Conversations". In *Sylvia Wynter: On Being Human as Praxis*, edited by Katherine McKittrick, 106–23. Durham, NC: Duke University Press.

Afterword

KEI MILLER

It is not a small task to be asked to write an afterword for the present volume. So many of the essays and papers collected here function, I believe, as their own "afterwords" to a strange and strangling network of silences that have often been imposed on queer subjects in the Caribbean. From rape to murder, from beatings to excommunication from families, the kinds of violence, both physical and emotional, that have been meted out onto the bodies and souls of gay women and men across these islands is almost unimaginable. But to the extent that it has been imagined, that imagination has been totalizing. It has proved difficult, if not impossible, for Caribbean LGBT people to consider, let alone talk about, our lives outside the some-times wearying and disempowering construct of victimhood. Attempts to do this are often met with scepticism or the explicit attempt to silence and sideline any narrative that suggests our bodies have agency and are not merely things acted upon. This is what happened in 2009 when J-FLAG wrote to Michael Petrelis, the organizer of the ill-conceived Boycott Jamaica campaign and Petrelis expressed doubt that a letter so eloquent could have been written by queer people living in Jamaica. While homophobia has undoubtedly limited the lives of gay people in the region, the refusal to allow narratives outside of that construct represents its own silencing and its own violence.

Forgive me then if I take serious liberties in this "afterword" to a volume of astonishing and incredibly important "afterwords", by which I mean words that have come afterwards and have come to break and disrupt any totalizing silence, words that had been held back because we had lacked the courage, agency or the very words themselves to say them when we should have. I would like to think about one such moment in my own life to finally correct that silence, and in so doing, offer both an afterword to it and to this book.

It is the winter of 2004 and I am behind the till of a shop in northern England. Besides Ahmil, the manager, the shop assistants are all students studying at one of the nearby universities, the University of Manchester or Manchester Metropolitan. There are no benefits to this kind of hourly work – no maternity leave, or pension, or holidays – but this one concession is made, and it makes the job bearable: according to a carefully designed roster, each shop assistant has DJ rights for an hour – we can stream our music through the store's speakers. It is a win-win arrangement. It is that kind of shop that tries to be a little bit funky and casual enough to draw in a student clientele. The music played is usually the standard pop songs climbing the charts on any given week, but there is an hour every week when the sounds of Jamaica fill that shop, like an antidote to the cold.

It is possible to say that in that winter of 2004, I had escaped the homophobia of Jamaica. It is not how I felt. It is not how I imagined my year as a postgraduate student in England. I only acknowledge the possibility to say such a thing because such a thing was often said or inquired of me, as if the only way to understand my presence in England that year – the presence of a queer Caribbean body – was through the idea of *escape*. It was two years before Tim Padgett's now infamous "The Most Homophobic Place on Earth?" article in the *Time*, but already the conversations that would make such an article possible were swirling. As Thomas Glave points out in the foreword to this volume, there was indeed a time, and that time was not very long ago, when if one considered oneself Jamaican and queer, it was virtually impossible for the next thought not to be about the spectre of homophobia that was such an everyday part of our world, that sometimes showed itself in overtly threatening and dangerous ways but was also casual and quotidian so that we adjusted ourselves to fit into a world that did not want us to fit. It is important to say this, that to consider our lives beyond homophobia is not to deny homophobia or to pretend that that battle has been completely won, but it is to insist on our lives as broader and more complicated than the box Tim Padgett would consign us to. If I had escaped anything, it was a dead-end job at an advertising agency in Half-Way-Tree. It was the job I had escaped, not the island. Already, Jamaica was a place I was becoming homesick for, a place I would soon return to, and so that hour each week when I could listen to Bob Marley, and Morgan Heritage, and I-Wayne was one that I looked forward to. It made the bright smile required of those working behind a till sit more naturally on my face.

There are small moments in one's life that one can spend years reliving, refeeling, repondering; there are incidents, however seemingly small, that we can spend a lifetime deconstructing, pulling from it a mountain of bricks from which we reconstruct our own ethics and politics. This is one of them: in the winter of 2004, a woman enters a shop in Manchester, England. She carries with her the weight of some deep annoyance. At the till she is unimpressed by the man who smiles brightly at her and asks, as he has been taught to, "Anything else for you?" In fact, there is something about her eyes and the curl of her lips that seems almost disgusted by the man, but he does not feel this is directed toward him. How could it be? What could he have done to earn such a visceral reaction by a stranger? She does not answer, but by a sort of twitch of the head she signals, "no, no . . . nothing else. I just want to leave!" As he scans and cashes her goods and sorts out her change, she finally cannot hold it in any longer. "For godsake could you turn that music off! Don't you know how hateful it is?" It is only then that I realize I have been humming along to the music; it is only then that I listen more intently to the words of I-Wane singing "Lava Ground".

> We stan up pon de lava groundnuff
> And nuff a dem ah look fi see I mawga down
> hype pon warrior cause dem have a gun
> but tell dem seh de warrior naah guh run (we naah guh run!)
> We stand up pon de lava ground.

What could possibly be hateful about this declaration of defiance, this insistence on standing one's ground, this refusal to be intimidated because someone comes to us with a gun or with the threat of violence – this stance that has in fact been the stance of so many heroic LGBT Jamaicans? It takes me a couple seconds – a couple seconds being reduced by her stare, her clear repulsion of me – to understand what she is hearing and under-standing. She understands the music is Jamaican and she understands that I, too, am Jamaican. She has observed me – my over-two-hundred-pound black male body, my dreadlocks – and what she understands of Jamaica is that it is one of the most homophobic places in the world, that the music of the island stridently advocates for this homophobia and so the big black man in front of her who is clearly the cause of this music and is singing along to it, must be humming a tune of hatred. If Jamaica is only defined by its homophobia, then every Jamaican must be either an agent or a victim of that hate. She must have some imagination of the broken, brown, queer body on whose behalf she now speaks. She does not imagine that the body before her is one such body. She does not understand that in this moment of encountering a brown, queer body from Jamaica, all she has done is to silence it. But because the customer is always white (or is it the customer is always right? I do not remember which except in that moment they meant the same thing). I turned off the radio and handed my DJ rights over to another student whose music would undoubtedly be less offensive.

I still remember how the woman left the shop – her walk, a sort of prac-tised wariness, as if already she was rehearsing the language her body would use whenever she recounted this story, her eyes raised in exasperation, a heavy sigh, "You just wouldn't believe", she might begin her own account of the terrible homophobes in this world. And I wondered how many bodies similar to hers would gasp in horror and would congratulate her on her bravery, the strength of her morals, and would find in it inspiration to start their own crusades against injustice in the world.

I did not know then the language of intersectionality. I did not understand then, as I profoundly understand now, how possible it is to advocate on behalf of people even as you silence them. I did not understand then, as I profoundly understand now, how easy it is to claim alliance, how easy it is to be involved in the world's various fights against inequality even as you reinscribe and fortify the privilege in which you yourself stand and speak. In that winter of 2004, I was not allowed to speak; I was not allowed a voice; I was not allowed any words in the aftermath. I claim those words now in this afterword.

To consider queer bodies in the Caribbean, and in Jamaica specially, is to consider bodies that are profoundly complex and whose various meanings are produced not only by their sexual orientation but by the intersections of gender, class, race, age and disability, to name a few. It is also to consider bodies that often experience belonging, community, friendship and triumph but are so often not allowed to tell these stories because they move so far beyond the narrative of homophobia – a narrative that will always be compelling and urgent but will never be complete.

The Beyond Homophobia conferences held at the Mona campus of the University of the West Indies and organized jointly by J-Flag and University of West Indies, Mona have finally offered a space where bodies that are so often spoken about can speak for themselves and articulate their own complexities. We must honour that space; we must honour the words collected here; we must think about how the necessary and still ongoing fight against homophobia can sometimes be totalizing and impose its own silence on queer bodies; we must honour this attempt to break such silences with the brave words that come after.

Contributors

Moji Anderson is a senior lecturer in the Department of Sociology, Psychology and Social Work at the University of the West Indies, Mona, Jamaica. She is co-founder of Beyond Homophobia.

Erin C. MacLeod teaches at Vanier College, Montreal, Canada. Her publications include *Visions of Zion: Ethiopians and Rastafari in the Search for the Promised Land* and (co-edited with Jahlani Niaah) *Let Us Start with Africa: Foundations of Rastafari Scholarship*. She is co-founder of Beyond Homophobia.

Nikoli Attai is a provost's postdoctoral fellow in women and gender studies at the University of Toronto, Canada.

Andre Bagoo is a Trinidadian poet and the author of four books of poems, including *Pitch Lake*, and the forthcoming essay collection *The Undiscovered Country*.

Vileitha Davis-Morrison is a lecturer in the School of Education at the University of the West Indies Mona, Jamaica.

Carol Hordatt Gentles is a senior lecturer in the School of Education at the University of the West Indies, Mona, Jamaica.

K. Nandini Ghisyawan is an independent scholar and former postdoctoral associate at Rutgers Advanced Institute for Critical Caribbean Studies, New Jersey. She is the author of the forthcoming book *Erotic Cartographies: The Decolonial Imaginaries of Queer Caribbean Subjects*.

Lyndon K. Gill is an associate professor in the Department of African and African Diaspora Studies, Department of Anthropology, and the Center for Women's and Gender Studies at the University of Texas at Austin. He is the author of *Erotic Islands: Art and Activism in the Queer Caribbean*.

Thomas Glave is a professor of English and creative writing at the State University of New York, Binghamton. His most recent book is *Among the Bloodpeople: Politics and Flesh*.

Rajanie Preity Kumar is a visiting assistant professor in the Department of Women's, Gender and Sexuality Studies at the College of New Jersey.

O'Neil Lawrence is an artist and chief curator of the National Gallery of Jamaica.

Nick Marsellas is a PhD candidate at the University of Pittsburgh, Pennsylvania.

Keith E. McNeal is an associate professor of anthropology in the Department of Comparative Cultural Studies at the University of Houston, Texas. He is author of *Trance and Modernity in the Southern Caribbean: African and Hindu Popular Religions in Trinidad and Tobago* and the forthcoming *Queering the Citizen: Dispatches from Trinidad and Tobago.*

Kei Miller is a professor of English at the University of Miami, Florida. His many publications include the novel *Augustown,* the poetry collection *In Nearby Bushes* and the forthcoming essay collection *It Is Always the Body.*

Carla Moore lectures at the Institute for Gender and Development Studies at the University of the West Indies, Mona, Jamaica.

Ajamu Nangwaya is a lecturer in the Institute of Caribbean Studies at the University of the West Indies, Mona, Jamaica. His recent publications include *Why Don't the Poor Rise Up?: Organizing the Twenty-First Century Resistance* (co-edited with Michael Truscello) and *Jackson Rising: The Struggle for Economic Democracy and Black Self-Determination in Jackson, Mississippi* (co-edited with Kali Akuno).

Adwoa Onuora is a lecturer in the Institute for Gender and Development Studies at the University of the West Indies, Mona, Jamaica. She is the author of *Anansesem: Telling Stories and Storytelling African Maternal Pedagogies.*

Anna Kasafi Perkins is a senior programme officer in the Quality Assurance Unit at the University of the West Indies, Mona, Jamaica. Her publications include *Quality in Higher Education in the Caribbean* and *Justice as Equality: Michael Manley's Caribbean Vision of Justice.*

Colin Robinson is director of imagination for CAISO: Sex and Gender Justice. His publications include the poetry collection *You Have You Father Hard Head* and the co-edited books *Other Countries: Black Gay Voices* and *Think Again.*

Dorothea Smartt is a poet and a fellow of the Royal Society of Literature. Her poetry collections are *Connecting Medium* and *Ship Shape.*

Rinaldo Walcott is a professor of Black Diaspora Cultural Studies at the University of Toronto, Canada. His many publications include *Black Like Who: Writing Black Canada, Rude: Contemporary Black Canadian Cultural Criticism* and *Queer Returns: Essays on Multiculturalism, Diaspora and Black Studies.*

www.ingramcontent.com/pod-product-compliance
Lightning Source LLC
Chambersburg PA
CBHW021346290326
41932CB00043B/157